DARK MATTER

Tony Watkins

Shedding Light on
Philip Pullman's Trilogy
His Dark Materials

IVP Books

An imprint of InterVarsity Press
Downers Grove, Illinois

InterVarsity Press
P.O. Box 1400, Downers Grove, IL 60515-1426
Internet: www.ivpress.com
E-mail: mail@ivpress.com

InterVarsity Press® is the book-publishing division of InterVarsity Christian Fellowship/USA®, a student movement
active on campus at hundreds of universities, colleges and schools of nursing in the United States of America,
and a member movement of the International Fellowship of Evangelical Students. For information about local and
regional activities, write Public Relations Dept., InterVarsity Christian Fellowship/USA, 6400 Schroeder Rd.,
P.O. Box 7895, Madison, WI 53707-7895, or visit the IVCF website at <www.intervarsity.org>.

Cover design: Cindy Kiple

Cover image: compass and spyglass: David Chasey/Getty Images
　　　　　　　frame: C Squared Studios/Getty Images
　　　　　　　knife: C Squared Stuidos/Getty Images
　　　　　　　Oxford: Max Dannenbaum/Getty Images

ISBN-10: 0-8308-3379-X
ISBN-13: 978-0-8308-3379-5

Printed in the United States of America ∞

Library of Congress Cataloging-in-Publication Data

Watkins, Tony, 1964-
　　Dark matter: shedding light on Philip Pullman's trilogy His dark
　materials / Tony Watkins.
　　　　p. cm.
　　Includes bibliographical references and index.
　　ISBN-13: 978-0-8308-3379-5 (pbk.: alk. paper)
　　ISBN-10: 0-8308-3379-X (pbk.: alk. paper)
　　1. Pullman, Philip, 1946-　. His dark materials. 2. Pullman,
　Philip,
　1946-　—Criticism and interpretation. 3. Fantasy fiction,
　English—History and criticism. 4. Young adult fiction,
　English—History and criticism. I. Title. PR6066.U44Z95 2006
　823'.914—dc22

　　　　　　　　　　　　　　　　　　　　　　　　　　　　　　　　　　　2005033148

P	19	18	17	16	15	14	13	12	11	10	9	8	7	6	5	4	3	2	1
Y	19	18	17	16	15	14	13	12	11	10	09	08	07	06					

Contents

PART THREE: SHEDDING LIGHT ON DARK MATTER

PREFACE

His Dark Materials is one of the most engaging stories I've ever read—it instantly drew me into its magical world and I quickly came to love its cast of vividly drawn characters. I found the gripping plot almost unrelenting in its demand that I keep on reading. The power and scope are quite simply breathtaking, and it seemed inevitable to me that *His Dark Materials* would become a huge influence in popular culture. But with such depth in the issues with which it grapples, and with such a range of sources from which Pullman drew inspiration, it was also clear that it would not simply become a bestseller but would also stimulate endless discussion. And it combines so many of the subjects I love—literature, physics, philosophy and theology— that I could not sit back and let other people contribute to the growing discourse without pitching in myself.

There are already two very helpful books on Philip Pullman and *His Dark Materials*—by Nicholas Tucker[1] and Claire Squires[2]—but I am coming at Pullman's work from a distinctively different perspective from them. I am unashamedly a fan, but I also take issue with Pullman on the question of his attack on God and Christianity.

In the chapters that follow I want to help you to understand and appreciate Pullman's work more fully, and also to analyze his underlying ideas and worldview. I do not assume or expect that you share my own Christian perspectives, but I do believe that it's helpful for all fans of Pullman's work— Christian or otherwise—to *understand* a Christian perspective on it. That does not mean there is an obviously Christian angle right through this book, or that it is consistently negative. And I am not presenting this book as the definitive way in which to read Pullman's work, so I don't expect you to agree with everything. As Pullman himself says:

> The last thing I want to say is you've got it wrong. Because then you enter a kind of fundamentalist mode where you're saying you've got to understand it this way, not that way . . . that's dreadful. People are at perfect liberty to find in my story whatever they want to find and I wouldn't dream of saying to someone they've got it wrong. I'm just very flattered and happy that lots of people are reading my books.[3]

In part one, I look at some of the background to Philip's writing: the things that have shaped Pullman himself; his career as a storyteller, including a brief look at his other work; and the major influences not just on *His Dark Materials* but on his wider thinking. In part two, I look in more detail at the narrative world of *The Golden Compass*, *The Subtle Knife*, *The Amber Spyglass* and *Lyra's Oxford*, to try and tease out some of the key strands of the story. In part three, I look at some of the big themes and issues that play a prominent part in the story: dæmons and the whole business of growing up; the nature of Dust and its connection with "original sin," the Fall and consciousness; truth and integrity; and finally the church, God and the republic of heaven. There's also an appendix on two aspects of the science that Pullman weaves into the story—my background as a physicist couldn't let that opportunity pass by. There are many omissions: themes I don't develop, wonderful passages from *His Dark Materials* that I don't even mention, perspectives I apparently ignore, great quotes from Pullman or others that are left behind, added to which I have given Pullman's other work only a fraction of the attention that it deserves and that I intended to give it. Restriction on space is a hard taskmaster and it makes a writer necessarily ruthless.

You will find some additional material, including a transcript of my interview with Philip Pullman, articles and study guides on some of his books, at www.damaris.org/pullman. I owe my sincere thanks to many people for their help while I was writing this book, not least Philip Pullman himself. He has been gracious in giving time to both talk with me and correspond by e-mail, and in allowing me to quote extensively from his work. I'm also grateful for his practical assistance in giving me a lift back to my mother-in-law's stranded car after it had suffered a puncture on my way to visit him. I'm sure contending with Oxford's rush-hour traffic was the last thing Philip wanted at the end of a busy day, but he was quick to volunteer and saved me a major headache.

I am grateful for the opportunity to engage with many groups and individuals on the subject of Pullman's books. Particular thanks to Wade Bradshaw for the first invitation to lecture on *His Dark Materials* at L'Abri in Hampshire, and to Alex Aldous for inviting me to sharpen my ideas with an audience of young fans at Oakham School. The CultureWatch Group (Damaris Study Group) in Southampton; Above Bar Church, Southampton; and various other groups around the country have also stimulated, challenged and shaped my thinking over the last two years. Thanks also to the enthusiasts who maintain various *His Dark Materials* websites—they have been an invaluable source of information. I must make particular mention of Merlyn and the rest of the team at Bridgetothestars.net, which was my first port of call on the Internet on many of my writing days.

Specific snippets of information came from many sources—my thanks to the many others who have not been mentioned here and my apologies for not mentioning you by name. Having valued David Wilkinson's books on science and faith over several years, I am particularly grateful for his time in bringing me back up to speed on cosmology. Thanks also to Gillian Hansford for information on South American shamans; David and Pippa Trollope, and Ruth Armstrong for transcribing my interview with Philip; and to Roger Eldridge and Richard Stuckey for photographs on the book cover.

Very special thanks must go to the team at Damaris for bearing with me in the months of working from home rather than in the office. Peter Williams and Caroline Puntis both made valuable comments on various sections of the manuscript of this book, and both have taken up some of the slack while I have devoted my energies to writing, as have others in the team. Caroline in particular has taken on the role of assistant CultureWatch editor in the last four months, which has been an enormous help. Of all the Damaris team, it is Steve Couch who earns most gratitude and admiration for editorially steering me to completion with his gentle prodding rather than beating me with a stick, and with metaphorical—though still edible— carrots (Turkish Delight, Stilton, good wine . . . time to start the next book!) to spur me on from stage to stage. He has been a model of encouragement, patience and (almost) impeccable pedantry. Pullman's editor David Fickling has three golden rules for editors: first, the author isn't always right; second, the book is the author's, not the editor's; third, neither rule works all the time. Steve has obeyed these rules to the letter and with great spirit. And finally, more thanks than I can express to my dearest friend—my wife, Jane, and to my three boys, Charlie, Oliver and Pip, who have endured my absorption in this project over months.

Tony Watkins
July 2004

Throughout this book, references to *The Golden Compass*, *The Subtle Knife*, *The Amber Spyglass* and *Lyra's Oxford* are given as abbreviations. All page numbers refer to the paperback editions published by Dell Yearling in 2001 (*The Golden Compass* and *The Subtle Knife*) and 2003 (*The Amber Spyglass*), except for *Lyra's Oxford*, which is the hardcover edition published by Knopf in 2003. All URLs for articles on the Internet, which are referenced in the notes, were accessible in October 2005.

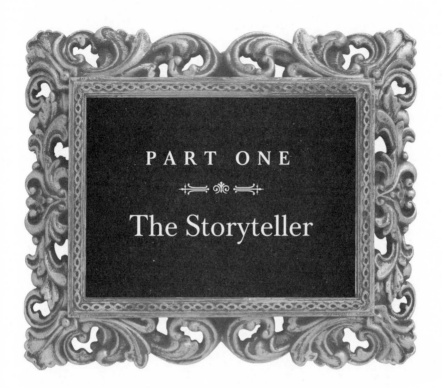

PART ONE

The Storyteller

1

THE ONCE UPON A TIME BUSINESS

"Pullman is a brilliant writer," wrote Nicholas Tucker, adding that he is "capable of lighting up the dullest day or greyest spirit with the incandescence of his imagination."[1] The British newspaper *The Observer* asked, "Is he the best storyteller ever?"[2] London's *Sunday Times* called him "inexhaustibly versatile" and a "prodigiously gifted author."[3]

But according to Peter Hitchens, Philip Pullman is "the most dangerous author in Britain."[4] The *Catholic Herald* is often quoted as saying that Pullman's books are "far more worthy of the bonfire than Harry Potter . . . and a million times more sinister." It is a reputation in which Pullman revels. He even stuck Hitchens's article on his study wall, saying, "It's a great compliment to me, isn't it?"[5] and, "Of course, I sent him a warm card of appreciation and thanks."[6] Controversy is good for a book's visibility—and sales. But Pullman enjoys comments like this for another reason. He openly admits, "I'm trying to undermine the basis of Christian belief."[7] Hitchens recognizes this and it distresses him. Leonie Caldecott, the *Catholic Herald* writer, recognizes it too, but her tongue was firmly in her cheek when she wrote the now infamous comment about bonfires. She was not actually saying that *any* books are worthy of the bonfire, but rather that the heated opposition to Harry Potter in some Christian circles in America was directed at a fairly insignificant target compared to what Pullman was writing.[8]

Why does Pullman's work excite people to such strong feelings? Most obvious is the sheer quality of his writing with its enchanting inventiveness, rich use of language, striking and well-honed phrases, vivid characterization and fast-paced, exhilarating plots. *Publishers Weekly* praised Pullman for being "a master at combining impeccable characterizations and seamless plotting, maintaining a crackling pace to create scene upon scene of almost unbearable tension,"[9] while Robert McCrum wrote in *The Observer*, "As well as giving his readers stories that tick with the precision, accuracy and grace of an eighteenth-century clock, he also writes like an angel."[10] According to Andrew Marr, the trilogy is destined to become a classic: "*His Dark Materials* will be being bought, and pulled dog-eared from family bookshelves, in 100 years' time. That is so because of a quality of writing that makes one think in turn of Milton . . . but also of Dickens and Tolkien."[11] Pullman is constantly compared with Tolkien, and also with C. S. Lewis. For many people *The Lord of the Rings* and the Chronicles of Narnia are the greatest British fantasy stories of the twentieth century. Pullman cannot bear either series, but to be considered at the same level shows how highly people think of him.

PARADISE RETOLD

Philip had already found success and acclaim as a children's author before anyone had heard of *His Dark Materials*. Fifteen of his books and two plays had been published before *The Golden Compass* hit the shelves in 1995. Since then, he's written six more books, besides *His Dark Materials* and *Lyra's Oxford*. He's become a major force in the literary world and in 2004 was named a Commander of the Order of the British Empire for his services to literature.[12] Two years previously he won the Eleanor Farjeon Award for his "crusading advocacy" of the children's book world. Pullman said: "I'm delighted by this prize because it's unlike other awards—it's not for a single book, but for something more long-term than that; and I'm honoured to be following in some highly distinguished footsteps. It's nice to get an award that doesn't always go to a writer, too—a general children's book world recognition."[13]

But in 1993, Philip had a conversation with his editor, David Fickling, then with Scholastic Publishing, which would eventually lead to Pullman's life being transformed. When he told Fickling that he wanted to do Milton's

Paradise Lost for teenagers, his editor immediately encouraged him to develop the idea. Pullman says:

> Off the top of my head I improvised a kind of fantasia on themes from Book 2 of *Paradise Lost*. And [Fickling] got quite excited because he loves *Paradise Lost* as well. By this time I knew the kind of thing I wanted to do—I knew the length, I knew it was going to be in three volumes and I knew it was going to be big and ambitious and enable me to say things I'd never been able to say in any other form.[14]

He began work on the first volume, *The Golden Compass*, and many ideas came together easily. But something about it was still not working as he redrafted the first chapter again and again, until "one day I found myself writing the words 'Lyra and her dæmon' and that was the key."[15] The first part of the story was published in 1995 as *Northern Lights* in the United Kingdom and as *The Golden Compass* in the United States.[16]

It was a huge success with readers and critics alike, attracting readers of all ages and in many countries. *The Guardian* describes it as "an eye-widening fantasy, a scorching thriller and a thought-provoking reflection on the human condition." Pullman was already hard at work on the second volume, *The Subtle Knife*, which followed two years later. By this time many fans were desperate to get their hands on the third volume of the trilogy,[17] *The Amber Spyglass*. Eventually one of them sent Pullman an anonymous letter with a picture of a squirrel and a note saying:

> I enclose a picture of a very cute squirrel.
> Please admire it.
> Now that you have admired it, I want you to remember your book, which the world has spent eons waiting for.
> Please admire the squirrel again.
> Cute squirrel, isn't it?
> Now, release your book or the squirrel dies.

Pullman finished the first draft of *The Amber Spyglass* in 1999, and it was published the following year. During a promotional tour following publication, Philip often told audiences about the letter. Several people approached him claiming to be the author of the note, or to be the author's friend. He didn't believe any of them until a teenager named Sophie spoke to him and asked why he had misquoted her letter—he had substituted the words "so long" for "eons" as he thought the word might not mean much to younger members of the audience. She presented him with a plastic squirrel with a knife through it, which he keeps on a shelf in his study.[18]

This shows the level of devotion that some people feel to Pullman, and especially to *His Dark Materials*. There is a global army of loyal fans—adults as well as teenagers—and a number of Internet fan sites delivering news, background information, discussion boards, fan art and more.[19] Then there are *His Dark Materials* related role-playing games[20] and fan sites in other languages (French, German, Portuguese and Russian at least).

Thanks to *His Dark Materials,* Pullman has become one of the most significant writers in the English-speaking world—a far cry from the obscurity of being a teacher in Oxford. He has sold more than seven million copies in thirty-seven languages as well as in audio books. BBC Radio 4 broadcast a major dramatization to considerable acclaim in 2003, and London's National Theatre staged an extraordinary two-part adaptation in late 2003 and 2004,[21] which the archbishop of Canterbury called "a near-miraculous triumph."[22] In the BBC's 2003 poll of Britain's favorite book, The Big Read, *His Dark Materials* came in at third place—the highest position for any living author.[23] *The Golden Compass* won the Guardian Children's Fiction Award and the Carnegie Medal.[24] *The Amber Spyglass* won the Children's Book of the Year[25] and the Whitbread Prize for 2001—the first time that a children's author had won this major literary award. Jon Snow, chair of the Whitbread judges' panel, said: "The wind was against Pullman, possibly because you feel that a literary prize is going to be for something exceptional, and you don't necessarily think of the children's genre as doing that."[26] But it only took the judges two minutes to unanimously agree that *The Amber Spyglass* deserved to win the overall prize. Boyd Tonkin, literary editor of *The Inde-*

pendent, said that "those two minutes will resonate in British publishing and literature for many decades."[27]

ALL-ENCOMPASSING

A key element in the appeal of *His Dark Materials* is the dazzling breadth of Pullman's story and its complexity. He weaves into the narrative powerful themes and big philosophical issues that engage any active mind: growing up, wisdom, separation, misuse of authority, freedom, responsibility, consciousness, God, the meaning of life and more besides. Millicent Lenz says:

> *His Dark Materials* interweaves an engrossing, breath-taking adventure story with a deeply felt examination of existential questions, such as Mrs. Coulter's anguished plea to know whether God is, as Nietzsche asserted, "dead," or why, if he still lives, he has grown mute. In his bold willingness to take on this and other "big" questions . . . Pullman differs from more timid contemporary writers.[28]

It has often been suggested that what marks out a literary novel is ambiguity—not tying everything up in a neat plot resolution, having gray areas as well as black and white. *His Dark Materials* delivers ambiguity in abundance. Think for instance of Lord Asriel's character, or even of Mrs. Coulter's in *The Amber Spyglass;* think of the veil Pullman draws over the grove where Lyra and Will express their love for each other; the mystery still surrounding Dust; or the questions about dæmons that persist even at the very end of the trilogy. For older readers there is plenty to reflect upon with these and many other issues.

The less satisfying elements are when Pullman leaves no ambiguity. The example most frequently commented on is his portrayal of the church as unremittingly awful. In London's *Sunday Times,* Nick Thorpe drew attention to "the almost pantomime evil of his churchmen, who are conspicuously lacking in . . . redeeming features."[29] Related to this, several critics have complained that *The Amber Spyglass* gets bogged down in the philosophical issues, and crosses the line from storytelling into propaganda for Pullman's atheistic worldview. Peter Hitchens commented that after the first two "captivating and clever" books, *The Amber Spyglass* is "a disappointing clunker . . . too loaded down with propaganda to leave enough room for the story."[30] Sarah Johnson called *His Dark Materials* "the most savage attack on organised religion I have ever seen."[31] Minette Marin sides with Pullman in calling herself a "godless scientific materialist," but laments, "This third book is frostbitten in parts by the freezing fingers of didacticism; overt didacticism is death to art; the magic of stories is too elusive for moralising."[32]

MIXED MESSAGES

Pullman denies that he is trying to communicate a moral or philosophical message:

> It's a story, not a treatise, not a sermon or a work of philosophy. . . . I'm showing various characters whom I've invented saying things and doing things and acting out beliefs which they have, and not necessarily which I have. The tendency of the whole thing might be this or it might be that, but what I'm doing is telling a story, not preaching a sermon.[33]

On his own website, Philip writes:

> As a passionate believer in the democracy of reading, I don't think it's the task of the author of a book to tell the reader what it means. The meaning of a story emerges in the meeting between the words on the page and the thoughts in the reader's mind. So when people ask me what I meant by this story, or what was the message I was trying to convey in that one, I have to explain that I'm not going to explain. Anyway, I'm not in the message business; I'm in the "Once upon a time" business.[34]

But he does admit that he is attempting to explore the big issues:

> In the hearts of many, many people there is a longing for significance, for meaning, for answers to the question, "Why? What's it all about? Why are we here? What have we got to do?" and so on. "What hap-

pens when we die?" and so on. In writing *[His Dark Materials]*, I was not trying to give answers to these questions, but to give expression to the questions. . . . Clearly this resonates with a lot of people.[35]

These protests highlight a tension in Pullman's comments on his work. On the one hand, he denies having a message; on the other, his uncompromising antireligious stance is far more explicit in *His Dark Materials* than in any of his previous books.

I think the resolution of this tension is probably to be found in the fact that writers always communicate their worldviews whether they intend to or not (unless, perhaps, they make a deliberate attempt to write from the perspective of another worldview). So Pullman, having decided to explore some of the great themes that were important to him from *Paradise Lost*, William Blake and other sources, wrote a story about a little girl who grows up *in the context of* a cosmic struggle against the idea of God. As the plot progresses, this becomes less of a background feature and more part of the plot itself. It is almost inevitable that Pullman would express some of his own animosity toward religion through the mouthpiece of his characters. He may not have *intended* to do so in such a blatant fashion, but he has nevertheless ended up with a story that expresses his worldview very clearly.

THE MAN WHO KILLED GOD

But who is the man behind the stories? Philip is tall, balding and middle-aged and still has the look of a teacher about him with his spectacles, sports jackets and penchant for vividly colored socks, shirts and ties. He and his wife, Jude, a former teacher turned hypnotherapist, have been married for over thirty years. They have two grown-up sons—Jamie, a professional viola player, and Tom, currently doing postgraduate studies in linguistics at Cambridge—and a grandson, Freddie. Philip is an unassuming, mild-mannered and genial man with a sharp mind and a lively curiosity about all kinds of things. It is partly this breadth of interest that makes his books so enjoyable. His enthusiasm is infectious when talking about something that particularly fascinates him.

When I talked with him we disagreed about a number of subjects, but he gave the impression of relishing the intellectual cut and thrust of our discussion. His deep antipathy toward Christianity does not seem to have come about as a result of a negative personal experience of the church. In childhood, at least, it was quite the reverse. Philip considers his grandfather, a Church of England rector, to be the most important influence on his life. In childhood he accepted everything his grandfather believed. But in time Philip lost any confidence he had in this: "As I grew up and began to look around and see how other people thought about things, and read books and so on, naturally I began to question this, as people do. And I eventually came—after a lot of swinging this way and that, and trying things out—to the position I hold now."[36]

Pullman acknowledges that God may be out there somewhere, but insists that he has seen no evidence for his existence:

> I'm caught between the words "atheistic" and "agnostic." I've got no evidence whatever for believing in a God. But I know that all the things I do know are very small compared with the things that I don't know. So maybe there is a God out there. All I know is that if there is, he hasn't shown himself on earth.
>
> But going further than that, I would say that those people who claim that they do know that there is a God have found this claim of theirs the most wonderful excuse for behaving extremely badly. So belief in a God does not seem to me to result automatically in behaving very well.[37]

This conviction that God is at best irrelevant to life, and that religious people have used their beliefs to justify intolerance and cruelty, drives much of the plot of *His Dark Materials* as well as at least part of Philip's real life—he is a supporter of the British Humanist Association and the National Secular Society. To say that Philip's naturalist worldview "drives much of the plot" suggests that I *do* see this as one of the central messages that come through *His Dark Materials*, despite Pullman's protests.[38] His comment quoted above that he is "trying to undermine the basis of Christian belief" would tend to confirm this, as would his statement "My books are about killing God."[39]

This is important in our reading, not just of *His Dark Materials,* but of Pullman's other works too, because it helps us as readers to see how Pullman expresses *himself.*[40] But it is equally important not to focus on this issue to the exclusion of others. I have already listed several themes that will be addressed in this book, and it is vital to let Pullman speak for himself on these issues rather than simply force them into the grid of his "anti-Christian agenda."

It is important that we allow Pullman's values to be seen—many of them, it turns out, are quite consistent with a Christian worldview. Philip says: "We must be cheerful and not go round with a face like a mourner at a funeral. It's difficult sometimes, but good will is not a luxury: it's an absolute necessity. It's a moral imperative."[41] Here he shows that, unlike many contemporary writers, Pullman is not a moral relativist. The centrality of values like these makes *His Dark Materials* a very life-affirming story in many ways. Another moral imperative for Pullman is to be hopeful. His optimism about people shines through: "When you look at the news sometimes, you despair. But then you look at the achievements of the human race and you feel optimistic again. . . . I think I'm 51 per cent optimistic. I think I have to be. . . . It's a moral duty, isn't it, to be optimistic?"[42]

2

PHILIP PULLMAN
Places and People

Philip Nicholas Outram Pullman was born on October 19, 1946, in Norwich, England, the son of an RAF fighter pilot, Alfred Pullman, and his wife, Audrey.[1] Although in many ways his childhood was very unsettled, he looks back on it with great warmth. He recalls vividly some of the experiences and places of his childhood. On his website he describes a moment of joy as a young child—an incident that he later worked into *The Broken Bridge*:

> My mother was hanging out some washing on a sunny day, and singing, as happy as a lark. The wind was chasing fat white clouds through the blue sky, and the sheets on the line billowed like the clouds, big fresh-smelling moist clouds that swelled and flapped and swung up high. The song my mother was singing filled the sheets and the clouds and the immense blue beaming sky, and I felt so light that I too might swing up and be blown along in the wild blue splendour; and she took me and swung me up, high up among the snowy-white sheets and the billowing clouds and the wind and the song and the endless dazzling sky, and I shouted and sang for joy.[2]

VOYAGES OF DISCOVERY
When Alfred Pullman was posted to Southern Rhodesia (now Zimbabwe), the family, including Philip's younger brother Francis, went too and some new experiences were lodged deep inside Philip's mind:

Sometimes my father would take us to the compound, where the Africans lived, to see a boxing match. . . . In the evening the most beautiful smell in the world, roasting mealies (corn on the cob), would drift out from the compound into the place where the white people lived. I loved that smell so much that when years and years later I happened to smell it unexpectedly in a street market in London, where someone was roasting mealies to sell, I found tears springing to my eyes.

Alfred Pullman died when Philip was just seven. His mother remarried two years later to another RAF officer and the family moved to Australia for eighteen months. This traveling gave him some great experiences:

I'm very thankful that I lived at a time before universal air travel meant that I didn't have a chance to realize how big the world is. . . . When you go by sea, you know how far it is, because it's taken you a long time to get there. And the weather changes on the way as you go over the Equator. It gets calmer, it gets hotter, the sea gets stiller, and you go down towards the Cape of Good Hope and the sea changes colour and it becomes green and blue and the waves change shape. There'll be much longer waves [so] that the ship plunges up and down as well as rocking from side to side. . . . If you have felt in your body the difference between the Southern Hemisphere and the Northern Hemisphere, you really have experienced it. And so a lot of my childhood was spent doing that.[3]

He recalls, "Nothing was more exciting than making a landfall."

After days of steadily beating through the sea, the ship would alter its motion; the ever-present creak would quieten; even the light would change; there'd be a different smell in the wind: trees, vegetation, swamp. We would all crowd to the rail and watch the line of land come closer and turn into a mountain, a city, a port—a foreign land! With foreign faces on the quayside, and a strange language in the air, and advertisements for unheard-of drinks and cigarettes on the hoard-

ings. They even rowed their boats around the harbours differently—
short choppy strokes in this place, long graceful sweeps in another.
We would go ashore and spend strange money on souvenirs of sewn
leather or carved wood, or ride in a taxi with open windows through
which boys threw flowers as they ran along beside us.[4]

LOVE OF THE LANDSCAPE

Returning to Britain meant new school experiences for Philip: first a prep
school in London, and then, when the family moved to Llanbedr in North
Wales, a school in Harlech. Ysgol Ardudwy is close to the beach and almost
opposite the imposing thirteenth-century Harlech Castle—a fantastic location to be at school. It was not easy being a new boy at school—he was
rather rootless after the various upheavals of his early childhood, and he got
into a fight on his first day because of his English accent. But he soon settled
in and looks back with great fondness for those carefree days:

My friends and I seemed to be free in those days to wander where we
liked: the woods, the wide hills, the miles of beach were open to us,
and the edge of our playground was the horizon. We roamed the hills
and broke into a derelict house where the last occupant had left a
Welsh Bible and a set of false teeth on the kitchen table. We made go-
carts, or trucks as we called them, and hauled them up slopes (there
were plenty of those) and hurtled down recklessly. We dared each
other to walk past the Hanging Tree in the clearing in the woods at
night. We swam in the sea; we swam in the river; we invented a new
sport, waterfall climbing. We put pennies on the railway line and re-
trieved them, flat and distorted and shiny, after the train had gone over
them. We hung about the bus shelters in the local town on Saturday
night, spying on the lovers. We went to the tiny cinema in the next village and came back on the last bus, running down to the bus stop
clutching bags of chips from the fish-and-chip shop, losing our foot-
ing, skidding along on the gravel with the chips held triumphantly to

our chests. We held spitting contests out the window of the school train. We held grass-bomb fights at night: a handful of grass and a careful tug, and you had a very satisfactory clump of earth to hurl through the air at the dimly seen enemy across the field. We teased the short-tempered pig in the farmyard by the river. We put fireworks on the roof of the ladies' toilets. We howled like banshees in the garden of cross old Mr Pugh till he came out and chased us away. . . .

I drew obsessively, the landscape, mainly: the massive rounded hills, the wide pearly estuary, the tumbled sand dunes, the dry stone walls, the ancient church half-buried in the sand. I learned that landscape by drawing it, and I came to care for it with a lover's devotion. Later in *The Broken Bridge* I wrote about a girl making the same discoveries, loving and drawing the same landscape. Many other strands went into the making of that book, but what lay at its heart was love; it's a love letter to a landscape.[5]

PHILIP'S OXFORD

After leaving school in 1965, Philip studied English at Exeter College, Oxford. It was the obvious thing to do after enjoying English at school and having such a flair for it. But he didn't enjoy studying English at Oxford at all. He says he never mastered the "coherent, focused, disciplined sort of reading which I imagine you need to do if you want an academic career. . . . I couldn't do it then, and I don't do it now."[6] In fact, discipline in studying doesn't seem to have been a strong point then at all, although he is an extremely disciplined writer now.

Although the academic side of university life was not a great success (he finished with a third-class degree, indicating that his grades were not high), the experience of being a student in Oxford made a huge impact on him. Writing about his time at Exeter College, Pullman says: "I had a group of idle friends who occupied their time and mine betting on horses, getting drunk, and sprawling about telling creepy tales."[7] Some aspects of his time there were later incorporated into *His Dark Materials*, and Lyra's origins in Oxford are an important part of her sense of identity. Exeter College formed the basis for the fictional Jordan College, although Pullman made Jordan the biggest, best and grandest of colleges. Lyra's rooftop escapades were based on real incidents, as Pullman recalls:

> In my second year I occupied the rooms at the top of staircase 8, next to the lodge tower, and one of the friends I mentioned, Jim Taylor, discovered that you could get out of the window and crawl along a very useful gutter behind the parapet. From there you could climb in through another window further along. I gave Lyra a better head for heights than I have, but I did the gutter crawl a number of times, usually when there was a party on the next staircase.[8]

SHED MASTER

The day after Philip Pullman graduated, he started work on his first novel. It was harder than he'd expected so he moved to London and worked for a time in the men's clothiers Moss Brothers, which was, he says, "an extraordinary experience." Each lunchtime he would cross the road to write poetry in the churchyard of St. Paul's Church. After eighteen months he took a new job at Charing Cross Library, but to progress as a librarian would mean taking a postgraduate diploma. By this time, Philip had met and married Jude (Judith) Speller, and their first son, Jamie, was born the following year. Since Jude was a teacher, Philip began to think for the first time about going into teaching himself. It seemed to offer "quite a nice life with long holidays" and scope for progressing with his writing. He chose to do his teacher training in Weymouth simply because he liked the place, then returned to Oxford, where he taught in two middle schools (ages nine to thirteen) until 1986. After twelve years in the classroom, Philip Pullman became a part-time senior lecturer in English at Westminster College, Oxford, and was involved in training a new generation of teachers for eight years. Eventually he was able to give himself entirely to the business of writing.

For years, Philip wrote in a shed at the bottom of his garden—he claims it was to escape the noise of his son playing the violin. The shed seemed to be becoming famous almost in its own right. Pullman described its contents:

> manuscripts, drawings, apple cores, spiders' webs, dust, books in tottering heaps all over the floor and on every horizontal surface, about a thousand jiffy bags . . . which I'm also too mean [stingy] to throw away, a six-foot-long stuffed rat . . . a saxophone, a guitar, dozens of masks of one sort or another . . . an old armchair filled to capacity with yet more books, a filing cabinet that I haven't managed to open for eighteen months because of all the jiffy bags and books which have fallen in front of it in a sort of landslide . . . bits of chewed carpet from when my young pug Hogarth comes to visit. . . . It is a filthy abominable tip [dump].[9]

By the time I visited Philip to interview him in the autumn of 2002, the shed was history—at least for him. He and Jude moved out of north Oxford to a nearby village—a move made desirable by the increasing numbers of people turning up on his doorstep, and made possible by the extraordinary sales of *His Dark Materials*. But although a roomy study within the new—and quiet—house made the shed redundant, Philip couldn't bear to just leave it behind. Instead, he gave it to his friend the writer/illustrator Ted Dewan on condition that it was passed on to another writer or artist at the end of its service to Ted.[10] Ted removed one of the windows to use as a frame for a montage of bits and pieces from the shed, including a scrap of curtain and some of the legions of Post-It notes. Philip's study was tidier than I'd expected after reading several accounts of the shed. The six-foot rat was nowhere in sight but the walls were lined with books, and around the room were all kinds of odds and ends, mementos and things that might stimulate another story one day. I suspect it may not always stay as tidy because, since I visited, Philip has apparently also moved some of his woodworking tools in. Working with wood is his passion—he has made a rocking horse for his young grandson. He loves drawing, too, and is delighted to be learning more and more about how to do it well. He was competent enough to draw the little illustrations at the start of the chapters in *The Golden Compass* and *The Subtle Knife*.[11] He's also musical, playing the guitar and the piano, and is a great fan of the music of Nicholai Medtner.[12] He writes three pages in longhand every morning, and then the first sentence of the page for the following day, just to get him started.

A "HALF ORPHAN"

It's not just places that have made a huge impact on Philip Pullman of course, but many people too. Philip recalls the birth of his baby brother as being a rather surprising event:

> One day when I was a little boy I went out for a walk with my grandmother. There was a big pile of dark brown earthenware pipes by the side of the road for the workmen to put underground, and Granny let me clamber about over them for a while and crawl inside and out the other end. But she was anxious to go back home, and I couldn't persuade her to stay, so I went with her, reluctantly; and when we got home, who could believe it? I had a new brother. A little crying baby, of all things. Where had he come from?[13]

When his father's tour of duty in Rhodesia ended, his mother, Audrey, and the two boys went to stay with her parents in Drayton, just outside Norwich in Norfolk. But while they were there in 1953, they received a telegram informing them that his father had been killed in an air crash while fighting Mau Mau terrorists in Kenya. They presumed that he had been shot down. Philip was just seven years old.

It's hard to imagine the impact this could have on a young boy, but Pullman claims that it hardly affected him at all. In interviews he maintains that he didn't see a great deal of his father anyway, so he didn't miss him much. On his website he writes,

> I suppose that my brother and I cried, though I didn't really feel sad. The fact was that we hadn't seen my father for a long time, and apart

from the glamour surrounding him, he was a figure who hadn't played much part in our lives. So my brother and I went back out to the sunny wall, where we'd been picking off the moss and throwing it at each other, and carried on.[14]

He told Sue Lawley something very similar on BBC Radio 4's *Desert Island Discs*:

It was a drama but it was offstage. . . . So we felt that something rather grand and important had happened to us, that we were almost orphaned! . . . I don't think it was dispassionate, but maybe part of me was already thinking "Ah, so this is what it feels like to be half an orphan. That's interesting, I'll make a note of that."[15]

But at other times, Philip has acknowledged that his father's death did have consequences for him. In an interview on Amazon.com, he says,

Peter Dickinson and I were talking one day and this subject came up and we agreed how strange it was that so many children's authors had lost one or both parents in their childhood. My father died in a plane crash when I was seven, and naturally I was preoccupied for a long time by the mystery of what he must have been like.[16]

Here Pullman hints at the possibility that losing a parent can be a factor in someone's becoming a children's author. Does writing about children provide an opportunity to reexamine the feelings and questions from all those years ago? Does it help a writer to feel that something positive has finally come about through the experience of losing one or both parents? Or does it simply give the writer a sensitivity to the joys and pains of childhood that many others would not have? These are speculations, but it is interesting that several of Pullman's protagonists have also lost one or both parents. In *His Dark Materials*, Lyra believes her parents were killed in an accident; Will's father is missing, presumed dead. Outside the trilogy, Sally Lockhart has just become an orphan at the start of *The Ruby in the Smoke;* the main character, Roger, in *I Was a Rat* knows nothing about his parents; *Count Karl-*

stein has two orphan girls at the center; *The Firework-Maker's Daughter* has lost her mother, as has Ginny in *The Broken Bridge*.

HEROIC FATHER

At the very least, Pullman concedes that a substantial period of time was spent thinking about the father he feels he never knew. His father was a mystery—one that he could not let go of for some time. That doesn't seem to quite fit with saying that his father's death barely affected him. Although his father may have been away for long periods of time, at least he was *somewhere*, and would come back to the family at intervals. One imagines it would have been exciting to have a fighter pilot as a father, and family times, although rare, would be very special to a seven-year-old. Not missing his presence in the home isn't the same as not grieving. Philip could easily have lamented the fact that he hardly knew his father before the crash, as well as the impossibility of now ever getting to know him. He *knew of him* as a glamorous hero (he was posthumously awarded the Distinguished Flying Cross) but could never *know him* intimately as a father. In one interview he said, "It is a traumatic thing, but also kind of a gift, because it enables you to imagine that the father who is missing is better than the one you end up with."[17]

Nearly forty years later, after his mother had died, Philip discovered some surprising facts about his father that shattered the impressions he had always had of him:

> He hadn't been shot down in battle; he had been drinking, and he'd crashed while practising for an air display. That was the first thing I found out, and the second was even more of a shock: I learned that it was generally known among his friends that he'd crashed his plane on purpose. He'd committed suicide. That had been covered up so that he could be awarded the medal and so that my mother could receive a widow's pension. Apparently he had been in all kinds of trouble: he'd borrowed money without being able to repay it, his affairs with other women were beginning to get out of his control, and he had had

to agree to a separation from my mother. I knew none of this while my mother was alive; I've found it all out in the past few years since she died. So all my life I've had the idea that my father was a hero cut down in his prime, a warrior, a man of shining glamour, and none of it was true. Sometimes I think he's really still alive somewhere, in hiding, with a different name. I'd love to meet him.[18]

In *The Subtle Knife*, Will is also preoccupied with the heroic father he had never known. Could something of Philip Pullman's own deep—even subconscious—longings be expressing themselves in Will's search for his father?

GLAMOROUS MOTHER

Both his parents were very glamorous in Philip's eyes:

There were two kinds of glamour: my mother's, which consisted of a scent called Blue Grass by Elizabeth Arden, and my father's, which was more complicated. There were cigarettes in it, and beer, and leather armchairs. The smell of my father's glamour was very strong in the Club, which we children were sometimes allowed in, but not to run around.

But after Alfred Pullman's death, it was Philip's grandparents (along with his great-aunt who lived with them) who provided the stability and emotional support needed by the two young boys: Philip and his brother lived with them while their mother went to work in London. Audrey's life there was remote from them in many ways, not simply in terms of geography but in terms of lifestyle too. Compared to their life in rural Norfolk in the mid-1950s, they perceived her life as very sophisticated:

She worked at the BBC and lived in a flat in Chelsea, and once or twice we went to stay with her and saw another dimension of glamour. She had lots of friends, and they were all young and pretty or handsome; the women wore hats and gloves to go to work, their dresses were long and flowery, and the men drove sports cars and smoked pipes, and there was always laughter, and the sun shone every day.[19]

Something feels a little Mrs. Coulterish in this comment from Pullman; was his mother's glamour part of what lies behind this extraordinary character? When Audrey remarried, it was to a pilot from the same squadron as his father (Pullman suspects they had been having an affair before his father's death). Although it took a while to adjust to the new situation, Philip warmed to his stepfather. He says, "I was very fond of him. He was a difficult man, but there was not one moment during my childhood when he made me think that I wasn't his son."[20]

BELOVED GRANDPA

The time spent living with his grandparents had a major impact on Philip because his grandfather, Sidney Merrifield, came to be the most significant figure in Philip's childhood. He was the father figure Philip needed so much:

> Both Granny and Auntie, and my brother and I, and everyone else for that matter, regarded Grandpa as the centre of the world. There was no one stronger than he was, or wiser, or kinder. People were always calling to see him, for a parish priest was an important man, after all. He led the church services in his cassock and white surplice; he took weddings and funerals and christenings; and he was the chaplain of Norwich Prison (though I didn't find out about the prison until much later, when I was old enough).[21] When I was young he was the sun at the centre of my life.[22]

Living with his grandfather meant that church played a big part in Philip's childhood:

> [It] involved, of course, going to church and going to Sunday School and listening to Bible stories and all the rest of it. He was a very good, old-fashioned country clergyman and a wonderful storyteller, too. He knew all the stories that one should know from the Bible. So it was a very familiar part of my background and it was something that one didn't question. Grandpa was the rector, Grandpa preached

a sermon and of course God existed—one didn't even thinking of questioning it.[23]

Later Pullman came to reject the faith that his grandfather stood for. He insists that his rejection of Christianity had nothing to do with the kind of man his grandfather was—it was not a reaction against him. "That would be preposterous. I've got nothing but love and affection for his memory."[24] He says, "He was the centre of my life. He was the sun around whom my emotional life revolved as a boy."[25]

INSPIRATIONAL TEACHER

One other influence on Philip must be mentioned—the teacher who had more impact than any other on the course of his life: his English teacher, Enid Jones. She introduced him to the Metaphysical Poets of the seventeenth century (John Donne, George Herbert, Andrew Marvell and others), to Wordsworth and especially to John Milton's epic poem, *Paradise Lost*. She encouraged him in his writing too and, in the acknowledgments at the end of *The Amber Spyglass*, Pullman writes that he owes to Enid Jones "the best that education can give, the notion that responsibility and delight can coexist" (*AS*, p. 521).

3

STORYTELLING AND OTHER STORIES

Philip Pullman says he's a storyteller more than a writer:

> For me the story is paramount and the actual literary texture is secondary. That's not to say that I think the literary features are not important, because I do take great care to use words properly and have a certain grace and rhythmic propulsion. But it would be flattering, for example, to think that I had made up a story which other people could tell in different words and which would still have whatever effect it has now. I'm aiming high, but Hans Christian Andersen's tales are just as effective, just as powerful, when told by other storytellers.[1]

He enjoys the process of writing and crafting his prose, but he's desperate to tell his story to anyone who'll listen, and he's not afraid of telling his stories very straightforwardly. When he wrote in a shed, Philip had a warning stuck over his desk: "Don't be afraid of the obvious." He despairs of writers (usually of adult fiction) who feel they have to write in such a clever way that the story itself is an emaciated thing with hardly any life in it. Pullman describes them as "picking up their stories with a pair of tongs," and says: "We shouldn't be afraid of the obvious, because stories are about life, and life is full of obvious things like food and sleep and love and courage which you don't stop needing just because you're a good reader."[2] It is one of the secrets of Pullman's enormous success—he gets on with the job of telling a great yarn, and people respond to it because we love stories. No, it's more than that—we *need* stories:

Stories are vital. Stories never fail us because, as Isaac Bashevis Singer says, "events never grow stale." There's more wisdom in a story than in volumes of philosophy. . . . We need stories so much that we're even willing to read bad books to get them, if the good books won't supply them. We all need stories, but children are more frank about it; cultured adults, on the other hand, those limp and jaded creatures who think it more important to seem sophisticated than to admit to simplicity, find it harder both to write and to read novels that don't come with a prophylactic garnish of irony.[3]

LUCK

Storytellers, in common with all artists and craftsmen, need three ingredients for success: "talent, hard work and luck,"[4] and Pullman has had a good measure of all of them. By "luck" he means the things that happened *to* him, rather than things within him (talent) or that he brought about (through his effort). For example, he frequently points back to the influence of his childhood on his future career, particularly the impact of living with his grandfather. Sidney Merrifield had an ability to tell stories that brought to life the places around their home near Norwich. His stories engaged the young Philip's mind so well that they have stayed with him:

> He took the simplest little event and made a story out of it. When he was a young man in Devonshire before the First World War he'd had a friend called Fred Austin, a fine horseman, a big strong man with a fierce moustache, and he and Grandpa had joined the army together to fight in France. When Fred came home to his farm after the end of the war, the baby he'd left behind was now a little girl who didn't know him and was frightened by this big dark laughing man who knelt and held out his enormous hands for her. She ran away and hid her face, but Fred was a wise man and didn't hurry. Little by little over the next days he coaxed her and was kind and gentle, and finally she came to him trustfully. When Grandpa told that story he said that God would appear to us like that; at first we'd be alarmed and frightened

by him, but eventually we'd come to trust in his love.

Well, many years later, when Grandpa and Fred Austin were both long dead, I used to tell the story of *The Iliad* to the children I taught; and there's a part of that story where the great Prince Hector goes up on the walls of Troy to watch the battle below and finds his little son Astyanax in the arms of his nurse. He reaches for the boy, but Astyanax is frightened by the great nodding plumes on his father's battle helmet and hides his face in the nurse's shoulder until Hector, laughing, takes off the helmet and reassures the little child. Whenever I told that story, I used to think of Grandpa's story about Fred Austin. Between my childhood and now, I've lost sight of God; but Hector the Trojan prince and Fred Austin the Devonshire soldier are still brightly alive to me; and so is Grandpa.[5]

Philip was also fortunate in spending eighteen months in Australia as a young boy—it introduced him to new and exciting ways of encountering stories. At that point television had not made much impact on Australia, but the gangster and cowboy serials on the radio held him spellbound, as did Superman. He then discovered Superman comics imported from the United States, and Batman, which was even better. He says, "Comic books changed my life because I saw for the first time an entirely new way of telling stories. The combination of words and pictures, of effortlessly vivid storytelling, made me want to tell stories more than anything else."[6] As well as stories being *accompanied* by illustrations (he remembers with special fondness Tove Janssen's *Moomin* books, *The Magic Pudding* by Norman Lindsey and *Emil and the Detectives* by Erich Kästner), he was discovering that they could be told *through* pictures. He felt the urge to tell stories himself, so each night, after lights out, he made up tales for his younger brother:

> I don't know whether he enjoyed it, or whether he even listened, but it wasn't for his benefit; it was for mine. I remember vividly the sense of diving into the dark as I began the story, with no idea at all what was going to happen or whether the story would "come out" as I called

it, by which I meant make sense or come to a neat end. I remember the exhilaration of the risk: Would I find something to say? Would I dry up? And I remember the thrill, the bliss, when, a minute ahead of getting there, I saw a twist I could give to the end, a clever way of bringing back that character who'd come into it earlier and vanished inconclusively, a neat phrase to tie it all up with.[7]

TALENT

Later, back in Britain, Philip's English teacher, Enid Jones, saw his talent and began to nurture it. He developed his skills through writing poetry, and though he later decided that his "real goal was not writing poetry but story-telling,"[8] it gave him solid foundations for being a first-class writer. Through writing poetry he developed discipline in writing, a feel for rhythm and a feel for the importance of word sounds. Philip sees his time studying English at Oxford University as a wrong move ("I should have gone to art college"). But, confident of his talent, his grand plan was to start a novel the day after his final exams and finish it within a couple of months. He thought it would be published quickly and make him a millionaire when the film rights were sold.

> So I bought a big book to write in: three hundred pages of beautiful smooth lined paper in a stout binding, like a family Bible; and I sat down on the first morning of my life-after-education and began to write. And before I'd got to the end of the first paragraph, I'd come up slap bang against a fundamental problem that still troubles me today whenever I begin a story, and it's this: where am I telling it from? Imagine the storytelling voice as being like a camera. A film director has to decide where to put the camera and what it's going to look at, and it's the same with the storytelling voice. . . .
>
> I was like the centipede who was asked which foot he put down first. I couldn't move. There were so many possibilities, and nothing to tell me which was the right one. What a shock! I had passed

through the entire British education system studying literature, culminating in three years of reading English at Oxford, and they'd never told me about something as basic as the importance of point of view in fiction! Well, no doubt it was my fault that I got a poor degree; but I do think someone might have pointed it out. Perhaps it had been covered in one of those lectures I hadn't found my way to.

What I couldn't help noticing was that I learned more about the novel in a morning by trying to write a page of one than I'd learned in seven years or so of trying to write criticism. From that moment on, my respect for novelists, even the humblest, has been considerably greater than my respect for critics, even the most distinguished.[9]

EFFORT

Once Philip had begun working at Moss Brothers, his writing was confined to the evenings and he began to learn the importance of serious, disciplined effort. It was at this time that he developed his practice of writing three pages every day. He eventually gave up on that first novel, but his second, *The Haunted Storm*, tied for first prize in a competition run by the publishers New English Library. It was published in 1972 when Philip was just twenty-five— he was very pleased with it: "I thought winning would change my life, but of course it didn't. Nothing happened. The book came out and it was completely ignored because it was terrible. I've kept quiet about it ever since."[10]

Claire Squires describes *The Haunted Storm* as "a weird narrative concerning murder and incest, and features a Gnostic cleric and a 23-year-old ridden by existential angst."[11] Pullman says he wrote it "out of a sense of duty, rather than conviction," and felt "glum and resentful" about it.[12] A second novel for adults, *Galatea* ("a picaresque, magic realist tale . . . populated by a profusion of characters including zombies, automata and 'Electric Whores'"),[13] followed in 1978, by which time Pullman was a teacher.

DEVELOPING HIS CRAFT

Teaching gave Philip the opportunity to develop the craft of storytelling, as well as familiarity with children's language, and insight into their emotional development. He realizes how fortunate he was to be teaching at a time when he was free to teach as he thought best without the constraints of Britain's National Curriculum, targets and testing.[14] "I was able to tell and learn and get to know dozens of myths and folk tales. It was the making of me as a storyteller."[15]

> I would tell them *The Iliad* and *The Odyssey*, all the way through. Whatever the children were getting out of it, I was getting several valuable things. Not least the thing that writers don't always have in a technical sense, which is a set of exercises—like a musical exercise. . . . There's no real equivalent in the literary arts. But I found one, and it's telling stories—the same stories, over and over, but not from the same words, always fresh, always speaking them—without a book or any props. . . .
>
> With storytelling you can learn so much about timing and also the kind of writer you are. You can find out what you're good at and what you're not. I'm not good, as I discovered, painfully, at telling funny stories that make people laugh—not aloud, that is. What I can do is evoke an atmosphere, I can paint a picture in the mind's eye. I can make it exciting, so that people will want to know what happened next. . . . That was the most valuable thing I ever got out of my years of teaching.[16]

One of his former pupils is poet Greta Stoddart, who recalls, "He had an extraordinary energy. And he didn't need books. He would come in and just launch into some story. He had this great mane of long, wavy hair that he would scrape back with his long fingernails—he kept them long to play the guitar. And he had that very direct stare that stays just a little longer than you'd expect. All of us girls were a bit in love with him."[17] On one Pullman family holiday, they ate in a restaurant each day. Each evening, as they waited for their meals to arrive, Philip told his second son, Tom, the story of *The Odyssey*. On the final evening Tom was so excited that he bit a chunk out of the glass he had been gripping, startling the poor waitress so much she dropped the food she was bringing to their table.

Teaching also gave Philip the chance to take his storytelling skills in a new direction—by writing plays for the pupils to perform. It was vital to him that they should entertain both children and parents; his ability to write for a wide audience is a large part of his appeal now. The first play was *Spring-Heeled Jack*, "a sort of melodrama, with an outrageous villain and larger-than-life heroes and comic policeman and that sort of thing."[18] He was beginning to find his groove as a writer: "I thought 'I am really enjoying this! I like this way of telling a story. It's grotesque, absurd and not realistic, but it is really good fun!' . . . This was where my imagination was active instead of sullen and glum."[19]

A little later Pullman realized that he could rework some of the plays into books—he was making his transition from being a writer of adult fiction to being a children's writer, though he insists that he tells stories for everyone:

> My ideal . . . is the old notion of sitting in a marketplace, where all kinds of other transactions are going on around me. People are buying food and selling food, and somebody doing tricks over there in the corner, and the pickpocket over there, and there's a public hanging over in the corner, all sorts of stuff. And there I am on a bit of carpet with a hat in front of me, telling a story. And whoever wants to stop and listen is welcome to do so. I do not put up a sign saying "this story is only for twelve-year-olds" or "no children welcome here" or "only women need be interested in this story" or anything like that. I don't want to exclude anyone, because as soon as you say "this story is for such and such a group," what you're actually saying as well is "this story is not for anybody else." I don't want to do that. I would like to tell the sort of story which brings children from play and old men from the chimney corners, as somebody used to say. I'd like to tell a story which is entertaining and interesting, in necessarily different ways, but nevertheless to all kinds of people and all different age groups.[20]

BROUGHT TO BOOK

The first play to become a book was *Count Karlstein or the Ride of the Demon*

Huntsman (1982). It was followed by *The Ruby in the Smoke* (1985)[21]—a reworking for older readers of a play called *The Curse of the Indian Rubies*. It was with this book that he "first found the voice that I now tell stories in,"[22] and he enjoyed the characters so much it became the first of the Sally Lockhart quartet.[23] His first play, *Spring-Heeled Jack*, was published four years later in 1989, and by that time a second story about Sally Lockhart had been published—*The Shadow in the North* (1986).

Pullman has a deep fascination with the nineteenth century, as these books show. He jumped at the opportunity of a part-time lectureship at Westminster College, Oxford, where he taught a course on Victorian novels. He is particularly drawn to the Victorian East End of London. It was a seedy area, which Pullman brings vividly to life—and you can't help feeling that he enjoys himself enormously as he does so. It forms the background for the Sally Lockhart stories, *Spring-Heeled Jack*, the two *New Cut Gang* books[24] and *I Was a Rat . . . or the Scarlet Slippers* (1999). "Wapping and Limehouse and so on are attractive because of their long-standing associations with crime, foreign sailors, sinister opium dens, etc."[25] The ominous-sounding (but apparently invented) location of Hangman's Wharf in Wapping appears in at least three unrelated books because it nicely captures the combination of crime and commerce.[26]

However, Philip's love of the nineteenth century is not confined to London's more violent neighborhoods. He is also drawn to German Romanticism, and this combines with both his love of folk tales and his enthusiasm for stories with pictures (two other courses he taught at Westminster) in *Count Karlstein* and *Clockwork or All Wound Up* (1996).[27] He refers to both of these as "fairy tales," though they are darker than the three classic fairy tales that he has retold for a new generation (*Aladdin and the Enchanted Lamp* [1995], *Mossycoat* [1998] and *Puss in Boots* [2001]). Pullman believes fairy tales (and myths) are vital because of what, and how, they teach us: "Fairy tales . . . are ways of telling us true things without labouring the point. They begin in delight, and they end in wisdom. But if you start with what you think is wisdom, you'll seldom end up with delight—it doesn't work that way round. You have to begin with fun."[28]

Pullman considers *Clockwork* to be the best of his short books.[29] The inspiration came from an old clock in London's Science Museum:

> I thought it would be fun to try and write a story in which one part turning this way connected to another part and made it turn that way, like the cogwheels of a clock. And when it was all fitted closely together, I could wind it up and set it going. . . . Of course, it had to be spooky too, because old clocks are, somehow.

The tale features a writer who abandons telling his story partway through, and an apprentice clockmaker who has been too lazy to produce the traditional final work of the apprenticeship—a new mechanical figure for the town clock. The writer's story and the reality of the apprentice's situation interlock in a very clever and creepy way. Pullman draws parallels between clocks and stories to talk about the business of storytelling,[30] and about "the inexorable nature of responsibility."[31] *Clockwork* touches on talent and luck as helping toward success, but stresses the effort involved: "Here's the truth: if you want something, you *can* have it, but only if you want everything that goes with it, including all the hard work and the despair, and only if you're willing to risk failure."[32]

Another of his fairy tales, *The Firework-Maker's Daughter* (1995), winner of the 1996 Smarties Book Prize Gold Award, also addresses these themes.[33] Like *Count Karlstein*, it started as a play.[34] Pullman always wanted to incorporate new theatrical tricks into his school plays, and one year decided he wanted fireworks (he's very enthusiastic about fireworks—in 2002 he had his stepfather's ashes scattered by launching them in forty rockets). Inspired by some stage designs he had seen in a library for a play called *The Elephant of Siam, or the Fire-Fiend* by nineteenth-century dramatist William Moncrieff, Philip constructed a story that gave him "bright lights and blazing rockets and loud bangs . . . gamelan music! Gongs and xylophones and lots of dancing—and masks—and an elephant!"[35] Later he revised the story and turned it into a book, and in doing so "realised the real meaning of the story. . . . I realised I was telling a story about the making of art."[36] The firework maker says, "You need talent and dedication and the favor of the gods before you can become a Firework-maker."[37]

TELL THEM STORIES

It is clear that Philip's passion for stories is not merely *why* he writes, but is also one of the key strands of *what* he writes. Like *Clockwork, I Was a Rat . . . or the Scarlet Slippers* is a story *about* stories, spinning off from the story of *Cinderella* and satirizing the media's sensationalist storytelling.[38] *Spring-Heeled Jack*, the two *New Cut Gang* books and the Sally Lockhart quartet are all inspired by the stories in Victorian "penny dreadfuls." They also feature in the Sally Lockhart books—one of the central characters, Jim Taylor, is a great fan of them.[39] *The Ruby in the Smoke* is the story of Sally Lockhart trying to piece together the story of her father's death, but in the process discovering shocking new stories about her own life. *The Shadow in the North* contrasts "spin" (public stories) with the real, behind-the-scenes stories of arms production and poverty. *The Tiger in the Well* sees Sally apparently defenseless against a maliciously untrue story, which results in her daughter being taken from her. *The Tiger in the Well* also has much to say about the political stories told about refugees, and one of the major characters, Daniel Goldberg, is a Jewish journalist. *The Tin Princess* revolves around the secret untold stories and the official cover-ups of a small central European principality.

Pullman's two books of teen fiction set in the contemporary world are also largely about stories. The plot of *The White Mercedes* turns on the stories that the key characters tell each other—as well as the stories they don't.[40] And the way that stories shape our lives is explored with great pathos in *The Broken Bridge*.[41] The central character, Ginny, has to reexamine her sense of who she is as a result of discovering that some of the stories of her early life are untrue. The stories that other people relate affect her deeply, and she fashions a story of her own to try to make sense of all she is discovering. But it is Pullman's most ambitious work, *His Dark Materials*, which explores the importance of stories and storytelling most fully.[42] Lyra is herself a consummate storyteller, and it is something very close to her heart. As she tells a story in the suburbs of the world of the dead, "part of her felt a little stream of pleasure rising upward in her breast like the bubbles in champagne" (*AS*, pp. 261-62). Whether or not Pullman feels this sensation, he relishes stories and storytelling. And he understands how vital they are to us. One of the messages of *The Amber Spyglass* is that we should live so that we have true and exciting stories to tell at life's end.

Pullman says, "Stories are the most important thing in the world. Without stories, we wouldn't be human beings at all."[43] Stories are how we construct our internal models of the world around us, whether they be creation myths or scientific theories.[44] Stories are how we make sense of who we are as people. Stories help us work out how to live:

> All stories teach, whether the storyteller intends them to or not. They teach the world we create. They teach the morality we live by. They teach it much more effectively than moral precepts and instructions. . . . We don't need lists of rights and wrongs, tables of do's and don'ts: we need books, time, and silence. "Thou shalt not" is soon forgotten, but "Once upon a time" lasts forever.[45]

4

HIS RAW MATERIALS

Philip Pullman's approach to writing is to "read like a butterfly, write like a bee."[1] He draws on many influences both consciously and unconsciously since all kinds of images and ideas lodge in a writer's mind to resurface years later. He gathers source material from all kinds of places, ranging from ancient esoteric beliefs to popular science, from Greek mythology to the popular Australian TV show *Neighbours*.

The esoteric beliefs have strongly influenced Pullman's portrayal of God and the angels. These are mainly Gnostic ideas (some shared with the Jewish cabala), especially as they have come to us through the Western esoteric tradition.[2] In contrast, the science is right up to date—dark matter, many worlds, the problem of consciousness, superstring theory, quantum entanglement and more—forming an important part of the background throughout *His Dark Materials*.[3] Greek myths show up particularly in the world of the dead with the boatman[4] and the harpies.[5] It's impossible to identify any specific *Neighbours* influences but Philip says:

> After lunch I always watch *Neighbours*. Soap operas are interesting because there's no limit to the length a story can have—it can go on for months, if it's got some life in it . . . it's fascinating to watch some characters gaining story-potency as others lose it, and to try and work out why it's happening. . . . It's all pure story: one thing following another.[6]

There are rather more sophisticated influences on *His Dark Materials*, including the Metaphysical Poets (especially George Herbert and Andrew

Marvell), Plato,[7] Augustine,[8] Dante,[9] Keats,[10] Byron,[11] Wagner,[12] Emily Dickinson[13] and plenty more. There are hints of voodoo (*zombis*, Specters and spy-flies) and many biblical ideas, the most significant being the Fall—the first rebellion of humanity against God. Pullman does not believe the Bible, but he values its language and stories nevertheless.[14] The exit from the world of the dead echoes Christ's harrowing of hell—a traditional Christian idea of Jesus descending to Hades after his crucifixion in order to proclaim redemption to the dead and to lead out the faithful to eternal life.[15] Pullman, however, inverts this by portraying "the faithful" as so deluded that they would rather stay in the world of the dead (*AS*, p. 321).

However, there are three key influences on much of Pullman's work that he draws attention to in the acknowledgments at the end of *The Amber Spyglass*: Heinrich von Kleist's essay *On the Marionette Theatre*, John Milton's *Paradise Lost* and the works of William Blake.

John Milton (1608-1674): *Paradise Lost*

Pullman was sixteen, studying for his college entrance exams, when he first read *Paradise Lost*.[16] He immediately fell in love with it: "I found it intensely enthralling, not only the actual story . . . but also the landscapes, the power of the poetry and the extraordinary majesty of the language."[17]

Paradise Lost is a landmark in the development of English literature. No one had written this kind of epic poem in English before. It's a huge poem written by a blind man as he witnessed the failure of a dream—Milton had supported Cromwell's Protectorate, and passionately opposed the restoration of the monarchy. In that context, Milton wanted to remind people of why the world was in the state it was: life is a mess because it's a fallen world, and it's fallen because there is an enemy both of God and of humanity.

Milton retells the story of the first three chapters of Genesis, focusing particularly on the actions of Satan in rebelling against God and instigating the Fall of Adam and Eve. It opens in hell where Satan, once a great angel named Lucifer, and his rebel army are licking their wounds after their rebellion was defeated. They decide that their best strategy is to take revenge by sabotaging the new world that God has created. Satan finds his way to the Garden of Eden—Paradise—and spies on Adam and Eve. He becomes jealous and decides to corrupt them. Having failed to get into the garden once, he enters a snake so that he can gain access undetected by the angel guards. Once inside, he tempts Eve to eat the one fruit that is off-limits to them. Adam follows suit and they immediately become aware and ashamed of their nakedness. Sin and Death, Satan's children, learn of his success so they build a bridge from hell to earth. Now under God's judgment, Adam and Eve are banished from the garden. The archangel Michael explains to them the consequences of their sin for the world, and also the reality of a coming Savior who will rectify the relationship between God and his people. Angels guard the entrance to prevent Adam's and Eve's return.

First disobedience. These themes of rebellion and fall are of enormous importance to Pullman. Given his love of *Paradise Lost* from his teenage years, it is no surprise that he eventually wanted to work it into a story. Dark matter was going to be a major part of his trilogy, so when he was scanning *Paradise Lost* for a phrase that would make a good title, "His dark materials" leaped out at him.[18] Milton's story of the angelic rebellion against God is the most important element in the backstory of *His Dark Materials*. Lord Asriel is explicitly attempting to conclude what he sees as unfinished business. The trilogy never addresses the question of what has happened to the character of Satan. Pullman's alternative "creation myth" casts the Sophia—Wisdom— as the instigator of the initial rebellion.[19] This seems to be because Pullman has taken Milton's story and mixed it with the Gnostic ideas of Sophia. In any event, Satan's role is shared by both Lord Asriel and Mary Malone.

Asriel plays the Satanic role of rebel leader, though this time the rebels are not just angels. King Ogunwe says, "This is the last rebellion. Never before have humans and angels, and beings from all the worlds, made a common cause. This is the greatest force ever assembled" (*AS*, p. 210). However, we don't learn any of this until early in *The Subtle Knife*. Perhaps because of this, Milton's influence on the latter two volumes seems more obvious than it does on *The Golden Compass*. We begin *The Amber Spyglass* knowing that the great conflict is drawing near. When the storm does break, the focus is so much on the characters we have been following that the great battle is little more than a rather blurred background. We hear nothing more from the battle once Will and Lyra have escaped into the peace of another world.

Mary Malone, meanwhile, plays Satan's other role of tempter, in the gentle world of the mulefa. In a clever twist, Pullman has another character sneak into the world in an attempt to sabotage the second Fall, which is about to happen. Since Pullman unequivocally sees this second Fall as the *right* thing, the ghastly Father Gomez is perhaps more analogous to Satan's sabotaging of Paradise than Mary Malone is. Pullman has turned upside down Milton's sense of who the good guys are.

Satanic reverses. In interviews, Pullman loves to quote William Blake's comment on Milton: "The reason Milton wrote in fetters when he wrote of angels and God, and at liberty when of devils and hell, is because he was a true poet and of the devil's party without knowing it."[20] Blake felt that Milton's description of Satan in *Paradise* Lost was much more sympathetic than his description of God, though unwittingly so. Shelley and Byron later took up this idea themselves, as has Pullman, who enjoys adding, "I am of the Devil's party and I know it."[21]

The problem is that this reading of Milton focuses too strongly on the first four (of twelve) books of *Paradise Lost* (Pullman in fact only read Books I and II when he first encountered it and formed his basic opinions). The other eight books (especially Books V to VIII) significantly reverse the picture. Satan is portrayed in heroic terms—in Books I to IV he boasts about his part in the battle against the forces led by Michael, claiming to have almost defeated them. But in Books V and VI, we discover that he hadn't even come close to this— Milton is deliberately undercutting the heroic ideals. During the battle, an angel, Abdiel (like Balthamos, he is "not of a high order among angels"—*AS*, p. 11), confronts the vastly more powerful Satan and strikes a blow that makes Satan stagger back ten paces. The rebel angels are amazed and furious "to see / Thus foil'd thir mightiest" by a humble foot soldier.[22] Later, Satan meets Michael in combat. Michael's sword, "temperd so, that neither keen / Nor solid might resist that edge" (the inspiration for the subtle knife?) slices right through Satan and wounds him deeply—his first experience of intense pain. Rebel angels rush to his defense and carry him back to his chariot, and:

> there they him laid
> Gnashing for anguish and despite and shame
> To find himself not matchless, and his pride
> Humbl'd by such rebuke, so far beneath
> His confidence to equal God in power.[23]

C. S. Lewis[24] says that Satan undergoes "progressive degradation" during *Paradise Lost*:

> He begins by fighting for "liberty," however misconceived; but almost at once sinks to fighting for "Honour, Dominion, glorie and renoune" (VI, 422). Defeated in this, he sinks to . . . ruining two creatures who had never done him any harm, no longer in the serious hope of victory, but only to annoy the Enemy whom he cannot directly attack. . . . This brings him as a spy into the universe, and soon not even a political spy, but a mere Peeping Tom leering and writhing in prurience as he overlooks the privacy of the lovers, and there described . . . simply as "the Devil" (IV, 502)—the salacious grotesque, half bogey and half buffoon, of popular tradition. From hero to general, from general to politician, from politician to secret service agent, and thence to a thing that peers in at bedroom or bathroom windows, and thence to a toad, and finally to a snake—such is the progress of Satan.[25]

Given Milton's Christian faith, it seems much more likely that Milton initially *wanted* his readers to sympathize with Satan so that they see the attractiveness of rebellion against God, and how willingly we are led down that route, *so that* we see more clearly God's mercy to us.

WILLIAM BLAKE (1757-1827)

However, Blake's influence on Pullman goes much deeper than these views on Milton. The American edition of *The Amber Spyglass,* curiously, has a longer quotation from Blake's *America: A Prophecy* in place of the hymn lines from Robert Grant. Pullman says: "I love Blake in the way I love all great poetry—because of the sound it makes, and because of the meanings that follow the sound. I love the *Songs of Innocence and Experience,* and *The Marriage of Heaven and Hell,* and some passages from the Prophetic Books."[26]

Songs of Innocence and Experience is probably Blake's most accessible work. The move from innocence to experience is central in *His Dark Materials,* but it is important to realize that Pullman doesn't mean quite the same thing by the words. Blake's world of *Innocence* is pleasant, sunny, pastoral— it's safe. *Experience,* however, is dark, wild or urban, and hostile. The landscapes of *The Golden Compass* fit more naturally with Blake's world of *Experience* than with *Innocence* (it's an adventure story so there has to be danger after all). There are several nighttime scenes: the retiring room, Lyra being secretly summoned to the Master's study, escaping from Mrs. Coulter, finding Tony Makarios, and the escape from Bolvangar. Other landscapes echo *Experience* in their wildness—from the remote fens of East Anglia,[27] through the dark forests of the north, to the wildness of Svalbard. In contrast, the landscape of the mulefa in *The Amber Spyglass* feels distinctly pastoral—it's a gentle, safe world (barring occasional tualapi attacks), which seems to echo the world of *Innocence.*

But for Blake, it's not so much the settings themselves that show the difference between *Innocence* and *Experience*—it's how things are *perceived.* In "Little Girl Lost" and "Little Girl Found," for example, the lost girl Lyca and her parents respond to wild animals in opposite ways.[28] She sleeps contentedly while the lion "gambolled round," whereas her parents are terrified until they come to see the lion with fresh vision. It's perhaps comparable to the ways in which Lyra and the gyptian leaders initially view Iorek Byrnison. Lyra is completely trusting of him, whereas John Faa and even Farder Coram are inclined to believe the story that "he's a dangerous rogue" (*GC,* p. 190). Similarly, when the alethiometer tells Lyra that Will "is a murderer" (*SK,* p. 28)—which would put most people off—Lyra's perception is that *therefore* she can trust him. And when Lyra realizes that her enemies perceive Dust as bad, she concludes that *therefore* it "must be good" (*GC*, p. 397). Perception is also important in, among other things, Lyra's reading of the alethiometer, Will's use of the knife and Mary's seeing of her dæmon in which she has to maintain a special state of mind combined with "ordinary seeing at the same time" (*AS*, p. 505)—a double vision that Blake strongly believed in.

Violent authority. Which brings us to another key difference: in *Innocence*, authority is protective; in *Experience*, it is cruel and repressive. Although Blake's passionate sense of solidarity with the oppressed leads him to attack several targets (not least commercial interests and the state), it is the church that bears the brunt of his stinging criticism. Blake portrays it as authoritarian and hypocritical, and he has a deep antipathy to God (at least as Blake sees him expressed in the Old Testament). Like Milton, he focuses especially on the Fall. He often highlights God's punishment of Adam and Eve, not their rebellion, and seems to put the blame for the rift between God and humanity firmly on God. Blake's poem "Earth's Answer" portrays God as the "selfish father of men" characterized by "cruel jealous selfish fear," who makes life on earth "dread and drear."[29] It sees his punishment of Adam and Eve as an "eternal bane" that puts "free love" into bondage. "A Poison Tree" goes further to suggest that God was secretly hostile to humanity, and deliberately set a trap into which Adam and Eve would inevitably walk so that he could blame and punish them.[30]

In his "Prophetic Books," Blake developed an alternative creation myth in which he presented God as a vicious tyrant.[31] It may well be that the breadth and complexity of this radical perspective lodged in Pullman's mind, later resulting in him developing an alternative myth of his own. In these books, Blake has two key characters, Urizen (who represents God) and Orc: "On the one side stands Urizen, a violent, destructive tyrant; on the other side Orc, a violent, destructive rebel."[32] They could very easily be the Authority and Lord Asriel. Pullman says, "I certainly wouldn't model any of my characters on any of [Blake's], or on anyone else's for that matter. It would be too limiting. In Blake's own words, 'I must create my own system, or be enslaved by another man's.'"[33]

Tyranny and freedom. However, while he may not have modeled his characters on Blake's, nevertheless his perspective closely matches Blake's, and he is open about Blake's influence on him. The parallel between Asriel and Orc extends to the deep ambiguity of character that some people have been surprised at in Lord Asriel. Pullman clearly sees Asriel as on the "right side"—working to establish the republic of heaven by overthrowing the Authority and his kingdom. Yet at the same time he is just as cold and ruthless as the agents of the Authority—he is prepared to go to any lengths to achieve his goal, including sacrificing Roger. Like the Authority he opposes, Lord Asriel is violent and destructive and arrogant. Like Orc, he also carries within him the seed of tyranny that would have expressed itself had he survived the great battle. He has the makings of a megalomaniac when he claims to Mrs. Coulter, "You and I could take the universe to pieces and put it together again" (*GC*, p. 396). And Thorold doesn't exactly present him as egalitarian in response to Serafina Pekkala's question about Lord Asriel's intentions: "You don't think he told me, do you? . . . I'm his manservant, that's all. . . . He wouldn't confide in me any more than in his shaving mug" (*SK*, p. 45).

Blake attacks the church for its complicity in tolerating injustice—in "The Chimney Sweeper," for example, in which a child sweep complains that "God and His priest . . . make up a heaven of our misery."[34] In other words, the church promises heaven to us if we put up with misery now. "The Garden of Love" focuses on the loss of innocence at the hands of the church:

> I went to the Garden of Love.
> And saw what I never had seen;
> A Chapel was built in the midst,
> Where I used to play on the green. [35]

It starts with the "innocent, uninhibited discovery of sexuality between children. However, the speaker is now aware of Church law, and sex is surrounded by bans, punishment and statutes which are enforced by a watchful priesthood."[36] Now the garden "that so many sweet flowers bore" has at its center a closed chapel with "Thou shalt not" written over the door. The rest of the garden is full of graves,

> And priests in black gowns were walking their rounds,
> And binding with briars my joys and desires.

The feeling of joyless, authoritarian lifelessness is unmistakable. The church's repressive attitude to sexuality is something with which Blake takes particular issue. In response, in *The Marriage of Heaven and Hell*, Blake orders "the cherub with his flaming sword[37] . . . to leave his guard at [the] tree of life."[38] He wants to return us to the state of affairs before the Fall—a state of sexual freedom that "will come to pass by an improvement of sensual enjoyment." Other poems ("The Blossom" and "The Sick Rose," for example) make the same point that natural sexuality, free from prudery and religious constraints, is something to be desired.

The echoes of Blake are easily discernible within Pullman's work. Like Blake, Pullman attacks what he sees as a repressive and cruel church, which feeds people a lie about heaven in order to keep them quiet.[39] He rails against a vicious God who imposes arbitrary and unnatural restrictions on humanity—and especially on our sexuality. It's no accident that Will and Lyra finally express their love for each other in a world where there is no church, and after the death of the Authority.

HEINRICH VON KLEIST (1777-1811): ON THE MARIONETTE THEATRE

Heinrich von Kleist was born in Frankfurt into a family of Prussian soldiers. He dutifully joined the army but left after five years to study science, philosophy and literature. Kleist's confidence in reason was shattered when he discovered the writing of Immanuel Kant, who maintained that human reason cannot discover the true nature of things—we can only rely on appearances. Kleist wrote plays (mostly tragedies) and short stories, but found little recognition. A business failure ruined him, and, with no one producing his plays and the army refusing to take him back, he committed suicide.[40]

A year previously, in 1810, Kleist published his essay *On the Marionette Theatre*.[41] It is a conversation about grace,[42] self-consciousness and the Fall. The narrator of the story[43] meets a friend who is a dancer, and expresses surprise at the dancer's interest in the marionette theatre, calling it a "vulgar species of an art form."[44] But the dancer asserts that puppets are more graceful than human dancers. Their advantage, he says, is that the arms and legs are lifeless pendulums, which simply follow the movement of the puppet's center of gravity—they can therefore never be guilty of affectation. A human, however, is so self-conscious that it's impossible to do anything without some measure of artificiality. The narrator recalls a very graceful teenage boy he had known. The boy had noticed a similarity between his posture and a certain statue, but when the narrator laughed at this he became self-conscious for the first time and soon all his grace was gone. But still the narrator protests that a puppet could never be more graceful than a person. "[The dancer] countered this by saying that, where grace is concerned, it is impossible for man to come anywhere near a puppet. Only a god can equal inanimate matter in this respect."[45]

To make his point about the benefits of lacking self-consciousness, the dancer recalls a time when he beat a friend in a fencing match. The friend challenged him to try fencing with a bear that was being reared on the friend's farm. The bear was an extraordinary opponent:

> It wasn't merely that he parried my thrusts like the finest fencer in the world; when I feinted to deceive him he made no move at all. No human fencer could equal his perception in this respect. He stood upright, his paw raised ready for battle, his eye fixed on mine as if he could read my soul there, and when my thrusts were not meant seriously he did not move.[46]

From this the dancer makes the point that "as thought grows dimmer and weaker, grace emerges more brilliantly and decisively."[47] The bear is more "graceful" because it has no self-consciousness. The less self-consciousness there is, the more gracefulness there can be: "Grace appears most purely in that human form which either has no consciousness or an infinite consciousness. That is, in the puppet or in the god." This was Pullman's inspiration for Iorek's demonstration that bears cannot be tricked (*GC*, pp. 226-27). Iorek, of course, is not just any old bear—he is fully conscious, but perhaps (since he has no soul) he is not self-conscious like a human would be.

The dancer says that this problem of self-consciousness is unavoidable "now that we've eaten of the tree of knowledge.[48] But Paradise is locked and bolted, and the cherubim stands behind us. We have to go on and make the journey round the world to see if it is perhaps open somewhere at the back."[49] In other words, now that we have partial knowledge and self-consciousness, there is no way back; all we can do is continue pursuing knowledge until it is total. Blake has the same idea when he says, "If the fool would persist in his folly he would become wise."[50] "Only a god can equal inanimate matter," says the dancer, because "this is the point where the two ends of the circular world meet." The narrator asks if this means "that we must eat again of the tree of knowledge in order to return to the state of innocence?" "Of course," replies the dancer, "but that's the final chapter in the history of the world."[51]

FULL CIRCLE

The incompatibility of grace and self-consciousness appears again at the end of the trilogy, after Lyra has become the second Eve and brought about a second Fall. Lyra has reached a new level of consciousness about herself—and her skill with the alethiometer deserts her. Xaphania tells Lyra that she has read it by grace; now she must learn all over again through hard work: "But your reading will be even better then, after a lifetime of thought and effort, because it will come from conscious understanding. Grace attained like that is deeper and fuller than grace that comes freely, and furthermore, once you've gained it, it will never leave you" (*AS*, p. 491). Here Pullman seems to mix up the way Kleist uses the word "grace" (talking of a natural ease of doing something) with its theological sense of the undeserved kindness of God. Reading the alethiometer *by grace* sounds theological—and in a sense it is, though Dust, rather than God, has given Lyra her ability. But grace in this sense cannot be earned or worked at; grace in Kleist's sense can be, and he relates this to the Fall. Pullman says:

> Grace is a mysterious quality which is inexplicable in its appearance and disappearance. It's disappearance in Lyra's case symbolizes the loss of innocence but the fact that she can regain it through work and study symbolizes the fact that only when we lose our innocence, can we take our first steps towards gaining wisdom.[52]

In other words, having lost her innocence she has lost her grace.[53] When Lyra returns to Oxford the Master recognizes that her "unconscious grace had gone, and how she was awkward in her growing body" (*AS*, p. 514). But by a lifetime of effort she can regain it in a new and better way—she can come back to paradise by the back door.

PART TWO

The World(s) of
His Dark Materials

5

THE GOLDEN COMPASS

The opening of *The Golden Compass* is instantly gripping: "Lyra and her dæmon moved through the darkening hall, taking care to keep to one side, out of sight of the kitchen" (p. 3). So many questions clamor for attention within the very first sentence. Who's Lyra? What's a dæmon? Where is this hall? Why is she so furtive? From the outset there's an air of mystery and adventure. And the mention of the dæmon is unsettling—does it mean "demon"? Is it evil or good? Why is it "*her* dæmon"? This one sentence is enough to set the tone of the trilogy and give us the sense that Lyra's world is not like ours.

Lyra is "a barbarian" (p. 34), "a coarse and greedy little savage," and like "a half-wild cat" (p. 36) who prefers adventuring on college roofs, disturbing tutorials, stealing apples and waging war against the more civilized aspects of life in an Oxford college. She's a typical child, living for the moment and full of curiosity. But Lyra is approaching puberty and *His Dark Materials* is, more than anything else, a story about growing up. It's about moving from innocence to experience, and taking responsibility for our actions and destinies. It's about becoming fully conscious and finding true knowledge.

LYRA THE LIAR

Lyra's character, though not her name or any details, had been in Pullman's mind for years. As a child he read *A Hundred Million Francs* by Paul Berna, and was struck by a drawing of some of the characters—including a young girl:

> She was a tough-looking, very French sort of character, with a leather jacket and socks rolled down to her ankles and blonde hair and black

eyes, and altogether I thought she was the girl for me. I wouldn't be at all surprised—in fact, now I think about it, it's obvious—to find that the girl on page 34 of *A Hundred Million Francs* is the girl who four decades later turned up in my own book *Northern Lights* [*The Golden Compass*] . . . where she was called Lyra.[1]

Pullman says Lyra "had her name from the very beginning. I don't know where it came from."[2] But perhaps its subconscious origins are, at least partly, from Lyca, the subject of William Blake's poems "The Little Girl Lost" and "The Little Girl Found."[3] The similarity of sound between "Lyra" and "liar" becomes critical in one of the most important moments in Lyra's life in *The Amber Spyglass*. It's entirely appropriate because Lyra sees spinning tales as her greatest talent. She uses this skill to escape the ire of scholars and college servants, as well as to enthrall the gang of kids with whom she fights townies, brick burners or gyptians. Her flair for lying becomes invaluable when she finds herself under the watchful eyes of Mrs. Coulter and her golden monkey dæmon, then later at Bolvangar and on Svalbard. But once away from Oxford, Lyra seems to respond very positively to integrity when she perceives it in others. She feels that John Faa and Farder Coram must be told only the truth, and she quickly realizes that trying to deceive Iorek Byrnison is futile. It is ironic that Lyra the liar is the one entrusted with an instrument for finding the truth, the alethiometer. It is partly through her encounters with the consciousness behind this instrument that she eventually grows to value truth so highly.[4]

Lyra's moral engagement with the world seems to be complicated by her having a dæmon—though we come to realize that their relationship externalizes the internal dialogues that we all experience. Pantalaimon functions in some ways like Lyra's conscience—that's certainly how he comes across at the beginning of the trilogy. But it's not that simple—Lyra has to challenge Pantalaimon's ethics when he advocates keeping their noses out of any attempt to poison Lord Asriel. She tells Pan they have a duty to stay now that they know what the Master intends to do, and asks him, "You're supposed to know about conscience, aren't you?" (p. 9). Without being explicitly told, we realize that Lyra and Pan are one, and yet distinct. They are two aspects of one person, one shared consciousness, knowing each other's thoughts and feelings, and yet in some ways they are two separate beings.[5] Pantalaimon has almost magical shape-shifting abilities[6]—one of many ways in which metamorphosis runs through the story. But hanging over Lyra and Pan is an impending reality that, like Peter Pan, they are not yet ready to face: the time is soon coming when Pan's form will become fixed and Lyra will no longer be a child.

PLAYING WITH WORLDS AND WORDS

Dæmons are the biggest difference between Lyra's world and our own, but there are many more and Pullman has plenty of fun with them. Her home is "the grandest and richest of all the colleges in Oxford" (p. 34). Pullman writes:

> Jordan College occupies the same physical space in Lyra's Oxford . . . as Exeter College occupies in real life, though rather more of it. I didn't see why I shouldn't make my college the biggest of them all. Jordan . . . has developed in a haphazard, piecemeal way, and for all its wealth, some part of it is always about to fall down, and is consequently covered in scaffolding; it has an air of jumbled and squalid grandeur.[7]

The name Jordan was prompted by an area of our Oxford called Jericho, past which flows the Oxford Canal. Pullman says that although real-life Jericho is "thoroughly respectable," it "has always struck me as having a hidden character, more raffish and jaunty altogether, with an air of horse-trading, minor crime, and a sort of fairground Bohemianism. That is the Jericho I describe in the story."[8] The gyptians who ply the canal and hold fairs at Jericho get their name from *Egyptian* because gypsies (in our world) were first believed to have come from Egypt. Pullman plays a number of similar games with words. For example, Lyra is fond of drinking *chocolatl*—many dictionaries will tell you that this is how the Aztecs pronounced their word for the drink made of cacao beans;[9] synthetic materials (derived from fossil fuel

products) are referred to as coal silk; the underground in London is called
the *chthonic* railway—*chthonic* means "relating to the underworld." A more
involved example is *anbaric* lighting (the main power source being *atom-craft*—nuclear energy), which is supplanting traditional naphtha lamps.[10]
It's obvious that *anbaric* means *electric*—but why? Our word *electricity* comes
from *electrum*, the Latin name for amber (used in early experiments with
static electricity). In Lyra's world they continue to use this Latin name, *electrum*, for amber (*SK*, p. 57). But their word for electricity derives from *anbar*,
the Arabic word, which came into English as *amber*. The two root words
have been used in opposite ways in the two worlds. There are many more
examples, some of which are documented on various Internet fan sites.[11]

One place in Jordan College where naphtha lighting will definitely not be
replaced is the Retiring Room into which Lyra's curiosity finally takes her. It's
a comfortable, well-furnished room, full of traditions: "only Scholars and
their guests were allowed in here, and never females" (p. 4); here the Master
cooks after-dinner poppy for the scholars.[12]

Lyra barely has time to look around before she is hiding first behind a
chair, then in the Retiring Room wardrobe. This was the first idea Philip
Pullman had for the story: "I started with a picture of Lyra hiding in the
wardrobe, and overhearing things that she wasn't meant to hear. And I had
pictures of other things in the story—the bear in armour, and the witches
coming up through the clouds."[13] A number of critics have commented on
the parallel between this scene and Lucy hiding in a wardrobe in *The Lion,
the Witch and the Wardrobe*.[14] Pullman, who is vehement in his criticism of
the Chronicles of Narnia, insists that it was accidental: "I didn't notice the
parallel till it was too late to do much about it. Actually I didn't mind, because you could see this story as being a sort of riposte to the worldview
Lewis puts in front of us in Narnia."[15]

INNOCENCE MEETS EXPERIENCE

Lyra, of course, doesn't go through the wardrobe into another world. But as
she stays within it and attends closely to the evening's activities, another

world begins to open up—thanks to the arrival of Lord Asriel. Lyra believes him to be her uncle—her only relative after the death of her parents in an air accident. Like Pullman's father, a remote yet glamorous fighter pilot, Lord Asriel is an occasional figure in Lyra's life, but with a very definite air of glamour. Asriel is described as "a tall man with powerful shoulders, a fierce dark face, and eyes that seemed to flash and glitter with savage laughter. It was a face to be dominated by, or to fight: never a face to patronize or pity. All his movements were large and perfectly balanced, like those of a wild animal, and when he appeared in a room like this, he seemed a wild animal held in a cage too small for it" (p. 13). He's a "high-spirited man, quick to anger, a passionate man" (p. 121). His dæmon, Stelmaria, is a snow leopard: exotic, powerful, graceful and dangerous.[16] Asriel is an explorer, a scientist and a member of the Cabinet Council advising the Prime Minister (p. 10). He cares nothing for social status or rank—the gyptians owe him their allegiance because of his help politically, and because of his heroism in saving the lives of two gyptian children (p. 135).

Lord Asriel's affair with the high-spirited and passionate Mrs. Coulter, and his attempt to hush up the birth of their child, led to him killing Edward Coulter—apparently with scarcely a second thought (p. 132). This coldness is a key ingredient in his character. There's no warmth in his interactions with Lyra at Jordan College—perhaps just the barest hint when he tells her about the vast area of college below the ground. The one time in *The Golden Compass* when it matters to him that Lyra is his daughter is when she arrives at his house on Svalbard. He is horrified to see her, crying, "No! No! . . . Get out! Turn around, get out, go! *I did not send for you!*" (p. 364). But although he is dismayed, we somehow can't escape the feeling that if Roger wasn't with her, Lord Asriel would even sacrifice his own daughter to make his bridge possible. Nothing and no one will divert him from his great task, though the nature of his mission only becomes clear in *The Subtle Knife*.

Lyra had "always had a dim sense that . . . somewhere in her life there was a connection with the high world of politics represented by Lord Asriel" (p. 36). But in the Retiring Room wardrobe her curiosity is aroused by the over-

heard conversation, which touches on the biggest issues of the day. Politically, Lyra's world is radically different from our own. Tartars[17] from Siberia
are pushing westward and have invaded Muscovy[18] (p. 10); there have recently been the Skraeling wars[19] (*SK*, p. 121) in Beringland (Alaska in our
world); and warfare in Tunguska (p. 193), which is in Siberia (Iorek Byrnison and Lee Scoresby had fought there together). But the political landscape
is dominated by the church. In Lyra's world the Reformation never happened; instead of John Calvin becoming one of the most influential reformers of the sixteenth century, he became pope:

> Ever since Pope John Calvin had moved the seat of the Papacy to
> Geneva and set up the Consistorial Court of Discipline, the Church's
> power over every aspect of life had been absolute. The Papacy itself
> had been abolished after Calvin's death, and a tangle of courts, col-
> leges, and councils, collectively known as the Magisterium,[20] had
> grown up in its place. (p. 30)

The Magisterium has a very Jesuit feel to it. The dominant force within it
is the Consistorial Court of Discipline, but it's the new General Oblation
Board ("a semi-private initiative" directed by Mrs. Coulter), which we hear
most about in *The Golden Compass*. The Magisterium is the government, at
least in Europe, and controls almost everything with an iron fist.[21] Even science is under church control: physics is called experimental theology[22] and
radical theories are treated as heresy by the church.

Lord Asriel causes a stir with his "photograms" of streams of Dust and of
the Aurora (pp. 21-22). It's immediately apparent that Dust is a controversial
subject. Asriel's slides are also controversial because they clearly show the
existence of another world. This is an abhorrent idea to the Magisterium,
which refers to it as the "Barnard-Stokes" heresy after the two "renegade" experimental theologians who proposed that such worlds must exist (p. 30).
By coolly showing his two slides made using the special Dust-sensitive
emulsion, Lord Asriel puts himself right at the center of the controversy and
divides the scholars. His slides demonstrate that there is a connection be-

tween the Dust the Magisterium so fears and the heresy of other worlds that it refuses to countenance.

SEVERING AND SEPARATION

Lyra's insatiable curiosity has taken her to the edges of enormous political and theological turmoil. In her naiveté she finds it all terribly exciting and wants to join Lord Asriel as he leaves for the north. He refuses, telling her "the times are too dangerous" (p. 28). But it's not until the General Oblation Board swings into operation that Lyra realizes just how close to home danger will come. Children disappearing in other parts of the country makes the basis for a good game, but then Billy Costa disappears, and by the time Lyra and others have spent hours searching, Roger too has gone. Before Pullman tells us about this he introduces us to the work of the Gobblers, or of one in particular—a beautiful woman with a golden monkey dæmon enticing Tony Makarios away from his home and befuddled mother.

This is the point at which Pullman introduces a key strand that runs right through *His Dark Materials*—separation and division. Marina Warner, in her book *Fantastic Metamorphoses, Other Worlds*,[23] says that there are four kinds of metamorphosis in myths, fairy tales and fantasy: *mutating* (a key ability of dæmons), *hatching* (which only happens with Gallivespian dragonflies in *His Dark Materials*), *doubling* (Pullman doubles individuals by giving them dæmons; the Specters are also doubled when the subtle knife cuts between worlds) and *splitting*. This is the transformation which Pullman makes most use of—he calls it "binary fission" and says it is "something in the whole nature of the story, as well as in the underlying structural pattern."[24]

Again and again, the narrative is pushed on by some form of splitting. At this stage of *The Golden Compass* it introduces the clear and present danger of the Gobblers, separating prepubescent children from their homes and families for reasons we cannot yet begin to guess. Pullman takes time to show us how located Tony Makarios is—Limehouse is his home; his mother may not know what's going on, but she remains his mother; running errands and stealing from market traders is his life. But he is torn away from all this forever, thanks to the magnetism of the woman.[25] Ironically, it is the Master's concern to protect Lyra from the danger of the Gobblers that results in both her own separation from home and substitute families, and her movement toward the heart of the danger. Later at Mrs. Coulter's party, Lyra overhears that her new guardian is behind the Gobblers and she flees, separating herself from her new life and, though she doesn't know it, from her mother. Eventually we find out the gruesome nature of the General Oblation Board's experiment at Bolvangar and see that it is splitting once again—the wonderful shape shifting of the dæmons cruelly cut off by the process of "intercision." Each person whose dæmon has been severed has either died or "has— the well-known consequences of splitting—been evacuated of selfhood and become a zombie."[26] What the Board doesn't know—but Lord Asriel does— is that this process of severance releases vast amounts of energy. He uses this energy to bridge to another world (another example of "doubling") and in doing so not only separates himself from his world and his manservant, he also separates Roger from life and Lyra from her friend. It's the pain of this which ultimately drives Lyra to the world of the dead and her own agonizing disconnection from Pantalaimon.

THE POWER OF STORIES

While she's at Bolvangar, Lyra reflects that one of the zombie nurses "would be able to stitch a wound or change a bandage, but never to tell a story" (p. 238). She contrasts starkly with Lyra's life and energy and storytelling talent. As we saw in chapter three, Pullman enjoys putting storytelling in the foreground of his stories, and this is true of *His Dark Materials* too, not least by making his main protagonist an accomplished storyteller herself. In chapter three of *The Golden Compass*, Pullman describes how the story of the Gobblers grows and develops and mutates once children have begun to disappear (p. 45). However, the focus on stories within *The Golden Compass* is found in the section covering Lyra's time with the gyptians.

The day after Tony Costa and Kerim rescue Lyra from the Turk traders and she is safe on the Costas' boat, she "clumsily collected her story and shook it into order as if she were settling a pack of cards ready for dealing" (p. 107). As Lyra begins her story, Tony cuts in with his own stories of the terrors of the north—Tartars eating children, Nälkäinens, Breathless Ones and *panserbjørne*.[27] At the Roping, Lyra gets to meet John Faa,[28] lord of the western gyptians, and Farder Coram. Lord Faa is a man with innate authority and great reserves of strength. Lyra recognizes in him something of the qualities she has seen in the Master of Jordan and Lord Asriel, and instantly respects him. He may not be educated but he is a wise, brave and effective leader. Farder Coram, Lord Faa's adviser, seems to have little physical strength left, but is knowledgeable and very wise. The depths of Farder Coram are reflected in the extraordinary coat of his cat-dæmon, Sophonax. They believe it's important that Lyra knows her own story: "I'm a going to tell you a story, a true story. I know it's true, because a gyptian woman told me, and they all tell the truth to John Faa and Farder Coram. So this is the truth about yourself, Lyra" (p. 121).

Why Lord Asriel had wanted Lyra to know nothing of her true origins is unclear—perhaps just part of his attempt to keep her away from Mrs. Coulter. But as a result of the untrue story that Asriel made people tell Lyra, she grew up entirely unaware of her parents and of how much she owed to Ma Costa and other gyptians. Now "Lyra had to adjust to her new sense of her own story, and that couldn't be done in a day" (p. 130). There are echoes of Pullman's own story here. He started writing *The Golden Compass* in the early 1990s, sometime around, or soon after, the death of his mother. It was while he was subsequently sorting through her papers that Philip unearthed things about his parents that he had never known. His discoveries were not on the scale of what Lyra is told, but something of the same reorientation of perspectives must have taken place.

GRACE AND AUTHENTICITY

While Lyra is coming to terms with new stories about herself, she is also coming to terms with the alethiometer. In a sense the alethiometer is a story-telling instrument. As Lyra frames a question in her mind by pointing three of the arrows to symbols, the alethiometer responds by indicating a sequence of symbols and the appropriate level of meaning. From the sequence, Lyra can discern the meaning—a message from the conscious matter of the universe that tells her about past, present or future. It's an extraordinary experience for Lyra—"a sensation of such grace and power that Lyra, sharing it, felt like a young bird learning to fly" (p. 151). It's more than just a feeling of grace; she is reading it *by* grace (as we saw in chapter four). Dust is communicating freely with Lyra by enabling her to see the meanings in a way that is easy, natural, graceful. Instinctively Lyra knows that the alethiometer tells only the truth, and she argues the point passionately when the gyptian leaders are reluctant to try to employ Iorek Byrnison.

Our first encounter with the bear is full of tension:

> Lyra had an impression of bloodstained muzzle and face, small malevolent black eyes, and an immensity of dirty matted yellowish fur. As it gnawed, hideous growling, crunching, sucking noises came from it.
> . . . Lyra's heart was thumping hard, because something in the bear's presence made her feel close to coldness, danger, brutal power, but a power controlled by intelligence; and not a human intelligence, nothing like a human. (p. 179)

The pitiful circumstances in which Lyra finds Iorek once again has to do with separation. He is divided from his home and his rightful kingdom; even worse, he is cut off from his armor and thus his sense of purpose and dignity. But he is still a creature of integrity and has an extraordinary awareness of the properties of metal, manipulating it with graceful ease. Lyra again witnesses the grace of the bear when she fences with him. We see it again in his confrontation with Iofur Raknison who is marked not by grace but by affectation. Iofur coveted everything about human society—wealth, grandeur, learning—and yearned to have a dæmon. Not for him the uncomplicated life of a *panserbjørn* who makes his own soul by fashioning his armor out of sky (meteoritic) metal. He wanted a dæmon so badly that he carried around a doll as a substitute. Pullman draws very starkly the incongruity of this by his attention to the filth and stench and the uncertain behavior of Iofur's subjects. Iofur Raknison's pretensions to be human moved him from grace to self-consciousness, and so made him vulnerable to being tricked. The clash of Iorek and Iofur is much more than Iorek regaining his throne, and the way Pullman describes the conflict draws attention to its significance.[29] Here are two competing stories about what armored bears are, "two futures, two destinies" (p. 349). This is Kleist's contrast of grace versus artificiality—or truth versus lies: "Iorek Byrnison . . . was more powerful, more graceful, and his armor was real armor, rust-colored, bloodstained, dented with combat, not elegant, enameled, and decorative like most of what she saw around her now" (p. 326).

The contrast of authentic with inauthentic is an issue to which Pullman turns again and again. Central to the whole story is the inauthentic authority of the Magisterium and ultimately of the Authority himself. In *The Golden Compass*, we only see that of the Magisterium, and this is set off in opposition to two groups of people: the gyptians and the witches.

Gyptians are strong, tough and principled. They are on the fringes of society with their own secret ways and rich traditions, and so they are no friends of the Magisterium. Instead they have a deep goodness, which transcends the moral character of every Magisterium representative we see in the story. As do the witches, who also add to the mix an alternative spirituality: one which is bound up with the natural world. In their extraordinary but unaging beauty, minimalist clothing despite the cold, unrefined adornment of "a simple chain of red flowers" and effortless flying (on branches not broomsticks), everything about the witches speaks of grace. Gyptians and witches (and perhaps even the *panserbjørne* under Iorek's kingship) serve a similar purpose in the story. Pullman wants us to see them as genuine, open, unaffected, wholesome, pure. They have authentic traditions that go back centuries to a time before—in Pullman's view—all the extraneous nonsense of Christianity came in and cut people off from their deep roots. They all show that it's possible—even desirable—to live good lives of integrity entirely independent of such things.

Lyra is without her parents, she's away from the Master and the scholars, so representatives of gyptians and witches provide Lyra with what she needs as she grows up: surrogate parents, role models and perspectives. John Faa and Farder Coram give her new perspectives that enable Lyra to grow up with a true understanding of her past. Serafina Pekkala knows the prophecy about Lyra's future. She cannot tell Lyra, but once they have met, Serafina will do everything in her power to protect Lyra and help her to fulfill the prophecy. It is important that they meet again at the end of the trilogy so that they can testify both to the growth that has taken place and to the fulfillment of destiny.

6

THE SUBTLE KNIFE

Reading chapter one of *The Subtle Knife* straight after *The Golden Compass* might induce a sense of lostness. The grandeur of Jordan College, the cold beauty of the north and the feisty young heroine with her extraordinary friends are all missing. Instead we find ourselves in a Winchester residential development with a boy we've never heard of, struggling to cope with his unbalanced mother. He hasn't even got a dæmon! After one book within an alternative world, Pullman takes us back into "the universe we know"[1]—and in some ways it feels alien. We've grown used to dæmons communicating personality, but in our world they're nowhere to be seen. And in contrast to Lyra's magical world, Winchester residential developments are, frankly, dull.[2] Chapter two comes as a relief (despite its sinister beginning): Serafina Pekkala brings a sense of normality, and she goes on to play a major role in this book.

WILL POWER

Will Parry is a troubled, serious boy who is old beyond his years. We first meet him taking his mother to the home of Mrs. Cooper. She's a kind old lady who realizes that Will needs help and, in the face of his solemn determination, trusts that he is acting for the best. Clearly Will's mother has mental health problems. She appears to be psychotic,[3] believing that enemies watch her every move. Her psychosis seems to stem from severe depression as a result of her husband, John, disappearing when Will was a baby. Will was just seven when he first realized that he had to look after his mother.

Now, five years on, it's part of life—but something is different. He has discovered there *is* real danger and it's not entirely in her mind.

Will doesn't remember his father, but he is a very glamorous figure in Will's mind. A handsome ex-Royal Marine officer who turned to leading scientific expeditions in remote corners of the world, John Parry is the stuff of boyhood heroes. In the hours playing alone acting out dangerous expeditions and daring rescues, Will's father was his imaginary friend. As Will grew, so did the desire to know more about him. There were many unanswered questions: Why had he disappeared? Why are these mysterious men so eager to know about him? Part of the answer is in the writing case where Mrs. Parry keeps letters from her husband. But Will doesn't know where she hides it. He wakes in the night, suddenly knowing both that there are intruders in the house, and where the writing case is. This is one of several examples of characters having some extraordinary intuition. This is Dust in action, steering human thinking and attention onto things that are more critical than they realize at the time.[4]

WORLDS APART

Having killed one of the intruders, Will flees to Oxford to search for answers. He is confident in his skill at being unobtrusive during the day, but Will knows he must avoid the town center at night or he will draw attention to himself. He heads toward north Oxford where his attention is drawn to a cat, which behaves strangely before disappearing altogether. Like Will's flash of intuition the previous night, he is receiving a gift of guidance from the Dust:

> Will knew without the slightest doubt that that patch of grass on the other side was in a different world. . . . He was looking at something profoundly alien. . . . What he saw made his head swim and his heart thump harder, but he didn't hesitate: he pushed his tote bag through, and then scrambled through himself, through the hole in the fabric of this world and into another. (*SK*, pp. 15-16)

We know about the existence of other worlds from *The Golden Compass*—

Jordan scholars whisper nervously about the Barnard-Stokes heresy. But until Lord Asriel's audacious experiment with the aurora, it was thought to be mere speculation of a kind the Magisterium is determined to stamp out. Now we realize that Asriel had only found a new—and catastrophic—means of passing between worlds.

Will finds himself in Cittàgazze, the City of Magpies, in precisely the right place for Lyra to literally bump into him. Pullman uses their encounter to further explore the idea of alternative worlds. Although in *The Golden Compass* we have seen many ways in which Lyra's world differs from ours, now we see from the other direction: our world and its inhabitants are very strange in Lyra's eyes. She is shocked that Will has no dæmon, and when she enters his world she finds it bewilderingly different. In the center of Oxford she finds things that are comfortingly familiar—including, apparently, Simon Parslow's initials carved in a stone—but no Jordan College. She feels disoriented, and a photograph in the museum of men identical to the Samoyed hunters who had captured her intensifies the feeling.[5] Lyra is off-guard, resulting in the odious Sir Charles Latrom spotting her.[6]

The alethiometer leads Lyra to Mary Malone, a researcher into dark matter.[7] Lyra is astonished but excited to find a female scholar who knows something about Dust. Mary is flabbergasted by Lyra—especially when she suggests Mary could reprogram "the Cave" to use words. But the alethiometer had instructed Lyra to give first priority to helping Will find his father. Until this point, Lyra and Will are just acquaintances—all they have in common is their age and the fact that they had met in an alien world. From now on their stories are intertwined. However, instead of obeying the alethiometer, Lyra continues with her own agenda and visits Mary again. This stubborn independence leads to Lyra's first major setback—she ends up alerting the security services to her interest in dark matter and her connection with Will, and, what's more, Sir Charles steals the alethiometer. She later confesses to Will that this was the consequence of her disobedience, and she submits herself to helping him. Will and Lyra are very much equals, but for now Will takes the lead; the new dynamic is part of Lyra's growing-up process.

A SPECTER CALLS

Cittàgazze is alien to both Will and Lyra. It is both beautiful (though decaying) and menacing.[8] It is apparently deserted, but soon they discover the gang of children who roam around free from adult supervision. Their hostility toward the cat Will had followed, and later toward Will and Lyra, seems extraordinary. Will, however, knows that it is common for people to feel threatened by, and hostile toward, what they don't understand.

The far greater menace of Cittàgazze is something they can't see: Specters that prey on adults, feeding on their "conscious and informed interest in the world" (p. 280), sucking the mental life out of them and leaving them as empty shells. Intriguingly, while Pullman was writing about Specters, J. K. Rowling was writing about dementors draining people of their will to live.[9] Both writers were expressing something of their experiences of depression, although Pullman says, "I prefer to call it melancholy, or melancholia. It's a horrible condition, I tried to describe it as accurately as I could."[10]

Pullman's fascination with voodoo may also in part lie behind the Specters. Anthropologist Zora Neale Hurston investigated voodoo in Jamaica and Haiti in the 1930s and questioned someone who described something very similar to a Specter attack:

> One day you see a man walking the road. . . . The next day you come to his yard and find him dead. . . . He is still and silent and does none of the things that he used to do. But you look upon him and you see that he has all the parts that the living have. Why is it that he cannot do what the living do? It is because the thing that gave power to these parts is no longer there. That is the duppy, and that is the most powerful part of any man.[11]

The man is now a zombie—undead—and has nothing to restrain him from evil. He will work as a slave for the sorcerer who took his spirit—though this idea seems closer to Bolvangar and the regiment of African *zombis* than to the Specters that independently feast on the "duppies" of living adults.

For the people of Cittàgazze, Specters are a terrifying mystery. They know what Specters do, but not why, nor where they come from. Angelica explains to Will and Lyra what happens when a Specter attacks someone:

> They eat the life out of them there and then. . . . At first they know it's happening, and they're afraid; they cry and cry. They try and look away and pretend it ain' happening, but it is. It's too late. And no one ain' gonna go near them, they on they own. Then they get pale and they stop moving. They still alive, but it's like they been eaten from inside. You look in they eyes, you see the back of they heads. Ain' nothing there. (p. 60)

Seeing right through to the back of the head is a child's embellishment, but it conveys the utter blankness of victims' expressions. Later, Serafina Pekkala and her companions watch Specters attack some travelers at a river crossing. The adults all fell victim to their shimmering fate (Serafina, being adult, could see the Specters), leaving one man standing waste deep in the river, his distraught child still clinging to his back. When the child falls, the father barely responds to the splash and can't engage at all with the reality of his child drowning. Joachim Lorenz, a rider with the party who fled in order to return and care for the children once danger was passed, tells Serafina that there are many more Specters than previously (p. 135). This is a consequence of Lord Asriel's experiment, as was the great storm, which happened in this world (p. 137). In *The Amber Spyglass*, we discover more about its devastating consequences—an environmental crisis in Lyra's world, and other worlds out of alignment with each other. Joachim describes his world as it had once been—a place of beauty, plenty and peace—and tells how it all changed three centuries previously. He clearly favors the explanation of Specters that puts the blame at the door of the Torre degli Angeli, and its guild of philosophers (p. 135). Angelica's similar explanation adds a little more detail:

> This Guild man hundreds of years ago was taking some metal apart. Lead. He was going to make it into gold. And he cut it and cut it

smaller and smaller till he came to the smallest piece he could get. There ain' nothing smaller than that. So small you couldn' see it, even. But he cut that, too, and inside the smallest little bit there was all the Specters packed in, twisted over and folded up so tight they took up no space at all. But once he cut it, bam! They whooshed out, and they been here ever since. (p. 146)

At this point Pullman is having fun weaving modern physics together with alchemy and the stuff of horror films to warn against the dangers of pursuing technological progress simply because we *can*, without considering the long-term consequences and whether we *should*. The alchemists sought to turn lead into gold, but without success, and before long the idea of chemical elements and atoms was established. In the twentieth century physicists succeeded in splitting the atom—an event that ultimately led to the horrors of Hiroshima and Nagasaki. Subsequent discoveries about subatomic particles led to theories that there are actually ten[12] or eleven[13] dimensions to reality, rather than the four (three plus time) with which we are familiar. These extra dimensions are "packed in twisted over and folded up so tight they [take] up no space at all." Pullman uses this idea to create a way for Specters to be unleashed by the subtle knife. Giacomo Paradisi admits that the creation of the knife was responsible. The Guild of the Torre degli Angeli had probed thoughtlessly into the bonds between the elementary particles, thinking that like financial bonds they were "negotiable" (p. 187).

Now, after three hundred years of coping with small numbers of Specters, the world is in chaos with a deluge of them. The Specters, the great storm and fog, as well as angels flying overhead, are making people anxious. Joachim speculates on what might be happening:

Something is happening, and we don't know down here what it may be. There could be a war breaking out. There was a war in heaven once, oh, thousands of years ago, immense ages back, but I don't know what the outcome was. It wouldn't be impossible if there was another. But the devastation would be enormous, and the consequences for us . . . I can't imagine it. Though . . . the end of it might be better than I fear. It might be that a war in heaven would sweep the Specters from this world altogether, and back into the pit they came from. What a blessing that would be, eh! How fresh and happy we could live, free of that fearful blight! (p. 138)

This confirms what Thorold told Serafina Pekkala on Svalbard—that Lord Asriel was intent on mounting a rebellion against the Authority (p. 46). Joachim's prophetic comments begin to help her (and us) realize that any war in heaven will have enormous repercussions.

SERAFINA'S PERSPECTIVE

It's worth noting at this point that, although Will is the hero of *The Subtle Knife*, Serafina is Pullman's focus in terms of understanding and explaining the cosmic events that are the backdrop to the story. After escaping from the ship where she has played the role of Yambe-Akka and killed the witch who was being tortured,[14] she begins to wonder what Lord Asriel is doing. She perceives that all the upheaval in the world is a direct result of his activities. The fog enveloping the north acts as a metaphor for the uncertainty everyone feels. To find some answers, Serafina first visits Dr. Lanselius in Trollesund. He tells her about the Magisterium "assembling the greatest army ever known" (p. 42), including a regiment of *zombis*. Then she discovers Asriel's intentions from Thorold. It's a long time before we're told explicitly what mission awaits the Magisterium's forces, but it is clear, once we know Asriel's plans, that these forces will be fighting him.

Thorold's information prompts Serafina to call a clan council. Two guests address the council: Ruta Skadi and Lee Scoresby, the Texan aeronaut.[15] Both expand Serafina's understanding. First, Ruta Skadi recognizes that war is imminent. She has no doubt that the witches should fight against the Magisterium (her stinging criticism is examined in chapter fourteen). Second, Lee speaks about Stanislaus Grumman's knowledge of an object that could give more protection to the one who holds it than anything else. He's determined to find it, whatever it may be, and bring Lyra under its protection. Since they all realize that Lyra is central to everything, protecting her is of immense importance. Serafina and twenty other witches head into the Cittàgazze world to find Lyra, while Lee sets off to find Grumman. From this point in the narrative Pullman divides the story into two main strands, one following Serafina who soon finds Lyra and Will, the other following Scoresby. Ruta Skadi sets off with Serafina, but soon leaves to join some angels heading toward Asriel's fortress. Later, after Serafina finds the children and pledges to help them find John Parry, Ruta returns with astonishing news:

> It is the greatest castle you can imagine: ramparts of basalt, rearing to the skies, with wide roads coming from every direction. . . . I think he must have been preparing this for a long time, for eons. . . . I think he commands time, he makes it run fast or slow according to his will. And coming to this fortress are warriors of every kind, from every world. (p. 270)

Ruta also has news for Serafina from an unexpected source—an overheard conversation between some cliff-ghasts. The oldest of all cliff-ghasts tells the others that the impending war will be the greatest ever. Lord Asriel's forces are greater than in the earlier rebellion and better led,[16] but the Authority has an army a hundred times bigger. Asriel has passion and daring and a sense of justice on his side, whereas the Authority's forces are frightened or complacent. But the old cliff-ghast knows of one thing that will mean defeat for the rebellion: "He hasn't got Æsahættr. Without Æsahættr, he and all his forces will go down to defeat" (p. 273).

Serafina recognizes that Æsahættr "sounds as if it means 'god-destroyer'" (p. 274)[17]—neither she nor Ruta Skadi knows who or what it could be, though they speculate that it might be Lyra. The carelessness of Lena Feldt, one of the witches, prevents Serafina from putting one more piece of the puzzle in place. While spying on Mrs. Coulter, she hears Sir Charles Latrom/ Lord Boreal telling Mrs. Coulter that the subtle knife is also known as *teleutaia makhaira* or Æsahættr, to which nothing whatsoever is invulnerable

(p. 312). But in her absorbed curiosity, Lena Feldt was not sufficiently alert and so fell victim to a Specter, now under Mrs. Coulter's command. Not only did this lapse prevent Serafina from understanding the riddle, it led to the killing of her companions and to Lyra's capture.

SHAMANIC POWERS

Meanwhile, Pullman has been developing another major strand of narrative—Lee Scoresby's search for Stanislaus Grumman. First he goes to Nova Zembla[18] to see what he can learn in the bar of the Samirsky Hotel from the trappers and hunters passing through. The more Lee discovers about Grumman, the more mysterious his quarry becomes. He learns that Grumman had been initiated into a Tartar tribe, the Yenisei Pakhtars,[19] and had his skull drilled because he was a shaman.[20] He's told that Grumman took a Tartar name, Jopari, but Lee discovers that it is not a Tartar name at all. He sets out for the Yenisei River to find Grumman or his tribe. When they finally meet, Grumman tells Lee that the name Jopari is simply the Tartars' attempt to pronounce his real name, John Parry. Grumman's revelation that he summoned Scoresby using a ring that had belonged to Lee's mother rattles the aeronaut. Lee demands to know how he had come by it, but Grumman declines to explain, except to say it was thanks to his shamanic powers.

Grumman tells Scoresby that he has learned about the subtle knife and the Specter-filled world by traveling there in spirit while in a trance.[21] But he is a sick man from living in an alien world. He intends to use his remaining strength to find the knife bearer, and Lee is to help him. During their journey, Lee witnesses some of Grumman's other shamanic powers, including summoning a wind to carry them into the other world. When they are pursued by zeppelins, Grumman conjures a thunderstorm that destroys one of them. During the night Lee dreams with a vivid intensity of the shaman's work—or perhaps he has some kind of out-of-body experience. He sees Grumman summoning a Specter to attack a zeppelin pilot who then crashes into the mountainside; then Lee feels himself joining a flock of birds that weigh down a third zeppelin until it crashes. All this seriously drains Grumman's reserves of strength—and profoundly unnerves Lee Scoresby. When the final zeppelin catches up with them at a ravine, Lee holds them off while Grumman goes on through. This Western-inspired last stand by the Texan is one of the great heartbreaking moments of the trilogy, as he and his scrawny, laid-back hare dæmon Hester face their imminent death—and separation. Their very last thought is that they were helping Lyra—by helping Grumman find the knife bearer, Lee believed he was helping the little girl he had come to love so much.

Grumman had made an oath to Scoresby that the knife would protect Lyra, but just hours later Grumman breaks his word. His commitment to Asriel's aims is so great that when the knife bearer blunders into him on top of a mountain in the dark of a wild and windy night, Grumman insists that he go to Lord Asriel to offer the services of the knife. The fight on the mountain is curious, echoing Jacob's nighttime fight with an angel in Genesis 32. Will struggles to escape, but although Grumman's strength is failing, he can still grip tightly—he must discover if this is the knife bearer. Once Grumman is sure, he urges the bearer to fight with the knife and kill the Authority. Will wants no part of it, but Grumman's words help to shape Will's sense of himself and his task for some time: "You're a warrior. That's what you are. Argue with anything else, but don't argue with your own nature" (p. 320). Will is reluctant to see himself in those terms but recognizes the truth in what the man says. Moments later, as Grumman strikes a match, father and son see each other for the first time in twelve years, and—another heartbreaking moment—at the very moment that recognition dawns, they too are separated by the arrow of the vengeful witch whose love Grumman had rejected. As Will descends to the camp, he discovers the two angels who had been protecting his father. The book finishes with another agonizing separation as Will finds that the witches are dead, and Lyra has gone.

ABSENT FATHERS
The Subtle Knife is in the difficult situation of being the middle part of a trilogy, with neither the thrill of the new, which comes with an opening volume,

nor with the climax of the closing part. It is a mark of Pullman's quality as a writer that he manages to introduce many new elements without losing the essential ingredients of *The Golden Compass*, and without the new elements overwhelming. The knife itself, of course, is central to the plot, but the Specters and the shaman have pivotal roles too. Pullman also wisely develops two of the key supporting characters from *The Golden Compass*—Serafina Pekkala and Lee Scoresby—to give them major roles. Pullman works with four separate strands of the story, which he intertwines at stages through the book. First, he connects the thread of Lyra looking for Dust, with the new strand of Will Parry searching for his father. Then he takes the Serafina and Scoresby threads in different directions in order to get two different perspectives on the events that are taking place. Serafina Pekkala gradually pieces together Lord Asriel's role in the impending cosmic conflict. Her story merges with that of Will and Lyra after they have recovered the alethiometer. Lee's story takes him to the mysterious Grumman in an attempt to find something that will protect Lyra, little realizing that it already is protecting her. Grumman brings a shaman's perspective on the knife and the part it will play. Lee's story fades into Grumman's, only to be cut off at the point where it connects with Will's. Pullman has begun to bring together the threads in preparation for the climax in *The Amber Spyglass*—but we've a long way to go yet, so he cleverly divides Will's and Lyra's stories again to leave us with an immense cliffhanger.

The various threads of this story suggest that in terms of theme if not of plot, the two fathers are central to *The Subtle Knife*. Yet Lord Asriel doesn't appear in person once, and Stanislaus Grumman doesn't appear until almost two-thirds of the way through. However, it is Lord Asriel's implacable opposition to the Authority that is driving the story, and Stanislaus Grumman is the character who most clearly understands what Asriel is doing and why it matters so much. There are some interesting parallels between them. Both were unknown to their children (at least, in Asriel's case, as a father), both have traveled in different worlds and are vehemently opposed to the Authority. Pullman also hints that Asriel, like Grumman, has special powers—recall him "sending for" a child at the end of *The Golden Compass* (*GC*, pp. 364, 379) and Ruta Skadi's comment about him commanding time. Pullman never develops this but he has nonetheless given these two extraordinary men pivotal roles, which will profoundly impact two critical moments in *The Amber Spyglass*.

7

THE AMBER SPYGLASS

The calm and tranquility of the opening paragraphs of *The Amber Spyglass* come as a surprise after the tension at the close of *The Subtle Knife*, and the trauma of Lyra's disappearance. It's a shift of focus comparable to that between the end of *The Golden Compass* and the beginning of *The Subtle Knife*. It reinforces the fact that this is a new book—the story continues, but the end of one volume and the beginning of the next isn't an arbitrary split in the middle of the action. Chapter two returns to the moments immediately after Will discovered Lyra's disappearance, but chapter one is days or weeks later. Lyra and Will remain the heroes since this is their story, but we are moving into a new phase. As I noted previously, Pullman has separated the strands of Lyra's and Will's stories in order to maintain tension, and to allow him to introduce new elements into the story. It's not until chapter twelve that they are reunited.

Pullman shifts focus so dramatically on the first page that we have no idea where we are or what's happening. The scene is a valley high in the mountains, near the snow line. There are few clues as to where these mountains are. One clue comes in the first sentence: the valley is shaded with rhododendrons. It's enough to locate us somewhere in central or eastern Asia—the Himalayas perhaps. The mention of "faded silken flags," barley cakes and dried tea confirm this impression. Pullman describes this peaceful valley at length, not simply to paint the background, but to make us uncertain about where we are in the story. Gradually he zooms in: a path—the deserted cave—a creature at the entrance—a golden monkey—Mrs. Coulter.

Now the tension rises as Pullman refrains from telling us about Lyra. We recall that when we last saw Mrs. Coulter, she had one of her tame Specters torture a witch into revealing Lyra's destiny as the second Eve. Once Mrs. Coulter had understood this, she realized that she had to destroy Lyra to prevent a second Fall. But now we find her camping in a mountain cave, with a village girl, Ama, bringing her food. Still Pullman remains quiet about Lyra; instead, Ama is passing on the villagers' worried rumors of Mrs. Coulter's dangerous companion. Finally we learn that Lyra is alive, though sleeping "under a spell" (p. 4).[1] We're not surprised to learn that in fact her mother is keeping her sedated. What *does* come as a surprise is the disagreement between Mrs. Coulter and her dæmon, and the fact that her actions are secret from the Magisterium. Perhaps most surprising is the internal turmoil in a woman who has previously been utterly single-minded.

Mrs. Coulter's geographical isolation reflects a more profound isolation. She still wants to prevent Lyra from being tempted. But faced with the prospect of annihilating her own daughter, Mrs. Coulter's maternal instincts are beginning to wake from their dormant state, and she wants to hide Lyra from the Magisterium (p. 140). We don't discover this until much later—and we will be unsure of her motives for a long time, since she becomes a double agent—but this is the first sign that Mrs. Coulter is distancing herself from the Magisterium. This takes us back to the theme of separation or binary fission, which we noted in chapter five. Already in chapter one of *The Amber Spyglass* we have Lyra separated from Will, and Mrs. Coulter separated from her former allies, as well as being at odds with herself and her dæmon. The first of Lyra's dream fragments (which appear between the first eight chapters) reminds us of another separation that becomes increasingly important in the first half of *The Amber Spyglass*: Roger is cut off from life (p. 9). This fragment plants the idea of the world of the dead into the reader's mind; it grows in power and inevitability until Lyra finally gets there.

ANGELS FROM THE REALMS OF STORY

Meanwhile, Will has also been finding out about the world of the dead from his new companions, the angels Baruch and Balthamos. They are part of Lord Asriel's coalition—fallen angels, rebels against the Authority. Pullman says: "There's been a long tradition of seeing the 'fallen' angels as being in some way on the 'right' side, and I'm just going along with Milton[2] and Blake as well as some Gnostic traditions."[3] Pullman presents them, especially Balthamos, as haughty and unfeeling. They indifferently allowed John Parry to be killed—having led them to the knife bearer, he was no longer useful. It makes for a bad start in their relationship with Will who is distressed at his father's death and Lyra's disappearance. Will, although just a boy, is unfazed by the angels, knowing that with the knife he can call the shots. He insists that they look for Lyra before he will comply with their request to go to Lord Asriel.

Unfortunately, an unfallen angel finds them and summons the Regent who is flying far overhead in "the Chariot." They narrowly avoid his spear by escaping to another world in which Baruch and Balthamos explain to Will that the Authority is not God, but merely the oldest of all angels, and Metatron is his Regent (pp. 31-32). Metatron is an archangel in Gnostic writings, and the subject of many legends that have come to us via the Western esoteric tradition. This is a rich source of inspiration for Pullman who incorporates several of the ideas into his story (see chapter fourteen). Pullman says, "I was guided by what I read of angelic lore in, for instance, Gustave Davidson's *A Dictionary of Angels*, and elsewhere; and also by the needs of the story. If I needed an angel to have been a man at some stage, hey presto! I invented the possibility. There's a lot of making-up in fiction, you know."[4] His latter comment is curious since one of the main legends about Metatron is that he was once the man Enoch, who the Bible tells us "walked with God; then he was no more, because God took him away" (Genesis 5:24). It is not, however, a biblical idea—the Bible always sees angels as entirely separate, spiritual beings.[5] In the Metatron legends he is the most powerful angel, so it was a natural step for Pullman to make him the Authority's Regent. It's worth noting in passing that Pullman ignores Jesus.[6] In speaking about Jesus, the Letter to the Hebrews asks,

To which of the angels did God ever say,

> "Sit at my right hand
> until I make your enemies
> a footstool for your feet"? (Hebrews 1:13)[7]

The implied answer is "none" since it is part of an argument for Jesus' superiority to angels.

Will's separation from his father prompts him to ask Baruch and Balthamos, "What happens when we die?" They tell him that ghosts go to "a prison camp"—the world of the dead—not to heaven, which even the churches don't realize is a deception (p. 33). Will finds "his imagination trembling" at this—if it's just another world, the knife can get him in.

Very soon another separation occurs: Baruch flies off to tell Lord Asriel what he and Balthamos had discovered in the Clouded Mountain. He arrives in bad shape but passes on news about Metatron's plans, as well as about the knife, its bearer and Lyra (pp. 60-63). When the draft from an opening door swirls the angel's loosening particles into the air, Balthamos is immediately aware of Baruch's death. Pullman touchingly conveys the agony of his grief (p. 93). The depth of their love for each other is very moving. Many reviewers assume—wrongly in my opinion—that the two angels are homosexual because they love each other "with a passion" (p. 26). Pullman himself is "constantly amazed at how literal-minded [people] are. People come up to him and say, 'Excuse me, those two angels in *The Amber Spyglass*, are they homosexual?' And he'll say, as evenly as he can, 'No, they love each other, I have no idea of their sexual orientation.'"[8] Since these are angels, it seems entirely reasonable for them to have a profound platonic love for each other at a level of intensity that is impossible for thoroughly sexual humans to understand.

ON THE KNIFE EDGE

Will and Balthamos press on toward Lyra and reach a town on a large river leading directly to the Himalayas.[9] It's here that Will meets Iorek Byrnison and the other armored bears trying to refuel for their journey in search of a new home. With extraordinary courage and presence of mind, Will races to confront the enormous bear. By slicing up Iorek's helmet, he succeeds in brokering a deal between townspeople and bears, preventing the people's anger from flaring up, and in making himself uninteresting to them afterward (pp. 107-8). Iorek is deeply impressed by the boy—and intrigued by the knife.

When Will eventually reaches the cave, his meeting with Mrs. Coulter unsettles him, partly because she dazzles him and partly because she brings his mother into the conversation. The rescue of Lyra becomes messy: the Magisterium's forces arrive by zeppelin to kill the girl; Lord Asriel's gyropters arrive to rescue her and his tiny Gallivespian spies fly in from the zeppelins on their dragonflies. Crucially, Will looks at Mrs. Coulter as he starts cutting a window and the blade shatters, preventing the obvious means of escape. The sight of Lyra's mother brings home to Will his separation from his own mother and breaks his detached yet focused frame of mind. It's too much, too emotional; he becomes disconnected from the knife rather than feeling as if he is at the very tip of it, cutting with his mind as well as the knife, as he had been taught (*SK*, p. 182).

When Will asks Iorek to mend the knife, the bear is reluctant. The ensuing discussion can be seen as an exploration of the ethics of technology, similar to the conversation with Giacomo Paradisi (*SK*, pp. 186-87), but going further in examining the implications. As with all technology, there are side effects that cannot always be anticipated. Iorek recognizes that the knife is too subtle to fully understand, telling Will that "the harm it can do is unlimited. It would have been infinitely better if it had never been made," because "the knife has intentions too" (pp. 180-81).

Lyra insists that, since the knife does exist, it's better to use it responsibly than to let it fall into the wrong hands. Iorek acquiesces, recognizing that the bears also use technology, albeit far simpler. But he insists that Lyra consult the alethiometer first since "full knowledge is better than half-knowledge. . . . Know what it is that you're asking" (p. 182)—a common theme in the trilogy. The alethiometer tells Lyra that the knife is extremely finely balanced;

whether the knife brings about good or ill hangs on Will's motives. Within the framework of *His Dark Materials*, this cause-and-effect relationship comes into play when Will cuts open a fallen crystal litter so he can help the frail old angel within (p. 410). Will hates killing and would never want to harm such a pathetic creature. So it is Will's motive of compassion that leads to the knife's fulfilling its name—Æsahættr, god destroyer (*SK*, p. 274)—as the Authority blows away. The scene feels curiously incidental, although the narrative has been heading resolutely in this direction.

After reuniting the knife shards, Iorek is troubled over the wisdom of his actions. Will confesses that he is torn between using the knife to be reunited with his mother and offering its services to Lord Asriel. Iorek warns him: "If you want to succeed in this task, you must no longer think about your mother. You must put her aside. If your mind is divided, the knife will break" (p. 194).

The World of the Dead

With the knife reforged, Will and Lyra, accompanied by the touchy hand-high spies Tialys and Salmakia, can start their journey to the world of the dead. The idea has been growing in Will for some time, and since Lyra had dreamed of finding Roger, they both see the journey as vital—they long to be reunited, even briefly, with Roger and John Parry. The alethiometer confirms their choice, and following its advice of "Follow the knife," Will cuts into a world where they find a dead man. He cuts again to escape approaching soldiers, but finds a new world identical in every respect to the one he's in—except for the dead man looking alive and well, though shell-shocked. The man is coming to terms with the fact that he is now a ghost; when he leaves they follow him, joining up with more and more ghosts. As they travel, their surroundings fade away as the ghosts forget the world of the living, which they have left forever.

The travelers arrive in the shantytown "holding area" of the suburbs of the dead, and find shelter in the home of Peter and his family. It's an awkward meeting since Will, Lyra and the spies arrive without their deaths, whereas they don't understand who the deaths are. Peter explains:

> What we found out when we come here . . . we all brought our deaths with us. . . . We had 'em all the time, and we never knew. See, everyone has a death. It goes everywhere with 'em all their life long, right close by. . . . The moment you're born, your death comes into the world with you, and it's your death that takes you out. (p. 260)

The grandmother's death explains that if they want to cross to the land of the dead, they must call up their deaths, "Say welcome, make friends, be kind, invite your deaths to come close to you, and see what you can get them to agree to" (p. 264). But when Lyra sees her death face to face she is terrified—especially that the time of parting from Pantalaimon is imminent. Her death agrees to guide her,[10] and the party comes at last to the jetty to await the boatman. The scene on the shore is one of the most traumatic in the trilogy as Lyra is compelled to leave Pantalaimon behind. The agony of this separation, for both human and dæmon, in which they feel literally torn in two, is horrendous. Lyra's companions fare no better—they discover as they cross the lake that they too are leaving part of themselves behind.

After disembarking, Lyra's torment continues as they are confronted by No-Name the harpy. The loathsome creatures with their foul stench are immune to Gallivespian stings, but no one is immune to their taunting. Lyra's usual strategy of fabrication only succeeds in enraging No-Name. Lyra is shattered by her failure, but has little time to dwell on this, as the little group of living beings is almost immediately surrounded by innumerable ghosts: "They had as much substance as fog, poor things. . . . They crammed forward, light and lifeless, to warm themselves at the flowing blood and the strong-beating hearts of the two travelers" (p. 296).

The desolation of the place is reinforced by Pullman describing their voices as "no louder than dry leaves falling" (p. 297),[11] and later the ghosts themselves as "dry leaves scattered by a sudden gust of wind" (p. 298). The ghosts agree to help the children find Roger and Will's father. The pity Lyra feels for the ghosts prompts her to suggest using the knife to free the ghosts.

The "true smile, so warm and happy" (p. 303) that Will gives her causes a surprising reaction within Lyra. It's her first sensation of falling in love, though she has no idea yet what it means. The harpies are furious that their role, despicable as it is, will be taken from them. In the light of the harpies' response to Lyra's truthful storytelling, the Gallivespians get them to agree to guide the ghosts to the way out in exchange for true stories. With the harpies leading the way, the four travelers, followed by all the ghosts, start out for the best place to cut through into another world.

DUST AND DESTRUCTION

Alongside this narrative, Pullman has been teasing out another thread of the story. We last saw Mary Malone stepping into Cittàgazze (*SK*, p. 254), and when we meet her again in *The Amber Spyglass*, she is being guided by the I Ching to yet another world. Everything about this world astounds her: the lavalike roads, the seedpods from the giant trees and most of all the mulefa with their curious diamond-framed skeleton—and wheels.[12] Having a scientist in this world gives Pullman the opportunity to explore the subject of evolution. Mary guesses that the various worlds have split off from each other in the past and that evolution had taken a very different course here.[13] Most intriguing is the interrelated evolution of seedpods, and the claw on the mulefa's legs—the mulefa make good use of the pods, but in return crack the pods by riding on them, and care for the seeds. Mary recognizes the centrality of the oil in this, and when the mulefa try to tell her that the oil is connected with wisdom, she begins to see a connection with her work in Oxford (p. 129). Tantalizingly, Pullman immediately steers away from making the connection, telling us instead about a tualapi attack. We learn nothing more for several chapters other than a brief comment that the trees are dying.

Mary is astonished to learn from her friend Atal that the mulefa can see shadow particles, or *sraf*. Inspired by Atal's description of what sraf looks like, and its similarity to light, Mary sets about making something that will enable her to see it. Through basic technology, craftsmanship and patience, together with some good advice and a little luck,[14] Mary succeeds in making her amber spyglass, which enables her to see with fresh vision. Mary's story seems quite separate from the other strands of the book until this discovery—now Mary can see Dust, the element that is at the center of all the events. Once she has reached this point, the mulefa, who have been waiting for it, ask for her help with the dying trees. She soon finds that it's connected with a flow of sraf out of the world (pp. 233-35)—but before she can find a solution the drift turns into a flood.

Mary has no idea why there has been a sudden change, she just sees the effect. Lyra and Will, however, have seen the cause but are unaware of the effect. In the Magisterium's quest to destroy Lyra, they have a two-pronged strategy. One approach is their secret assassin, Father Gomez, who is following Mary's trail. The other is more opportunistic, and comes as a result of Mrs. Coulter's visit to Geneva, since she carries some of Lyra's hair in a locket. Stealing it gives the Consistorial Court of Discipline the perfect chance to use a new bomb, which can locate the exact position of the rest of the hair, and somehow target colossal energy to it. The energy needs of the bomb are prodigious—a power station to begin the process, then the extraordinary amount of energy released by severing a dæmon. At the power station in the mountains, Mrs. Coulter and Lord Roke manage to create a sufficient diversion for her to escape from being put into the silver cage, and for the golden monkey to rescue all but one hair from the resonating chamber of the bomb. Just as Father MacPhail is preparing to sacrifice himself in the cage, Will is reunited with his father in the world of the dead. The shaman, aware of what is happening, urges Will to shave off the cut hairs from Lyra's head and put them into another world. Will pushes the hairs through a window just as MacPhail twists two wires together and severs his own dæmon. The explosion, which is felt in other worlds, opens up an abyss into which Dust now cascades.

RELEASED AND RESTORED

True to the alethiometer's prediction (p. 183), the knife has brought about the imminent death of Dust—all the consciousness will flood out of every world into the abyss. After a hazardous journey along the edge of the abyss, Will is eventually able to cut a window out of the world of the dead. The ghosts stream out excitedly and dissolve into the air. As with angels, Pullman's ghosts have *some* physical being—they are not spiritual and nonmaterial; they're still made of particles, but are *very* thin. Later, after dealing with the Specters in the great battle, Lee Scoresby finally allows himself to drift apart. At this point Pullman seems to go against the oblivion he had been advocating, as "the last of Lee" comes out "under the brilliant stars, where the atoms of his beloved dæmon, Hester, were waiting for him" (p. 418).

In an audacious attempt to keep Metatron from finding the children's dæmons, and thus controlling the knife bearer, Mrs. Coulter again borrows one of Lord Asriel's intention craft. She finds her way to the Regent in the Clouded Mountain and seduces him into following her to the abyss. Although I argued earlier that angels' relationships are platonic, Metatron is portrayed as an angel who had been a sex-crazed man. He longs for contact with human flesh again. Down at the edge of the abyss, she is reunited with Asriel and the two of them sacrifice themselves for Lyra by wrestling the great angel down into the abyss.

In the heat of the battle, Will and Lyra finally reach their dæmons, which are being protected from Specters by John Parry, Lee Scoresby and other warrior ghosts. They scoop them into their arms, suddenly realizing they have each other's dæmons, and cut through into another world—the world where Mary Malone is worrying over the ebbing tide of sraf. It's not long before they are with Mary in the mulefa village, beginning to recover from their ordeal, though their dæmons are not yet ready to be with them. Some mulefa discover the ghosts leaving the world of the dead and take Mary to see it. The ghost of an old woman tells Mary to "tell them stories" (p. 432) before she dissolves—an injunction that Mary takes to heart and puts into practice the following day. In recounting her own experiences, Mary fulfills her role of tempter without even realizing it. On the next day, as Will and Lyra search for their dæmons, they come to understand their love for each other, and Lyra fulfills her destiny as a second Eve (explored in chapter eleven). The flood of Dust is halted, and it reverts to its age-old patterns of drifting down from space into conscious minds. The knife has also fulfilled the alethiometer's other prediction that it would keep Dust alive.

STAR-CROSSED LOVERS

Almost as soon as Will and Lyra understand that they want to be with each other forever, they are united once more with their dæmons. But their dæmons bring terrible news: every window opened by the knife creates Specters, and causes Dust to leak away. They must all be closed—all except the one from the world of the dead. Lyra and Will realize with dismay that they can only live in their own worlds because their dæmons cannot survive in any other (p. 484). There are some joyful reunions—with Serafina Pekkala, John Faa and Farder Coram—but always tempered with the anguished realization: once they go home, and the windows are closed, the knife must be destroyed and they will never see each other again. Their final parting is as heartrending as any other scene in *His Dark Materials*, and the pain of their eternal separation shatters the subtle knife, never to be reforged. Nicholas Tucker comments: "By making Will and Lyra—like Romeo and Juliet—separate just as they have finally found each other, Pullman also ensures that this first vision of young love remains for ever unsullied by any of the practical difficulties or inevitable disagreements that creep into even the most ideal of human relationships."[15]

But it is not the ending of the story. Xaphania gives them a glimmer of hope, which they barely recognize—she tells them that it would be possible, though very hard work, for them to travel between worlds even without windows as Will's father had done. A friend "has already taken the first steps" (p. 495)—we presume Mary after her out-of-body experience. Meanwhile, Will and Mary head off for a good cup of tea before beginning the process of sorting out the messes of their respective situations. Lyra has dinner with the Master and Dame Hannah Relf, and willingly agrees to be-

come a student at St. Sophia's, where she can make new friends and begin
the process of relearning how to read the alethiometer. And in the final
scene in the Botanic Garden, Lyra and Pantalaimon reflect on what they—
and Philip Pullman—see as their greatest purpose: to build the republic of
heaven.

8

BEYOND *THE AMBER SPYGLASS*

His Dark Materials is developing a life of its own through media other than books. In audio books, apart from the unabridged reading of the trilogy by Pullman and a full cast (a wonderfully absorbing thirty-four hours),[1] the BBC also produced a radio dramatization in 2003 starring Terence Stamp as Lord Asriel and Emma Fielding as Mrs. Coulter.[2] The adaptation by Lavinia Murray got around some of the difficulties of condensing such an extraordinary story into six hours by using Balthamos as a narrator. One small change from the books, which raised some eyebrows among fans, was a name for Mrs. Coulter's dæmon—Ozymandias. Pullman wasn't thrilled: "I didn't choose that name and to be frank I don't think I would have done. I imagine that the scriptwriter did get it from Shelley's poem, but you'd really have to ask her why she went for that name."[3] Pullman's reason for not giving the golden monkey a name is "because every time I tried to think of one, he snarled and frightened me. What's more he hardly speaks either."[4]

STAGE AND SCREEN

Another adaptation of the trilogy, which shoehorned the story into six hours, was Nicholas Wright's for Britain's National Theatre.[5] Nick Hytner, the director of the National, said it was "pouring a petrol station into a pint pot."[6] But he "wanted to do a play that spoke as directly to a young audience as a movie at the local multiplex."[7] It seemed almost impossible to be able to stage such an extraordinary story, but Hytner hadn't even finished reading the trilogy when he decided that he had to do it. He said, "What seemed immediately stageable were the series of archetypal, highly emotional family conflicts, which I thought were powerful and dramatic and would hold a theatre full of people."[8] Philip Pullman responded to the news with amazement: "I was astonished. . . . I was absolutely thrilled, of course. Delighted. And simultaneously relieved that it wasn't me having to make it into a play. It was someone else."[9]

Pullman is quite relaxed about his story being retold in a different medium, and by someone else:

> Once a story leaves your desk it goes into the hands of the reader—they see things in it that you didn't think were there. So once you've published a book, you've lost control of it, and if you want to fret about that then don't publish it. But to do something major with it, the main thing was to make sure it got into the best hands. I couldn't think of any better hands than Nicholas Hytner and the National Theatre.[10]

And Pullman was immediately impressed with the actors:

> When I saw [Anna Maxwell Martin] at the read through I was utterly convinced that she was Lyra—she looks like the Lyra I had in my head and she is very clever in a streetwise way like Lyra. And Dominic Cooper, who plays Will, is brilliant.[11]

While they were still rehearsing, Rupert Kaye, chief executive of England's Association of Christian Teachers, denounced the National Theatre for staging the play at all, and especially at Christmas:

> The National Theatre as a national institution has a responsibility to put on a family play over the Christmas and New Year season which is uplifting, enjoyable and accessible to people of all ages and backgrounds. Philip Pullman's story is deeply disturbing—it is offensive to Christians and will shock and appal people of other faiths too.[12]

Hytner, however, was unrepentant:

> I have no problem at all with fundamentalists taking offence at Philip's construction of a very beautiful and profoundly good mythology. If

they find his ideas heretical, that's fine. Let's discuss it. But the notion of banning is completely unacceptable. . . . We are not a church. It's not the business of the National to celebrate Christmas.[13]

Fans are awaiting the film adaptation of *His Dark Materials* with a mixture of eager anticipation and apprehension. Scholastic bought the film rights very early on, and have partnered with New Line Productions to make the films. Pullman is very pleased that New Line is involved given their track record with another three-part epic fantasy, Tolkien's *The Lord of the Rings*. He was also pleased that Tom Stoppard was brought in to write the screenplay in late 2002. When asked for his thoughts about a director, Pullman said: "I hope it will be someone who will take the story seriously and not be intoxicated by all the opportunities for lots of action. At the centre of the story is a very simple thing: a girl and a boy growing up, who realize they love each other."[14]

Discussions are taking place with Chris Weitz, and there are rumors that he will write a new screenplay in place of Stoppard's. Weitz, with his brother Paul, is best known for producing light entertainment films such as *American Pie*. Their most serious film to date is perhaps *About a Boy,* based on Nick Hornby's novel. Empire Online points out that Peter Jackson would not have seemed an obvious choice to direct *The Lord of the Rings* beforehand, and goes on to point out how keen Weitz is:

> Chris is reportedly so keen to land this job that he wrote a long dissertation detailing how he would tackle the books, which range across several different realities and feature angels, ghosts, Furies, armoured polar bears, a dæmon familiar for every character and the stuff the universe is made of. Weitz' treatment obviously impressed the studio executives as well as author Philip Pullman and screenwriter Tom Stoppard and he is now deep in negotiations for the job.[15]

Pullman says: "I've seen some of what Chris Weitz has written, and although there are some small areas where we shall have to discuss things, I like the general tendency of what he says."[16]

THE BOOK OF DUST

Philip Pullman is, meanwhile, still hard at work—and has stopped giving interviews for a while so that he can get on with his writing. Now that he has finished *The Scarecrow and the Servant*, he is finally getting down to work on the long-awaited *The Book of Dust*. This will develop further some of the ideas in *His Dark Materials*. In particular, he sees it as a good opportunity to flesh out the "creation myth" that underpins the trilogy. This myth is the story of the origin of the Authority, the first angel to condense out of Dust, and his deception of the angels who came afterward. It talks about "the Sophia," the angel who became known as Wisdom, and her attempt to unmask the Authority, which resulted in the first angelic rebellion. It also describes how these rebel angels brought "enlightenment" to the conscious beings of every world, prompting them to declare their independence of God. The churches of every world are, according to the myth, the Authority's way of punishing and controlling the fallen beings. The myth ends at the point where *His Dark Materials* begins—with Lord Asriel preparing a second rebellion. How much more than this story will go into *The Book of Dust* remains to be seen—Pullman is characteristically secretive about its contents, claiming that when he talks too much about things he ends up not writing about them. However, he has said:

> *The Book of Dust* will not be a simple reference book—far from it. I want to go into the background of Lyra's world, and the creation myth that underpins the whole trilogy, and to say something about some of the other characters, and about the alethiometer and the history of the subtle knife, and so on. Furthermore I want it to be richly illustrated. It'll be story-driven, not reference-driven, and I'll need to brood over it in silence before I find the right form for it.[17]

Pullman has often said that there are plenty more stories from Lyra's world to be told. He would like to tell the story of Lee Scoresby and Iorek Byrnison fighting together in the Tunguska campaign, for example, and there's a story in the relationship between Serafina Pekkala and Farder Coram. The story about Lyra will be set about four years after the end of *The Amber Spyglass*."

LYRA'S OXFORD

However, while Pullman was working on material for *The Book of Dust*, he began to realize that it might be good to have some kind of steppingstone first. He says, "I thought it would be fun to put together some documents and bits and pieces from Lyra's world, such as a map of the Oxford she knows, and as I did, I found a story beginning to take shape."[18] The story that took shape is just one episode, which probably would have gone into *The Book of Dust*, but editor David Fickling encouraged him to do something more self-contained with it: "I asked Philip if he could do some bits and pieces around the idea of a map and this book grew out of it. He always told me he couldn't write short stories, but it isn't true. . . . In my view this new short story is one of the finest pieces of writing that Philip has ever produced."[19] The short story is called "Lyra and the Birds" and is found in the book *Lyra's Oxford*. It's set around two years after Lyra and Will part at the end of *The Amber Spyglass*. The story of Lyra in *The Book of Dust* is likely to be set another two years on again, so "Lyra and the Birds" looks back to the trilogy as well as ahead to the later work—it acts as "a sort of bridge."[20] After *The Book of Dust* Pullman says there will be only one more book about Lyra's world—at Fickling's suggestion there will be a "little dark-green book" to partner the little dark-red book of *Lyra's Oxford*.

But *Lyra's Oxford* is more than just a single short story: "We wanted to create an object that was both intriguing and beautiful, and—like the story—was both self-contained and full of references elsewhere. There [is] a map of Lyra's Oxford, like ours but different, and various other bits and pieces; and it [is] illustrated by John Lawrence, the great master of the woodcut."[21] At the British Book Trade Awards, the Nibbies, in March 2004, *Lyra's Oxford* deservedly won the award for design and production, and David Fickling was voted editor of the year. The "various other bits and pieces" include the map of Lyra's Oxford, a postcard and other material from Lyra's world. Pullman's delightfully enigmatic preface to *Lyra's Oxford* comments on them:

> The other things might be connected with the story, or they might not;
> they might be connected to stories that haven't appeared yet. It's not
> easy to tell.
>
> It's easy to imagine how they might have turned up, though. The
> world is full of things like that: old postcards, theatre programmes,
> leaflets about bomb-proofing your cellar, greetings cards, photograph
> albums, holiday brochures, instruction booklets for machine tools,
> maps, catalogues, railway timetables, menu cards from long-gone
> cruise liners—all kinds of things that once served a real and useful
> purpose, but have now become cut adrift from the things and the peo-
> ple they relate to.[22]

Some of the things clearly relate to Lyra's world, but others—the postcard
from Mary Malone, for one—are from ours. Who knows how these pieces
came together, but here they are, stuck together as if they had been tucked
into the book for safekeeping. "All these tattered old bits and pieces have a
history and a meaning," but that meaning is only apparent to the person
who put them into the book. The effect is as though we've picked up the
book in a secondhand bookshop and been intrigued at what else has come
along for the ride. That's exactly the effect Philip Pullman and David Fickling
wanted, of course—that's part of the reason why the book is clothbound,
and John Lawrence's superb woodcuts add to the feeling. It needs to *feel* like
a lovely, precious book into which you might tuck some of these things.

Pullman is having lots of fun here. On the reverse side of the map are various advertisements, including one for "books on travel, archaeology and related subjects." Several of these fictional publications have connections with
the trilogy: we see that Colonel Carborn, who "made the first balloon flight
over the North Pole" (*GC*, p. 76), has written a book about his adventure,
and that Dr. Broken Arrow is an anthropologist as well as an oceanographer
(*GC*, p. 76). We also discover that the talented Marisa Coulter is a published
author—bizarrely on "The Bronze Clocks of Benin," which seems to be very

far removed from the activities of the General Oblation Board. But we do know she spent time exploring in Africa—this is presumably where she came across *zombis* and the magic that created the spy-flies.[23] There's a book on "some curious anomalies in the mathematics" of the *Four Books of Architecture* by one of the world's greatest architects, Andrea Palladio (originator of the Palladian style). The book is by one Nicholas Outram—these are Philip's middle names. The final two books listed also hark back to *The Golden Compass*. Jotham Santelia recovered his mind enough to write up his experiences on Svalbard as *A Prisoner of the Bears*,[24] while his Jordan colleague Trelawney is the author of *Fraud: An Exposure of a Scientific Imposture*—rather ironic given Santelia's outburst about him (*GC*, p. 329).

Perhaps most tantalizing of all the extras is the information about the cruise of the S.S. *Zenobia* through the Mediterranean to the Levant (the old name for the countries at the eastern end of the Mediterranean: Lebanon, Israel and parts of Syria and Turkey). Is this something that will play a part in *The Book of Dust*? We'll have to wait and see. The item that Pullman draws most attention to in the preface is the postcard. It features a very odd collection of images—as its sender, Mary Malone, acknowledges when she writes, "Such a beautiful city, and they produce a card like this!"[25] Observant readers of the trilogy immediately recognize the hornbeam trees in Sunderland Avenue from Pullman's little drawing for the first chapter in *The Subtle Knife*. We understand the significance of the bench in the Botanic Gardens, and the science building in which Mary works. The picture of a house in Norham Gardens doesn't obviously fit, but Mary says it's round the corner from her flat. Pullman writes:

> It might not have occurred to [Mary Malone] . . . when she sent a postcard to an old friend shortly after arriving in Oxford for the first time, that that card itself would trace part of a story that hadn't yet happened when she wrote it. Perhaps some particles move backwards in time; perhaps the future affects the past in some way we don't understand; or perhaps the universe is simply more aware than we are.[26]

It is perhaps significant that the preface to *Lyra's Oxford* isn't signed—it doesn't need to be signed, but it often would be. Maybe it only becomes significant because it follows the quotation from Oscar Baedecker. This quotation seems to have the same status as those at the beginning of *The Golden Compass* and *The Amber Spyglass*—passages from other writing that influence or shed light on what is to follow. The Baedecker quotation functions in the same way, but it is as much part of the fiction as the story of Lyra and the birds. There is no reference to him anywhere—not even in the British Library or the American Library of Congress. What finally gives the game away is the reference to him on the page apparently from an old Oxford guidebook (inserted just after page 30 of *Lyra's Oxford*) where Baedecker is quoted as referring to "the coastline Oxford shares with Bohemia." Perhaps Baedecker is not even of Lyra's world—he certainly isn't from ours. So the preface, sandwiched between fictions, seems to be as fictional as the rest.

THE SEARCH FOR MEANING

The question that keeps coming back while pondering on all these bits and pieces is "What does it all mean?" How does it all fit together? As the preface concludes, "There are many things we haven't yet learned how to read. The story in this book is partly about that very process." Is Pullman suggesting that *everything* has some meaning if only we can discern it? Lyra soon confirms this. The story begins with Lyra on the roof of Jordan College again, watching a vast flock of starlings swooping around above the Oxford skyline before roosting in the Botanic Garden. She and Pantalaimon speculate on whether or not their complicated flight path might have some meaning. Pan suggests that it might mean nothing, "It just is" (*LO*, p. 5), but Lyra is adamant that "Everything means something. We just have to find out how to read it" (pp. 5-6). After her experiences with the alethiometer, and with the loops and swirls on Mary Malone's computer, perhaps it's not surprising that she holds this conviction so fiercely.

As they ponder this question, the flock begins to attack something. Lyra and Pantalaimon are shocked to realize that it's a witch's dæmon. They help him to escape through the trapdoor into Jordan College and away from the starlings' fury. It transpires that the dæmon is looking for Lyra to get her help in searching for a man called Sebastian Makepeace. The dæmon's witch is sick and needs help from Makepeace. As Lyra investigates the whereabouts of Makepeace, she discovers that he is an alchemist and a former scholar of Merton. Jordan scholar Dr. Polstead dismisses him as a nut case: "He devoted himself to alchemy—in this day and age!" (p. 18). At dinner in St. Sophia's,[27] Lyra quizzes an elderly history scholar about alchemy and why it was no longer practiced, and is told that Makepeace is the only serious alchemist in two and a half centuries. Lyra's two informants both make connections to the theme of meaning. Dr. Polstead believes that, because Sebastian Makepeace is mad, his work and his mumblings to himself have no meaning. The scholar, Miss Greenwood, tells Lyra that the alchemist's name is "ironic," as he "was said to be very violent" (p. 22)—his name means the opposite of his character.

Lyra and Pantalaimon take the dæmon to Jericho after dinner—but they feel uneasy. There are too many uncertain aspects of what's going on for them to understand. They are suspicious of Makepeace because "alchemy's nonsense" (p. 26). They are suspicious of the witch's dæmon, though they have no real reason beyond the fact that they had never heard of the "birch-oath," which the dæmon had mentioned to them (p. 15). And it's a mystery to them why birds keep attacking the dæmon. When they press him to tell them the truth, he explains that Makepeace is the only one who can cure the new sickness that is killing witches but not their dæmons. Lyra's heart goes out to the dæmon, though she suppresses the questions and doubts that still fill her mind. Pullman comments that "since she and Will had parted two years before, the slightest thing had the power to move her to pity and distress; it felt as if her heart were bruised forever" (p. 30).

When they reach the alchemist's house, Lyra and Pan finally become aware that they are walking into a trap. While Pan struggles with the witch's dæmon, Lyra prepares to face the witch, thinking through how Will, the natural fighter, would act in the situation. She is saved by the extraordinary intervention of another bird, as a swan flies at full speed into the witch, breaking her back. Makepeace and the witch had been lovers; their son had died in the recent war and the witch held Lyra responsible as it was said that the war was fought over Lyra. Lyra claims it had nothing to do with her—it seems that even now she doesn't realize how central a role she played. As they reflect back on the odd behavior of the birds, Pan realizes that it wasn't random behavior, but rather they were protecting Lyra. Makepeace confirms this, saying, "Everything has a meaning, if only we could read it" (p. 45). The alchemist cannot discern the meaning, but he does tell them, "It means something about you, and something about the city. You'll find the meaning if you search for it" (p. 46). As they return to St. Sophia's, they hear a nightingale singing—a sign of peace after the turmoil of the previous hours—and they try to work out the meaning of it all. Pan says, "It feels as if the whole city's looking after us. So what we feel is part of the meaning, isn't it?'

The story is like the book as a whole—there are several elements that don't seem to fit in or make sense, at least initially. Some of them only make sense when looked at in a different way. Some look back to events that have already taken place, some anticipate events still to come and we won't see the significance of these for some time. It seems highly likely that Sebastian Makepeace (who seems, in the end, to be both sane and peaceful) will play a significant role in *The Book of Dust*;[28] perhaps Dr. Polstead and Miss Greenwood will too. Why the city should be looking after Lyra at all remains a mystery—the all-pervasive Dust must still have some purpose in mind for Lyra. Back in *The Amber Spyglass*, as Mary Malone surveys the wreck of her fallen tree, she too is searching for some meaning and finds it in the love of matter for Dust. Pullman's message seems to be that we must search for meaning in this world, our home, and in the matter and consciousness of which it is composed. Lyra's relationship with Oxford seems to be a metaphor for the relationship Pullman thinks we should have with the physical world in which we live: "The city, their city—*belonging* was one of the meanings of that, and *protection*, and *home*" (p. 48). We'll explore what kinds of meanings Pullman sees in the world and expresses through his books in part three.

PART THREE

Shedding Light
on Dark Matter

9

DÆMONS AND GROWING UP

Perhaps the most harrowing moment of *His Dark Materials* is when Lyra leaves Pantalaimon to travel to the world of the dead:

> [Lyra] looked back again at the foul and dismal shore, so bleak and blasted with disease and poison, and thought of her dear Pan waiting there alone, her heart's companion, watching her disappear into the mist, and she fell into a storm of weeping. Her passionate sobs didn't echo, because the mist muffled them, but all along the shore in innumerable ponds and shallows, in wretched broken tree stumps, the damaged creatures that lurked there heard her full-hearted cry and drew themselves a little closer to the ground, afraid of such passion. . . .
>
> Lyra was doing the cruellest thing she had ever done, hating herself, hating the deed, suffering for Pan and with Pan and because of Pan; trying to put him down on the cold path, disengaging his cat-claws from her clothes, weeping, weeping. Will closed his ears: the sound was too unhappy to bear. Time after time she pushed her dæmon away, and still he cried and tried to cling. . . .
>
> And she pushed him away, so that he crouched bitter and cold and frightened on the muddy ground. (*AS*, pp. 282-84)

We can't quite imagine the depth of pain Lyra experiences because we have no conception of what it means to be inextricably bound up with a creature that is external to us, and yet part of us. I can imagine the pain of leaving the person I most love, possibly never to see them again. But that person is still *not me;* I know what it's like to be away from them; I know that the person exists independently of me. It's the finality of parting that would cause the anguish. But to be sundered from a *part of me*—what would that be like?

THE UNITY OF HUMAN AND DÆMON

It's perhaps at this point that we understand even more fully how terrible a place Bolvangar was. Back in *The Golden Compass* we realized that to separate a child from his or her dæmon was a terrible thing; we could see Lyra's distress over it. But nearly eight hundred pages later we are so much more engaged with Lyra and Pantalaimon that we feel the trauma intensely. The oneness of girl and dæmon has become normal to us, as indeed, it has to Will.

We have come to realize that Lyra's sense of herself is as much bound up with Pan as with her own body. She feels no less integrated as a person than Will, who has no visible dæmon. It is Lyra's sense of Will being just as complete as she is that enables her to reason that his dæmon must be inside him. Will is completely unaware of this other part of him—until he discovers "an agony building inside him" as he leaves the desolate shore with Lyra. He realizes that he does have a dæmon—and he, too, is being torn apart from himself:

> Part of it was physical. It felt as if an iron hand had gripped his heart and was pulling it out between his ribs, so that he pressed his hands to the place and vainly tried to hold it in. It was far deeper and far worse than the pain of losing his fingers. But it was mental, too: something secret and private was being dragged into the open, where it had no wish to be, and Will was nearly overcome by a mixture of pain and shame and fear and self-reproach, because he himself had caused it.
>
> And it was worse than that. It was as if he'd said, "No, don't kill me, I'm frightened; kill my mother instead; she doesn't matter, I don't love her," and as if she'd heard him say it, and pretended she hadn't so as to spare his feelings, and offered herself in his place anyway because

of her love for him. He felt as bad as that. There was nothing worse to feel. (*AS*, p. 285)

Toward the end of *The Amber Spyglass*, Will gets to meet his dæmon, Kirjava,[1] for the first time. He realizes that he'll never forget that meeting, nor the feeling of having Kirjava ripped apart from him before he even knew of her existence.

Dæmons, then, make for a very powerful narrative device within *His Dark Materials*, but what are they?

TRUE COMPANIONS

Philip Pullman uses the dæmons to great effect within *His Dark Materials*, but the idea isn't entirely original to him as he concedes: "Dæmons came into my head suddenly and unexpectedly, but they do have a sort of provenance. One clear origin is Socrates' daimon. Another is the old idea of the guardian angel."[2] As Pullman says, the concept of dæmon goes back to the Greeks. A dæmon in that classical sense is "a spirit, or immaterial being, holding a middle place between men and deities in pagan mythology" or "one's genius; a tutelary spirit or internal voice; as, the dæmon of Socrates."[3] You sometimes find dæmon in this classical sense spelt as "daimon" or "demon" but there are no evil overtones to this concept. Over time the meaning (and spelling) of the word shifted to have the sense that it does today—an evil spirit. But Pullman draws on the earlier idea and turns it into something visible—the companion animal. Toward the end of *The Amber Spyglass*, Serafina Pekkala reminds Pantalaimon what the primary function of a dæmon is: "One thing hasn't changed: you must help your humans, not hinder them. You must help them and guide them and encourage them toward wisdom. That's what dæmons are for" (*AS*, p. 473).

The idea of companion animals who are more than simply animals is an important part of shamanism and witchcraft. Animal familiars are often thought to be able to change shape and to be spirit guides. In tribal shamanism, the spirit traveling while in a trance (*SK*, p. 215) is often believed to be in an animal form. In his 1992 television series, *Millennium: Tribal Wisdom and the Modern World*,[4] anthropologist David Maybury-Lewis described how Ignacion, a Makuna shaman, became a spirit jaguar under the influence of a hallucinogenic drug. Sir James Frazer, in his famous 1922 book, *The Golden Bough*, also talks about various tribal cultures that believed in the idea of an external soul in animals or even stones. Often they believed that the death of the animal entailed the death of the human and vice versa.[5] However, neither this nor the Greek idea of dæmons is quite how Philip Pullman uses dæmons in *His Dark Materials*, but these things underpin his invention.

Sally Vincent, writing in the Manchester, England, newspaper *The Guardian*, says:

> Your dæmon . . . is the creature of your deepest essence; a bird, reptile, insect or animal, attached to you by an inevitable thread, like an externalised soul. It is your guardian angel, your confidante, your conscience, your representative. In childhood, while you make the choices that form your character, your dæmon changes; when you become an adult, it is what you have created, and it stays like that until you die. A slimy snake, a sly monkey, a fierce tiger, an obedient dog, a pussy cat: it's yours. It's you. You're never alone with a dæmon.[6]

These descriptions—*externalized soul, guardian angel, confidante, conscience, representative*—are partly, but not entirely, right. *Externalized soul* is probably the best description, as Iorek Byrnison makes clear when he tells Lyra that "a bear's armor is his soul, just as your dæmon is your soul" (*GC*, pp. 196-97). But it doesn't seem to be the case that the human has no soul and no conscience apart from the dæmon. That would make Lyra's separation from Pantalaimon a very different affair. Neither is it quite right that the dæmon is a guardian angel, despite Pullman referring to the idea (he does, of course, include angels as beings in their own right). *Guardian angels* is suggestive of entirely separate beings with a responsibility for watching over and protecting humans. And the dæmon isn't quite a *representative* of the human—except in the case of witches and shamans, whose dæmons can travel far from their humans—although it does represent something about the human. Human and dæmon are fuzzy, overlapping parts of the same thing, two facets of one being.

And yet they also have some measure of independence. They are physically, although invisibly, bound together. But a dæmon can be active while the human is still, and can move some distance from the human. A child's dæmon can change shape, while the human obviously can't. The human and dæmon are mentally bound together—they each know what the other is thinking ("[Lyra] and Pantalaimon could feel each other's thoughts"; *GC*, p. 234), and yet they can also think differently. Think back, for example, to the opening scene when Lyra and Pantalaimon sneak into the Retiring Room and see the Master poison the Tokay. Pan argues that "it's none of our business. And I think it would be the silliest thing you've ever done in a lifetime of silly things to interfere" (*GC*, p. 8). Lyra doesn't see that they have a choice anymore and accusingly says to Pan, "You're supposed to know about conscience, aren't you?" Pantalaimon realizes that he hadn't spotted Lyra's intention of hiding and watching. Lyra tells him off for nagging. There's a suggestion here that the dæmon is, to some extent, the voice of conscience, but clearly Lyra is not without a conscience, despite disagreeing with Pan.

A human and dæmon share physical experiences and are also emotionally bound together, feeling the same way much of the time but not all of it. In the incident just referred to, Lyra and Pantalaimon end up feeling cross, but they are cross with *each other*. Before they are reunited after their agonizing separation, Lyra longs to see Pan and to hold him, but her dæmon keeps his distance from her as a punishment (*AS*, p. 474).

THE DIVINE PARADOX

Like the overlapping circles of a Venn diagram, a human and dæmon partly share a consciousness, and partly have separate consciousnesses. Given Philip Pullman's antipathy to Christianity, the great irony of his invention of the dæmon (and the Death) is that he has constructed a rather good model of the Trinity of God. The Trinity is a very difficult concept. It expresses the

Christian belief that there is one God, and yet we see God in the Bible in three persons: Father, Son (Jesus Christ) and Holy Spirit. Each of these three persons is fully God, but their unity is such that we cannot say they are three Gods. People often claim that these two aspects of God's nature are contradictory—God cannot be both one and three at the same time. But this isn't the case.

First, it may not be a contradiction but a paradox. A paradox *appears* contradictory but actually expresses some truth that is not obvious. Second, if God is infinite, then we should expect to find aspects of his nature and being that are beyond our ability to understand. If everything about God were easily comprehended by my limited human mind I would be more likely to agree with those people who argue that Christianity is merely human invention. Third, we accept paradox in other aspects of life, such as the wave-particle duality within modern physics. This holds that electromagnetic waves such as light behave both like waves *and* like particles. And so do particles like electrons or protons. It all depends on what kind of experiments you do.[7] It goes against common sense, but the physics forces us to see things in this way. It's much the same with God and our understanding of his three-in-one nature.

Pullman's wonderful idea of a human and a dæmon inextricably connected with—indeed, part of—each other is not too dissimilar an idea. When you first read *The Golden Compass* the connectedness of Lyra and Pantalaimon (and Pan's shape-changing abilities) seems extraordinary. As we discover more about the way they are two parts of one being, the harder it becomes to understand but the more normal it seems. As I commented above, by the time Lyra is being ferried to the world of the dead, their unity is something we barely stop to think about. The tearing apart of Will's united self brings it home to us forcefully.

The ghosts add yet another level to the person. Pullman says, "[Lyra] can think about her body and she can think about her dæmon. Now there must be a third part of her to be doing the thinking, and this is the part I call the ghost. . . . The ghost is the part that survives death."[8] Although we can distinguish among the three parts of her—human, dæmon, ghost—we have to recognize that together they are one being. It's not a perfect model of the Trinity by any means, but it's not a million miles away from it either.

DÆMONIC PURPOSES

One of the other ways in which Pullman sometimes uses dæmons—perhaps unconsciously—is to indicate the value he puts on a character, or their potential for redemption. Lord Asriel has Stelmaria, the stunning, graceful and exotic snow leopard; Mrs. Coulter has the beautiful but cruel golden monkey; Farder Coram has the double-size cat Sophonax with her fur of extraordinary richness; Stanislaus Grumman has the magnificent osprey Sayan Kötör. By contrast it is revealing that all of the religious characters in *His Dark Materials* have cold-blooded dæmons.[9]

Pullman also uses dæmons to say something about the pain of separation, about depression and about death. It's a rich metaphor, which he uses very creatively. He says, "Right at the end of *Amber Spyglass*, after 1200 or more pages, I was still discovering new things I could do with this human-dæmon link."[10] While there may be no simple way of describing what a dæmon is, what we can say is that a dæmon is a visible, external part of a person that represents facets of the person's character. They are, perhaps, physical representations of what Stanislaus Grumman calls "a silent voice in the mind" (*SK*, p. 213). These facets of character are not tangible in human beings in our world—we deduce them from a person's actions and words. But Pullman uses this companion creature to bring some aspects of personality to the surface. The existence of dæmons "was the richest idea I've ever had," says Philip Pullman. "There were so many different things I could do with it. But it works, and it's actually saying something about the business of being human—it's not just decorative."[11]

KNOW YOURSELF

Jerry, the able seaman on the voyage to Trollesund, tells Lyra that the form of a dæmon tells someone what kind of person he or she is:

Take old Belisaria. She's a seagull, and that means I'm a kind of seagull too. I'm not grand and splendid nor beautiful, but I'm a tough old thing and I can survive anywhere and always find a bit of food and company. That's worth knowing, that is. And when your dæmon settles, you'll know the sort of person you are. . . . There's plenty of folk as'd like to have a lion as a dæmon and they end up with a poodle. And till they learn to be satisfied with what they are, they're going to be fretful about it. Waste of feeling, that is. (*GC*, pp. 167-68)

Pullman says:

You cannot choose your dæmon, and so no matter how much I might like to have a bird or a cat or something graceful or elegant, I'd probably turn out to have a crab or a slug. . . . Somebody criticized me for being terribly class-ridden and British and snobbish because all servants are people whose dæmons are dogs. This critic thought that I was saying if your dæmon's a dog you have to be a servant. It's not like that at all, as Lyra explains elsewhere to Will (who doesn't know about dæmons). "If your dæmon turns out to be a dog, that means you're the sort of person (and there are plenty of those about) who enjoys knowing where they are in a hierarchy, who enjoys following orders and pleasing the person in charge." There are people like that, and they make good servants. We don't have servants any more in our society but we do in Lyra's world. If your dæmon is a dog that is a sign to you that that'd be a career that you'd enjoy doing and that you'd be good at. . . . The way to find out what your dæmon is, is to ask your friends to write it down anonymously. Then you will find out.[12]

Elsewhere he suggests what his own dæmon might be: "I think she's probably a magpie or a jackdaw, one of these birds that pick up bright shining things and doesn't distinguish in terms of shininess between the diamond ring and the Kit Kat wrapper—just as I don't distinguish in terms of 'storyness' between Shakespeare and *Neighbours*."[13]

Dæmons are usually of the opposite sex—a consequence of the fact that we all have aspects of our personalities that can be thought of as primarily masculine and some that are primarily feminine. In *The Subtle Knife* Stanislaus Grumman tells Lee Scoresby of the time when he first entered Lee's world and saw his dæmon for the first time: "I hadn't known of Sayan Kötör here till I entered [your world].[14] People here cannot conceive of worlds where dæmons are a silent voice in the mind and no more. Can you imagine my astonishment, in turn, at learning that part of my own nature was female, and bird-formed, and beautiful?" (*SK*, pp. 213-14). The discovery helped him to become more aware of aspects of his personality that he had sensed only dimly, if at all. Bernie Johansen, the pastry cook at Jordan College, is one of the few people with a dæmon of the same sex. Pullman says: "Occasionally, no doubt, people do have a dæmon of the same sex; that might indicate homosexuality, or it might indicate some other sort of gift or quality, such as second sight. I do not know. But I don't have to know everything about what I write."[15]

GROWING UP

Pivotal to *The Golden Compass* is the fact that Pantalaimon is able to change his shape—he can be a moth one moment and a wildcat the next and then a sparrow. He can do this because Lyra is still a child. But adolescence is not far off for Lyra and she knows the time will soon come when Pan will change less and less until finally settling into one form for the rest of their life.

This transition from having a dæmon that can change to having a settled dæmon says something about "the business of being human"—in particular about the business of growing up. For Pullman, this is the central theme of *His Dark Materials*: "I suddenly realized that of course what the whole story is about is growing up. It's about the difference between innocence and experience, between childhood and adulthood."

Lyra asks Jerry the sailor why dæmons have to settle. "Ah, they always have settled, and they always will," he replies. "That's part of growing up. There'll come a time when you'll be tired of his changing about, and you'll want a settled kind of form for him" (*GC*, p. 167). Lyra can't believe she would ever want this to happen, but it is inevitable if she is going to stop being a child. The sailor explains that settling dæmons help children develop their self-awareness as they pass through adolescence. Pullman says that dæmons "symbolise the difference between the infinite plasticity, the infinite potentiality and mutability of childhood and the fixed nature of adulthood."[16] Millicent Lenz writes, "Being an adult entails accepting the narrowing of one's potential possible 'shapes,' learning to live with a diminishment of the protean possibilities inherent in the child. As the wise seaman implies, there may be some comfort to an adult in having a firmer basis for self-trust and a clearer awareness of limits."[17] There is, however, a danger that fixed dæmons and this stress on "the fixed nature of adulthood" shuts down the potential for substantial change of character as an adult. Mrs. Coulter goes through something of that process in this story. The Christian experience of conversion is often one of a profound change in character and outlook.

Lyra is very much a self-obsessed child when we first meet her. Her life revolves around escapades on the roofs and in the lanes of Oxford, a constantly shifting array of enemies and allies, and avoiding being worked too hard by her reluctant tutors, the Jordan scholars. She believes that telling an inventive lie is far more satisfying and useful than the truth could ever be. She's a typical child in that she doesn't really know herself—who she is, or what kind of person she is, or what really matters in her life. The changeability of her dæmon reflects the uncertainty, the unsettledness in Lyra.

But as she approaches adolescence—and faces some extremely challenging circumstances—she gets more of a sense of herself. Although she doesn't know what the future has in store for her when she returns to Jordan College at the end of *The Amber Spyglass*, she has some direction and some mature perspectives on life. She has grown up and is rapidly moving toward adulthood. The surprise for me is that this change seems to happen in early adolescence, whereas many adolescents in our world seem to be more confused about their identity and direction in life than they ever were before the onset of puberty.

EMBRACING CHANGE

Like the heroes of so many—perhaps all—great stories, Lyra and Will are on a journey of self-discovery. They set out on their quests as children—extraordinary, strong-willed, resourceful kids maybe, but still children—and in the process of pursuing their goals find something more valuable that they hadn't been looking for: self-knowledge and maturity. The tumultuous events in which they are caught up happen at just the right time for them as they begin to make the transition into adolescence. Of course, this great change in life is also concerned with reaching sexual maturity—something the church feared but that Lyra and Will embraced (we'll return to this in chapter ten). For Pullman this transition is perhaps the most important stage of life, in which we move from innocence to experience, childhood to adulthood. And this, more than anything else, is beautifully represented by the imagery of dæmons.

> Will put his hand on hers. A new mood had taken hold of him, and he felt resolute and peaceful. Knowing exactly what he was doing and exactly what it would mean, he moved his hand from Lyra's wrist and stroked the red-gold fur of her dæmon.
>
> Lyra gasped. But her surprise was mixed with a pleasure so like the joy that flooded through her when she had put the fruit to his lips that she couldn't protest, because she was breathless. With a racing heart she responded in the same way: she put her hand on the silky warmth of Will's dæmon, and as her fingers tightened in the fur she knew that Will was feeling exactly what she was.
>
> And she knew, too, that neither dæmon would change now, having felt a lover's hands on them. These were their shapes for life: they would want no other.
>
> So, wondering whether any lovers before them had made this blissful discovery, they lay together as the earth turned slowly and the moon and stars blazed above them. (*AS*, pp. 498-99)

10

DUST, SIN AND THE FALL

At the heart of the plot of *His Dark Materials* is the existence of some very mysterious particles. We first learn about them when Lord Asriel shows some photograms of his recent arctic expedition to the scholars of Jordan College:

> [Lord Asriel] lifted out the first slide and dropped another into the frame. This was much darker; it was as if the moonlight had been filtered out. . . . But the man had altogether changed: he was bathed in light, and a fountain of glowing particles seemed to be streaming from his upraised hand.
>
> "That light," said the Chaplain, "is it going up or coming down?"
>
> "It's coming down," said Lord Asriel, "but it isn't light. It's Dust."
>
> Something in the way he said it made Lyra imagine *dust* with a capital letter, as if this wasn't ordinary dust. The reaction of the Scholars confirmed her feeling, because Lord Asriel's words caused a sudden collective silence, followed by gasps of incredulity. (*GC*, pp. 20-21)

What a great reaction—exactly what Lord Asriel expected. But why do the scholars react like this? It's not simply that they're seeing an image of something that had previously been invisible, but that what they're seeing is extremely controversial. Dust has recently become the subject of intense speculation among experimental theologians (physicists), having been discovered by a Muscovite named Rusakov some years before. Rusakov found that there was a constant flow of previously unknown particles coming from space.[1]

These particles interacted with matter in a radically different way from anything that had been studied previously. In particular, he noticed that human beings seemed to attract the particles—but the effect was much stronger in adults than in children. Lord Asriel's photogram shows this clearly:

> [Lord Asriel] indicated the blurred shape of the smaller figure.
>
> "I thought that was the man's dæmon," said the Enquirer.
>
> "No. His dæmon was at the time coiled around his neck in the form of a snake. That shape you can dimly see is a child."
>
> "A severed child—?" said someone, and the way he stopped showed that he knew this was something that shouldn't have been voiced.
>
> There was an intense silence.
>
> Then Lord Asriel said calmly, "An entire child. Which, given the nature of Dust, is precisely the point, is it not?" (*GC*, p. 21)

DUST AND SIN

Rusakov's discovery was deeply disturbing to the church authorities—though Pullman doesn't really spell out why. When Lord Asriel explains all this to Lyra, he simply comments that "discoveries of this sort . . . have a bearing on the doctrines of the church" (*GC*, p. 370). But why does the existence of these particles have anything to do with church doctrine? Rusakov has, apparently, only four significant facts about the particles:

1. They exist.
2. They are elementary particles (they can't be broken down any further).
3. They are attracted to human beings.
4. They are attracted to adults much more than children.

Which of these would cause the Magisterium to suspect Rusakov of possession by an evil spirit (*GC*, p. 371)? The mere existence of a new type of elementary particle would hardly do so. However, the fact that the particles are attracted to humans means that they must be bound up with the nature of humanity—and that does relate to theology. What it means to be human is, it seems, something that must be tightly defined in the Magisterium's official doctrines. But again, the simple existence of Rusakov particles reveals little of any consequence about human nature. Only by understanding what those particles are, and the way they affect people, could experimental theologians say anything of note.

The one really significant insight that comes from the discovery of Rusakov particles is that they indicate a major difference between children and adults. Though, since everyone knows that dæmons lose their shape-shifting ability during adolescence, even this is hardly earth-shattering news. However, the Rusakov particles do begin to look like a good candidate for an explanation of *why* dæmons settle. The ambitious Mrs. Coulter was the one to guess that there was a connection (*GC*, p. 375). Even so, without knowing much more about the nature and action of these particles, there's nothing in this to really make anyone worry. The Magisterium, though, is dogmatic, unthinking and close-minded—it is no surprise that they responded like this (we'll look more fully at Pullman's portrayal of the church in chapter thirteen).

GENESIS RELOADED

After their knee-jerk response to Rusakov's work, the Magisterium needed to work out how it fitted in with their doctrines. The answer seemed obvious: these particles were the physical evidence for original sin. Lord Asriel explains this to Lyra by referring her to Genesis 3. He reads the passage in which Adam and Eve, having been tempted by the serpent, break God's command not to eat from the tree of the knowledge of good and evil. Theologians call this first rebellion against God "the Fall."

What Asriel reads is very different from the real text of Genesis 3. In Lyra's world everyone has a dæmon, so Pullman inserts new material and changes a little of the original to reflect this. He uses the 1611 Authorized Version of the Bible because he loves its rich and poetic language.[2] Here is the passage in question—the material deleted from the real Genesis 3 is shown with a line through it, and Pullman's inserted text is in italics:

And the woman said unto the serpent, We may eat of the fruit of the trees of the garden:

But of the fruit of the tree which is in the midst of the garden, God hath said, Ye shall not eat of it, neither shall ye touch it, lest ye die.

And the serpent said unto the woman, Ye shall not surely die:

For God doth know that in the day ye eat thereof, then your eyes shall be opened, *and your dæmons shall assume their true forms,* and ye shall be as gods, knowing good and evil.

And when the woman saw that the tree was good for food, and that it was pleasant to the eyes, and a tree to be desired to ~~make one wise~~ *reveal the true form of one's dæmon,* she took of the fruit thereof, and did eat, and gave also unto her husband with her; and he did eat.

And the eyes of them both were opened, ~~and they knew that they were naked~~ *and they saw the true form of their dæmons, and spoke with them.*

But when the man and the woman knew their own dæmons, they knew that a great change had come upon them, for until that moment it had seemed that they were at one with all the creatures of the earth and the air, and there was no difference between them:

And they saw the difference, and they knew good and evil; and they were ashamed, and they sewed fig leaves together, ~~and made themselves aprons~~ *to cover their nakedness.*[3] (Genesis 3:2-7)

Inserting around 50 percent more material is a fairly significant alteration to the original. Since many young people reading *His Dark Materials* have no idea what Genesis 3 actually says, I can't help wondering how many of them either begin to wonder whether dæmons are real but invisible, as for Will, or assume that Pullman has invented the whole quotation! This tampering with the text is a difficult issue for many Christians. They believe the Bible to be communication from God himself and as such it has a very special status—it should be left with nothing added and nothing taken away. Philip Pullman, of course, values the Bible as nothing more than a work of literature. He doesn't especially revere it, and so feels no qualms about changing it to suit his purposes. Christians may not like it, but it's unreasonable to expect an atheist to worry about this—especially since this passage is part of a work of fantasy fiction, and is set in another world.

Returning to the point Lord Asriel was making, his theology is correct when he tells Lyra, that this "was how sin came into the world . . . sin and shame and death." But he also tells her it was "the moment their dæmons became fixed." In other words, there is a connection between sin and settled dæmons. As far as the Magisterium is concerned, if dæmons first settled when humans first fell, then a settled dæmon *must* have something to do with sin. And if Rusakov particles cluster around adults with settled dæmons, then *they* must have to do with sin too.

ORIGINAL SIN

However, the phrase "original sin" doesn't simply refer to the first human act of rebellion against God. It is the belief that every human being since is caught up in it. Christians disagree about how this actually works[4] but they agree that, since Adam, sin—rebellion—is part of our *nature*, not just what we *do*. Sin is a word that many people misunderstand. It has connotations of Victorian morality, or of "naughty" things we do (which we find rather enjoyable). In fact, *sins* are specific acts (or thoughts), which are contrary to God's nature as utterly pure and holy. *Sin* is a fundamental, innate attitude of rebellion against God. As the Reformers said, we are not sinners because we sin, we sin because we are sinners. "[Christians] agree on the universality, solidarity, stubbornness and historical momentum of sin. That is to say, all serious Christians subscribe to the generic doctrine of corruption, the centrepiece of which is the claim that even when they are good in important ways, human beings are not *sound*."[5] That doesn't mean that there's no good in us—Christians also believe that humans are made in the image of God, and therefore it is also in our nature to be good. In a sense, good is more fundamentally part of our nature than bad, but both are very much part of life for every one of us. These parallel convictions of goodness *and* sinfulness explain the paradox of human nature.

Since this affects *all* human beings, there is no age distinction. We talk easily about the innocence of children—and at some levels they are innocent—but they already have this bias in their nature. Surely no one who has had children should be surprised at this—their capacity to do the wrong thing manifests itself at a remarkably young age.

Rebellion against God has consequences. The Bible's position is that there is no greater crime than to rebel against the creator and sustainer of the universe, whose very nature defines what is good. Adam's first sin brought about death—his spiritual death was immediate; his physical death came later on. Part of God's judgment on him (and all humanity) was that he would "return to the ground, since from it you were taken; for dust you are and to dust you will return" (Genesis 3:19). This phrase was the origin of the Magisterium's name for Rusakov particles: Dust. Incidentally, Lord Asriel's comments about this verse—that the translation is disputed because the text is corrupt, and that it could mean God is admitting his own sinfulness (*GC*, p. 373)—are unjustified. I have yet to find any commentator arguing for an alternative translation of "to dust you will return."[6] And the idea that this could have any reference at all to God's nature has no basis whatsoever outside Pullman's fictional world.

It's clear that the Magisterium is in error because it has misunderstood the doctrine of original sin—sin doesn't start at puberty, it is part of every human being long before then. Therefore, the fact that Dust is attracted to humans from adolescence onward shows not that it is evidence *for* original sin, but that it cannot have to do with original sin at all. The Magisterium had hastily jumped to a wrong conclusion about the nature of Rusakov particles. It was also wrong to give the name Dust to Rusakov particles, since Adam was made from the dust of the ground *before* the Fall, not from Dust falling from space. Having made these mistakes, the Magisterium has backed itself into a corner from which it can only ever view Dust as bound up with sin and evil.

SEVERING THE SIN PROBLEM

In the minds of the church authorities, then, the influx of Dust, the settling of a dæmon and sin itself are firmly linked with adolescence. And, therefore, they are implicitly linked with sexuality. Mrs. Coulter certainly hints strongly at this in what she tells Lyra at Bolvangar:

> Dust is something bad, something wrong, something evil and wicked. Grownups and their dæmons are infected with Dust so deeply that it's too late for them. They can't be helped. . . . Your dæmon's a wonderful friend and companion when you're young, but at the age we call puberty . . . dæmons bring all sort of troublesome thoughts and feelings, and that's what lets Dust in. (*GC*, pp. 282-84)

Having spotted the connection among dæmons, Dust and adolescence, Mrs. Coulter began to wonder whether children could be insulated from the effects of Dust before adolescence kicks in. If so, would that prevent them from becoming sinful? And if Dust is linked with a dæmon taking on its settled form, might the solution be to sever that powerful bond between human and dæmon? Mrs. Coulter certainly thought so, not least because of her experience of *zombis* in Africa—unquestioningly obedient slaves who have lost their own will as a result of being separated from their dæmons. She knew it was possible, she was desperate for power, and the Magisterium was frightened of what Rusakov had discovered. So they quickly took up her suggestion that a new body—the General Oblation Board—conduct some experiments on children.

As far as Mrs. Coulter was concerned, it is all in a good cause; the end justifies the means: "A quick operation on children means they're safe from it. Dust just won't stick to them ever again. They're safe and happy. . . . A quick little operation . . . and you're never troubled again. And your dæmon stays with you, only . . . just not connected. . . . Like a wonderful pet, if you like" (*GC*, pp. 283-84). However, her reaction when she finds her own daughter in the silver cage shows that the end she is pursuing is not altruistic but deeply personal. Mrs. Coulter wants power, status and influence rather than the ultimate good of the children—that is simply how she rationalizes it all to herself. Lyra spots the inconsistency and asks, "If it was so good, why'd you stop them doing it to me? If it was good you should've let them do it. You should have been glad" (*GC*, p. 283). Her mother never quite answers the question. It's clear that Mrs. Coulter is protecting her daughter from the very thing that she claims is so beneficial.

By now Lyra's conviction that Dust isn't actually bad is growing. She's seen her mother's double standards. She's seen what this terrible machinery has done to Tony Makarios, and knows it's all wrong. She's seen the vapid nurses with their "blank and incurious" dæmons, who contrast sharply with the powerful, intelligent, energetic people she admires so much—John Faa, Farder Coram, Lord Asriel, even Mrs. Coulter (though Lyra's former admiration for her has evaporated by this point in the narrative). She has no clue as to the real nature of Dust, but it seems nobody else has either. At the end of *The Golden Compass*, Lyra realizes that if everyone she *doesn't* trust perceives Dust to be a *bad* thing, it's probably the opposite—and she and Pantalaimon set out to search for it.

The Magisterium becomes aware of Lyra and learns about the witches' prophecy. But it takes them until *The Amber Spyglass* before they finally have the all-important detail: "The child . . . is in the position of Eve, the wife of Adam, the mother of us all, and the cause of all sin. . . . If it comes about that the child is tempted, as Eve was, then she is likely to fall. On the outcome will depend . . . everything. And if this temptation does take place, and if the child gives in, then Dust and sin will triumph" (*AS*, pp. 67-68). For the Magisterium, this is unmitigatedly terrible. Having made a connection between Dust and original sin, they can only see a "triumph" of Dust as the worst possible outcome. And now that they know that Lyra is to reprise Eve's role, they perceive that they are facing the most critical moment in the world's history since the first Fall. Their solution is as callous as Bolvangar: Lyra must be stopped at all costs.

OFF THE LEASH

We, of course, have known about Lyra's destiny since the witch Lena Feldt confessed it to Mrs. Coulter (*SK*, p. 314). If it is true that Lyra is a second

Eve, then it looks rather as if the Magisterium was right after all: Dust has to do with sin. But if Dust is good, and Dust is sin, then doesn't that mean that "sin" is also good?

This takes us right to the heart of the reversal that underpins the whole of *His Dark Materials*. Philip Pullman portrays the Magisterium and God as unremittingly bad, and he sees all that the Magisterium opposes as wholesome and good. In Christian thinking, the Fall was the undoing of humanity—the moment at which we rebelled against God and became outcasts. Pullman doesn't accept the account of the Fall as historical, but it *represents*, for him, one of the greatest moments in human history. Like Lord Asriel, he thinks of Adam and Eve "like an imaginary number, like the square root of minus one: you can never see any concrete proof that it exists, but if you include it in your equations, you can calculate all manner of things that couldn't be imagined without it" (*GC*, pp. 372-73).[7] During an Australian radio discussion he said, "I just reversed [the traditional view of the Fall]. I thought wasn't it a good thing that Eve did? Isn't curiosity a valuable quality? Shouldn't she be praised for risking this? It wasn't, after all, that she was after money or gold or anything—she was after knowledge. What could possibly be wrong with that?"[8] Pullman sees Adam and Eve before the Fall as God's lapdogs,[9] clever pets that trot around the Garden of Eden doing exactly as they're told, with no freedom and no will of their own. In contrast, the act of taking the fruit was an act of self-determination, of freedom. This was the moment at which humanity took responsibility for itself and its destiny. This was the moment at which we cast off God's shackles and grew up so that we could stand on our own two feet. This was the moment at which we became wise.

FREEDOM AND CONSTRAINT

Pullman's characterization of what happened is partly right but he also misreads the situation. The world in which Adam and Eve lived was not one of constraints, but one of great freedom:

> The LORD God took the man and put him in the Garden of Eden to

work it and take care of it. And the LORD God commanded the man, "You are free to eat from any tree in the garden; but you must not eat from the tree of the knowledge of good and evil, for when you eat of it you will surely die." (Genesis 2:15-17)

It is clear that those first people had some positive responsibilities—work and caring for their environment is mentioned in this extract. They are also responsible to rule in God's place—to be stewards of the earth (Genesis 1:26), to be fruitful (1:28), to investigate and develop (2:19-20). All of this suggests very strongly that Adam and Eve were being treated like responsible and capable adults, not like lapdogs. They had enormous freedom and only one restriction: "You must not eat from the tree of the knowledge of good and evil." The very fact that God gives them this command is evidence that they had the ultimate freedom of choosing whether to listen to God or to some other voice. They aren't *prevented* from eating from the tree of the knowledge of good and evil, or *programmed* not to do so, but *commanded* not to—it's their moral choice to obey or not. There may be nothing special about the tree apart from the fact that this was the one they shouldn't eat from—a test case tree.[10] It was the *disobedient act* of eating from the tree that brought them knowledge of good and evil, not some supernatural property of the fruit itself.

The serpent first put doubts into Eve's mind, asking her, "Did God really say, 'You must not eat from any tree in the garden'?" (Genesis 3:1). This is not at all what God said—the restriction was eating from *one* tree, not *any* tree. Eve answers him correctly at first, but then for some reason adds her own exclusion on top: ". . . and you must not touch it, or you will die" (verse 3). Then the serpent moves to a flat denial of what God had said—"You will not surely die" (verse 4)—before finally misrepresenting God and his motivations: "For God knows that when you eat of it your eyes will be opened, and you will be like God, knowing good and evil" (verse 5). This is partially true: God did know that their eyes would be opened and that they would know good and evil. But they would not be like God because they would neither see like he sees, nor know good and evil like he does. Their eyes were opened—to see their nakedness, and they were ashamed of it. Until then human relations had been characterized by absolute openness, honesty and love—they could be free to be naked as they had nothing to hide. From that point on, relationships would be characterized by shame, deception, blame and exploitation—and their impulse to cover themselves was the sign of their new situation. They did come to know good and evil—but from the inside, experientially, because they had embraced evil—that which is inconsistent with God's utterly pure and holy nature.

Adam and Eve fell for the skepticism, the denial and the misrepresentation. For the first time they perceived themselves as cheated out of some freedom and insight, which they now felt ought to be theirs. They wanted complete autonomy—the absolute freedom to make their own choices, to decide for themselves what was right and wrong, to make themselves, rather than the God who made them, the center of their worlds. They wanted God's role for themselves. But it was the wrong kind of autonomy and freedom. They had been given so much, but by grasping after that little bit more, they threw away much of what they had. Human existence would never be the same again.

Pullman commends Eve for embracing freedom and knowledge, suggesting that her motivation was simple curiosity. But he ignores the fact that true freedom is structured and always at least a little constrained. To go beyond that is to embrace anarchy, which undermines the good that was already being appreciated. I could say that I resent the restriction my skeleton puts on my movements. I can't slide through narrow gaps or even touch my right elbow with my right wrist. But the restrictions go with the territory and my skeleton is in fact what liberates me. If I disposed of it and its constraints I would be a lump of quivering blubber on the floor.

By identifying Dust with sin, and then showing us that Dust is such a good thing, Philip Pullman turns the traditional understanding of sin on its head. Instead of its being the height of human arrogance—rebellion against God—it becomes something every wise person should embrace. It's still rebellion against God, but Pullman suggests that this is exactly the right thing to do. Like the serpent, Pullman has misrepresented God (a theme we'll return to in chapter thirteen) and encouraged us to wrest control away from him. Since Pullman frequently says, "I am of the Devil's party and I know it,"[11] I suspect he'd be rather pleased at the comparison.

11

CONSCIOUSNESS, WISDOM
AND THE SECOND FALL

In *The Subtle Knife*, the alethiometer leads Lyra to an Oxford physicist in our world who is researching dark matter. Dark matter is one of the great mysteries of modern physics—Pullman says it is "intoxicatingly exciting."[1] It's possible to calculate the mass of the universe—how much stuff there is—but most of it can't be accounted for. What this means is that we can see stars, planets and gas clouds, but not enough of them. If you calculate the mass of everything we can see, it only adds up to a fraction of what we know must be out there. This was first spotted in the 1930s but it was only in the 1970s that scientists started to realize that only seriously large amounts of hidden matter could account for some of their observations. Now astrophysicists are trying to find out what and where this mysterious missing mass is, because it will help to confirm theories about the universe's origins and structure. Estimates vary, but something between around 90 and 99 percent of the stuff in the universe is invisible. Nobel Prize winner Carlo Rubbia says, "All the visible objects in the Universe . . . only account for 0.5% of the total, so the Universe as we know it is only a side-show."[2]

SOME OF OUR UNIVERSE IS MISSING

This missing stuff is known as dark matter because there's no detectable light coming from it, whereas we see stars and galaxies by the light coming from them. At the end of the twentieth century, and in the first two or three years of the twenty-first century, the leading candidate—the one Pullman builds into *His Dark Materials*—was vast numbers of tiny particles. These particles hardly interact with the normal matter of which everything around us is made. This means that millions of them are passing through you each second. Coincidentally, I'm writing this chapter on the first anniversary of the opening of a major British research facility for detecting these particles: Boulby Underground Laboratory.[3] Its detectors are more than a kilometer underground, which it is hoped will soon yield some answers.[4]

Dr. Mary Malone is spared the rigors of going deep underground dressed in miner's gear to do her experiments. She and her colleague Oliver Payne have managed to solve the riddle of the missing matter in the comfort of their laboratory by using an electromagnetic field to deflect all the particles that they're not trying to detect. Dark matter particles aren't affected by electromagnetism so they get through. But their pioneering research has produced startling results: "Our particles are strange little devils, make no mistake. We call them shadow-particles, Shadows. . . . You know what? They're conscious. That's right. Shadows are particles of consciousness" (*SK*, p. 88). Here Philip Pullman has brilliantly woven two of the greatest puzzles of modern science—dark matter[5] and the nature of consciousness—into one very powerful element within his narrative. He has just enough of the real science to make it all sound quite plausible—but he says it's best not to research it too deeply because it would stop him feeling free to develop the ideas as he sees fit. To combine the two *and* link them with the difficult transition from childhood to adolescence is a stroke of genius, and one of the reasons why this trilogy works so incredibly well at several different levels.

The mystery about consciousness is that we really don't have much of a clue how it works. We know *that* we think and feel—but how? We understand a lot about the physical processes within brains, but very little about how those physical processes end up as thoughts. As I sit at my computer writing this chapter, electrical signals are buzzing around my brain, passing from neuron to neuron. We know that the signals in certain areas of the brain have predominantly to do with vision or fine motor control, and a scan of my brain would indicate high levels of activity in those regions as a result of what I'm seeing on screen and the movement of my fingers as I type. There would be activity over many other parts of the brain too. Some of this activity controls my body's basic functions and I'm never aware of it; some of it causes this chapter to form into words on the screen. But *how* electrical signals result in the business of thinking and actually result in a written chapter is an enigma. It's a mystery how this lump of soggy grey matter in my head gives me the sense of being me. Why is my brain conscious? This riddle is known as the mind-body problem—the mind is my experience, awareness and thought; the body includes my physical brain; the problem is because we can't understand how the two interact. This issue is profoundly interesting to brain scientists, psychologists, philosophers, cyberneticists and others.

For many scientists working in the area, the solution lies entirely within the physical structures and processes of the brain—a "materialist" approach. This is in sharp contrast to the traditional idea of the mind being closely connected with the soul, which is somehow separate from the brain—an approach known as dualism. Although Pullman believes that the physical universe is the only reality, his solution to the problem of consciousness in *His Dark Materials* is not materialistic as we might expect, but dualistic. To some extent, it's dualistic because of dæmons, though as we have seen in chapter nine, they can't really be thought of as being an external soul, despite many critics seeing them in this way. A far more significant way in which Pullman takes a dualistic line is his use of Dust. By making shadows the "particles of consciousness," he has a system in which consciousness comes from outside.

FOCUSED CONSCIOUSNESS

This understanding of consciousness does present a significant problem for the narrative, however. If Dust is the stuff of consciousness and cascades down on humans in far greater quantities *after* adolescence, the implication would appear to be that children are not fully conscious *until* adolescence. At that point these particles of consciousness start streaming into them, and their dæmons settle into a fixed form. As far as Dust is concerned, that's when the person really seems to come alive. But on that basis we would expect children to have more in common with an adult whose dæmon has been severed—we would expect them to be zombies. The reality is very different of course. Lyra and Will are as conscious and as fully alive as any adult. Stanislaus Grumman helps to make it a little clearer when he explains to Lee Scoresby the Specters' lack of interest in children: "The Specters feast as vampires feast on blood, but the Specters' food is attention. A conscious and informed interest in the world. The immaturity of children is less attractive to them" (*SK*, p. 280). Pullman explains, "Of course children are conscious. But I think that a different kind of self-awareness, self-consciousness, comes to us all at adolescence. It's partly sexual in origin, of course. But it coincides with a sudden and passionate interest in other things—science, poetry, art, music, religion, politics."[6] Reaching adolescence in Cittàgazze was an altogether deadlier process than it was in Lyra's Oxford, but the underlying change is the same. In one world a dæmon becomes fixed; in another the Specters have something new to feed on. Behind both of these phenomena lies the huge increase in Dust settling on the person. As the adolescent matures, "a conscious and informed interest in the world" grows. Unlike the child whose attention is drawn in many different directions, the adult is more focused. When Mary Malone first sees sraf, she sees a golden haze around all of the mulefa's objects and a slightly stronger haze around one of the mulefa children. What marked him out was that the golden sparkles were in little currents and eddies that swirled around him. His mother, however, had much stronger currents that were "more settled and powerful" (*AS*, p. 231). So Dust may be the stuff of consciousness, but there's clearly a high value on directed consciousness.

This raises the question of which comes first—a rising influx of Dust, or a focused consciousness? Does the increase in Dust change someone, and make them mature? Or does a maturing person attract more Dust? If Dust is particles of consciousness, it would suggest that the Dust must come first. But at the end of *The Amber Spyglass*, the angel Xaphania tells Lyra and Will that conscious minds produce Dust: "'Understand this,' said Xaphania:

'Dust is not a constant. There's not a fixed quantity that has always been the same. Conscious beings make Dust—they renew it all the time, by thinking and feeling and reflecting, by gaining wisdom and passing it on'" (AS, p. 491). We also know that Dust remains associated with objects that have been changed in some way by conscious beings—the trepanned skulls in the museum, for example. So Dust collects around people, especially adults with focused minds; it lingers on objects produced by them; and more Dust is produced by them. In other words, it's a symbiotic relationship between conscious beings and Dust. This becomes very clear when we discover about the mulefa's symbiotic relationship with the wheel trees. When Mary Malone tries to explain her work to Atal, she is astonished to discover that her mulefa friend is well ahead of her. Mary asks if the mulefa know where it comes from. "From us, and from the oil," replies Atal, adding, "Without the trees it would just vanish again. With the wheels and the oil, it stays among us" (AS, p. 223). After explaining the mulefa version of the Fall, Atal makes the symbiosis very explicit: "When the children were old enough to ride the wheels, they began to generate the sraf as well, and the sraf came back with the oil and stayed with them" (AS, p. 224). Pullman confirms the intertwined nature of conscious beings and Dust:

> Dust permeates everything in the universe, and existed before we individuals did and will continue after us. Dust enriches us and is nurtured in turn by us; it brings wisdom and it is kept alive by love and curiosity and diligent inquiry and kindness and patience and hope. The relationship we have with Dust is mutually beneficial. Instead of being the dependent children of an all-powerful king, we are partners and equals with Dust in the great project of keeping the universe alive. It's a republican relationship, if you like, not a monarchical one.[7]

IT'S ALIVE!

It's clear both from these comments, and from many incidents in the trilogy, that the particles of Dust are not simply the raw materials of consciousness, but are conscious themselves. The particles seem to have a kind of collective consciousness, rather than at an individual level (and given the vast numbers of Rusakov particles, it's probably as well). Dust can think for itself and interact with intelligent brains in a number of ways. The most obvious of all examples of this within *His Dark Materials* is the alethiometer. Lyra begins to suspect that it works by Dust while watching the Aurora at Trollesund (*GC*, p. 184). It's Dust that directs the swinging needle in its journey around the symbols that decorate the alethiometer's rim.

Mary Malone deduces that her "shadows" are conscious (*SK*, p. 88), but is shocked when, at Lyra's suggestion, she reconfigures the software of her computer, the Cave, and gets messages in English directly from the particles she is investigating (*SK*, pp. 247-51).[8] Later, in the mulefa's world, Mary realizes that the I Ching is another means of communication from this mysterious consciousness (*AS*, pp. 80-81), though Lyra worked that out very quickly when she visited Mary's office and saw the chart on the door (*SK*, p. 95).

Pullman makes the connection not only between the alethiometer and the I Ching, but with other methods of divination. He says: "The alethiometer comes about because of my fascination with symbolic images of the Renaissance and earlier. I thought it would be interesting to invent a little machine to come up with symbolic answers."[9] His ideas for the alethiometer were influenced by "the notion behind or underneath the Tarot":

> The notion that you can tell stories, you can ask and answer questions, and so on, by means of pictures. . . . What did influence [me] were those extraordinary devices they had about the middle of the sixteenth century—emblems, emblem books. There was a great vogue for these things. The first emblem book, I think, was published in 1544 in Italy. The idea was that you had a little moral . . . a little piece of wisdom encapsulated in a verse, usually Latin, usually doggerel, and a sort of motto, and illustrating those there was a picture. . . . They're all rather everyday little things, like "look before you leap," or, "penny wise, pound foolish" . . . but given this extraordinary semi-surrealist air by being pictured in emblem form in these rather curious little woodcuts.

. . . So I invented the alethiometer using a mixture of conventional symbols . . . and ones I made up. . . . And then I discovered, in a book of emblems in the Bodleian Library, something rather similar. It looked as though somebody had actually drawn the alethiometer. But what had happened was that in this particular emblem book, which was published in about 1620, somebody had invented a way of fortune-telling. You were supposed to cut this thing out, and you put a pencil or a stick through the middle of it, and you twirl it . . . and wherever it falls . . . refers you to a number inside the book, and you look that up, and that's the answer to your question. So people were using this sort of thing in that sort of way. And then, of course, there's the Tarot . . . there's the Chinese I Ching—all sorts of ways of divination. There are dozens and dozens of ways of interrogating the universe, basically, and the alethiometer is the one I made up for this book.[10]

When I asked Pullman to explain what he meant by "interrogating the universe," he replied:

Perhaps "interrogating" is too fierce a word (not least in view of the pictures we've seen from Iraq recently). I should have said something like "respectfully questioning." Human beings have got lots of ways of doing this; as well as the ones I mentioned, there is astrology, palm-reading, etc. I don't think these things give true answers; but what they might do—especially the more intellectually complex or enigmatic ones—is help you focus your question more precisely. So the answer you seem to be getting from them is actually coming from you. Probably.[11]

Within the context of *His Dark Materials*, all these are means by which Dust communicates. It's clear that Dust can also communicate more directly, though more intuitively. I commented earlier (chapter six) on Will's sudden intuition about the intruders in the house and the location of the writing case. Will seems to run into Lyra in Cittàgazze entirely by accident, but after the fight with Tullio on top of the Torre degli Angeli, we realize that something had brought him here. Giacomo Paradisi tells Will that he was destined to be the knife bearer. When we also learn the importance, both to the story and to Will, of Stanislaus Grumman, we again see some kind of invisible force at work. The force is, of course, Dust. It has guided Will using inquisitive cats, apparent accidents, even the theft of the alethiometer by Sir Charles Latrom, all to bind Will's path with Lyra's. And Dust guides them both on their path to growing maturity, reaching its zenith at the point at which they recognize their love for each other in the grove. Somehow this reverses the flow of Dust and revitalizes the vast multiplicity of worlds. We'll return to this shortly, but for now we need to note that expressing their love wasn't just focused attention, but a new level of self-consciousness.[12] It's this self-awareness that coincides with their dæmons fixing on their final forms—they know who they are and what they want in life.

A Second Fall

As we saw in chapter nine, the theme of growing up is very significant to Philip Pullman—it is a change from innocence to experience. This theme is central to much of Pullman's work. In *The Broken Bridge*, *The White Mercedes*, the Sally Lockhart quartet and even *The Firework-Maker's Daughter*, the central characters all leave a stage of innocence and find wisdom. In particular, they come to understand who they are and where they're going in life. Pullman often identifies this with a growing independence of thought, and in both *The White Mercedes* and *His Dark Materials*, he ties this in with the Fall.

We saw in the previous chapter that Pullman inverts the traditional understanding of the Fall, seeing it as a good thing. As he sees it, all Eve was after was knowledge, and "what could possibly be wrong with that?"[13] Throughout *His Dark Materials* we have a growing sense of Lyra having some cosmic significance, from the Master's dark hints (*GC*, p. 31), through to the moment when Father Gomez is dispatched to kill her (*AS*, pp. 71, 76-77). We learn that we are heading toward a second Fall—a second occasion in which the future of everything would hang in the balance. Pullman knew from the outset that he "would use a variation on the temptation motif, when Lyra falls in love . . . but here it's seen from another angle, through other eyes, this moment of revelation and sudden understanding, sudden self-consciousness, knowledge."[14] The moment itself is beautifully captured by Pullman, and yet is also an anticlimax, considering that the entire trilogy has been building toward some critical point. There is drama—Father Gomez is heading in their direction, rifle in hand; if it wasn't for Balthamos's reappearance like Lee (Robert Vaughn) after regaining his nerve in *The Magnificent Seven*,[15] all would have been lost—but this is slightly removed from the "Fall" itself.

The moment of "temptation" is further removed—it happens the day before, when Mary describes her experience of falling in love. She remembered that as a child she had fallen in love with a boy who put some marzipan in her mouth.[16] Years later, as a nun researching physics, she had met, and enjoyed the company of, a man at a restaurant. Suddenly the taste of marzipan had brought her earlier experiences flooding back. It was the key to her starting a brief affair with the man and throwing off her Christianity. As she tells this story Lyra experiences some new sensations:

> She felt as if she had been handed the key to a great house she hadn't known was there, a house that was somehow inside her, and as she turned the key, she felt other doors opening deep in the darkness, and lights coming on. . . . She didn't know what it was, or what it meant, or where it had come from; so she sat hugging her knees, and tried to stop herself from trembling. Soon, she thought, soon I'll know. (*AS*, pp. 444, 447)

The following day, Lyra and Will go searching for their dæmons, taking a packed lunch including some "sweet, thirst-quenching red fruits" (*AS*, p. 456). When they stop to eat in a grove of trees, they are edgy and hesitant; the food has no taste to it—until Lyra deliberately takes one of the red fruits and, replaying both Mary's childhood incident and Eve offering fruit to Adam, puts it to Will's lips. It's all so lovely and natural—two young people who are growing up fast and who have been through hell together, falling in love. Pullman tells this story in a beautiful, tender way, and invests their first kiss with very powerful emotions. He is often asked if Lyra and Will made love, but he insists it is none of his business: "I don't know what they did. I wrote about the kiss—that's what I knew happened. I don't know what else they did. Maybe they did, maybe they didn't. I think they were rather young to, but still . . ."[17] Elsewhere he says, "My imagination withdrew at that point. If you want to follow them under the tree and watch what happens, you must bear the responsibility for what you see. Personally, I think privacy is a fine and gracious thing. I describe a kiss: and there are some turning-points in life for which a kiss is quite enough."[18]

INNOCENCE AND EXPERIENCE

In an interview for *Third Way*, he sets out the difference between the Fall of Will and Lyra, and the Fall of Adam and Eve:

> But of course the Satan figure is Mary Malone . . . and the temptation is wholly beneficent. She tells her story about how she fell in love, which gives Lyra the clue as to how to express what she's now beginning to feel about Will, and when it happens they both understand what's going on and are tempted and they (so to speak) fall—but it's a fall into grace, towards wisdom, not something that leads to sin, death, misery, hell—and Christianity.[19]

Perhaps this is why the "Second Fall" feels anticlimactic—for me, at least. The parallels aren't strong enough. Although Pullman says that Mary Malone is the "Satan figure," she doesn't quite *tempt* Lyra. The serpent of Genesis 3 questions and denies what God has said, and misrepresents God's character. Mary simply "tells them stories." By recounting her own emotional development, she gives Will and Lyra the insight that unlocks their own feelings for each other, and the freedom to express those feelings. For Eve, the fruit represented wisdom and autonomy; for Lyra, it represented the deepest feelings of her heart. Adam and Eve were knowingly acting in disobedience to God; Lyra and Will were simply acting out of love for each other. The Bible contrasts the initial innocence of Adam and Eve with their subsequent guilt; Pullman contrasts innocence with wisdom. He does the same in *The White Mercedes*:

> We're not innocent; we *know*. . . . The Garden of Eden—you know that
> story? The tree of knowledge of good and evil. . . . Before you eat the
> fruit you're innocent, whatever you do is innocent because you don't
> understand. Then you eat it. And you're never innocent again. You
> know now. And that's painful; it's a terrible thing . . . Losing that inno-
> cence is the first step on the road to real knowledge. To wisdom if you
> like. You can't get wisdom till you lose that innocence. (pp. 155-56)

Pullman says that before eating the fruit, we are innocent, naive and ig-
norant. Taking the step toward knowledge and wisdom may be very difficult
and painful (though not for Will and Lyra—their pain is still to come) but is
essential if we are ever going to find it. Here he is drawing on Kleist and
Blake (both discussed in chapter four). Will and Lyra are, metaphorically,
eating the fruit a second time and beginning the process of returning the
world to a state of innocence. Which brings us back to where we started this
chapter. Will and Lyra have turned their backs on innocence, and have
turned the ebbing tide of Dust, the myriad mysterious particles that are the
very stuff of consciousness. They are stepping over the threshold into maturity—Mary sees them as "children-no-longer-children" as they return to the
village (*AS*, p. 470). They have become fully self-conscious, their dæmons
are about to settle, and they have no doubt about what they want in life.
They don't yet realize that their deepest desire—to be together—will be
thwarted, but they know they must work at building the republic of heaven
wherever they are. Pullman thus equates this goal with their pursuit of wisdom. What this means in practice we will consider in chapter fourteen.

12

TRUTH, INTEGRITY AND
THE ALETHIOMETER

Philip Pullman has a passion for stories and storytelling as we saw in chapter three. But it is Pullman's most ambitious work, *His Dark Materials*, that explores their importance most fully. In particular, it is here that he makes the strongest and clearest case for the importance of *truthful* stories.

Truth seems to be something that Lyra doesn't initially value very highly. She talks her way out of trouble with the scholars and college servants. She lies to her Uncle Asriel when he comes to inquire about her progress, and where she plays. She maintains her position of power within the various games and feuds that shape her life by telling stories. For example, she convinces Roger that she is not afraid of Gobblers by telling him, "I'd just do what my uncle done last time he came to Jordan. I seen him. He was in the Retiring Room and there was this guest who weren't polite, and my uncle just give him a hard look and the man fell dead on the spot, with all foam and froth round his mouth" (*GC*, p. 46). When Roger is doubtful, having not heard about this in the kitchens, Lyra weaves another layer into her story, claiming Lord Asriel had done the same to some Tartars who had captured him and tied him up ready to "cut his guts out." Lyra tells such stories with glee, as well as a complete disregard for the truth. Roger isn't at all sure about it, which highlights the effect Lyra achieves with her stories. She uses them to exploit the fact that she connects with the worlds of academia and politics as well as with the worlds of the college servant children and the townies. Her fanciful stories about the dashing Lord Asriel enable her to reflect some of his glamour and mystique onto herself. Roger, and presumably others, strongly suspect that Lyra is making things up, but are not sure that they're in a position to disagree. Besides, it's more fun if such things *might* be true. In this incident, as probably in many others, the story is "too good to waste" (*GC*, p. 46), and they act it out using sherbet dip to get some authentic foaming at the mouth.

DECEPTION AND DISCRETION

At Mrs. Coulter's party Lyra finds telling half-truths harder than outright lies, but it's not long before she has to rely on her lying skills. Having escaped from the party, she finds herself the focus of attention of a man in a top hat. Lyra tells the man that she is going to meet her father, a murderer, and that she has his spare clothes in her bag. She manages to slip away into the crowd when she diverts the man's attention with her claim that her father is approaching and looking angry. Much later at Bolvangar, Lyra turns herself into Lizzie Brooks, a "slow and dim-witted and reluctant" (*GC*, p. 237) eleven year old. Now she is lying both with what she says and with her whole nature, using her small stature to make herself seem "shy and nervous and insignificant" (*GC*, p. 238). Lying is so habitual to Lyra that she often invents stories even when she doesn't need to. When Lyra, Will and the Gallivespians spend the night in the suburbs of the dead, Lyra embroiders one of her fanciful stories for her host in response to his question about their origins:

> "I'll tell you all about it," said Lyra.
>
> As she said that, as she took charge, part of her felt a little stream of pleasure rising upward in her breast like the bubbles in champagne. And she knew Will was watching, and she was happy that he could see her doing what she was best at, doing it for him and for all of them. (*AS*, pp. 261-62)

The only reason for Lyra to make up her extraordinary story is to avoid having to admit why she is trying to get to the world of the dead. The people and their deaths lap it up, and it's such an engaging tale that Will and the spies are drawn into colluding with the invention: Will affirms what Lyra says, and Salmakia adds details of her own. Chevalier Tialys eventually rebukes Lyra: "You're a thoughtless, irresponsible, lying child. Fantasy comes so easily to you that your whole nature is riddled with dishonesty" (AS, p. 265).

It's not that Lyra can't tell the truth, of course, just that Pullman presents her as instinctively lying in all kinds of situations. There are many times when we see Lyra telling the truth—very often, as we noted in chapter five, when she is speaking to people whom she senses have real integrity. This first happens after Lyra has been rescued by Billy Costa and Kerim, and Ma Costa wants to know what had happened to the young girl of whom she was so fond. All the enmity between Lyra and the gyptians—which she pretended was deadly serious, but was of course very playful—has gone, and Lyra responds to the down-to-earth goodness of the gyptian woman by telling the truth (or much of it).

FAA SIGHTED

Later, at the Byanroping, Lyra sees Lord Faa for the first time—a man with "nothing to mark him out but the air of strength and authority he had" (GC, p. 114). He's strong in every way, straightforward, perhaps even rough and ready. He doesn't have the learning of Farder Coram but he comes across powerfully as a man with great integrity, a man with a strong moral sense who encourages other gyptians to have the same standards. When Raymond van Gerrit questions rescuing the landloper children, John Faa makes clear the implications of what Raymond is asking and suggests that he is "a better man than that" (GC, p. 116). In the second assembly John Faa has to rebuke van Gerritt again, this time reminding him that Lyra is the daughter of Lord Asriel, a man to whom they owe much. Faa is a man to whom duty matters more than money, insisting that although there's a thousand-sovereign bounty for Lyra's capture, none of the gyptians should even think about handing her over: "Anyone tempted by those thousand sovereigns had better find a place neither on land nor on water. We en't giving her up" (GC, p. 115). John Faa shows his integrity, too, in conceding his ignorance about what the Gobblers are doing, and admitting that rescuing the children will be difficult and dangerous. When Lyra gets to talk to Lord Faa and Farder Coram in the parley room, she tells him everything "more slowly than she'd told the Costas but more honestly, too. She was afraid of John Faa, and what she was most afraid of was his kindness" (GC, p. 119). The delightful Farder Coram, and, indeed, the vast majority of the gyptians, are also presented as deeply honorable and trustworthy people.

Here, of course, Pullman is deliberately reacting against the stereotype many people in the real world have about gypsies, whether referring to travelers or true Romanies. Peter Hitchens, writing in the British magazine *The Spectator*, seems to imply that this is a mark of Pullman's leftist moral degeneracy, claiming that "much of his thinking could . . . have been taken from the pages of the *Guardian*, or from politically correct staffroom conversation in a thousand state schools. Among the good characters in his trilogy are gypsies, an African prince,[1] a homosexual angel and a renegade nun."[2] This extraordinary sweeping comment from Hitchens implies that the four good characters he mentions should all be considered bad. Whatever opinion one has on Africans and gypsies, homosexuality and apostasy,[3] it is a profoundly shallow view of human nature that sees the people concerned as only qualifying to be bad characters in a story.

Bear Necessities

When Lyra meets the witches' consul, Dr. Lanselius, she tells him the truth, not because of her sensing *his* integrity, but because she felt that his dæmon sensed the lack of honesty in what Farder Coram was saying (GC, p. 173). The dynamic in the development of her relationship with Iorek Byrnison includes both her responding to his integrity, and her feeling that he could see right through her. She quickly realizes the utmost faithfulness of the bear, even given the dreadful circumstances in which he finds himself ("I must work till sunset. . . . I gave my word this morning to the master here. I still owe a few more minutes' work"; GC, p. 197) and uses this to dissuade him from killing one of the sentries at the priest's house (GC, p. 200). Lee

Scoresby is in no doubt about the quality of Iorek's character: "All bears are true, but I've known Iorek for years, and nothing under the sky will make him break his word. Give him the charge to take care of [Lyra] and he'll do it, make no mistake" (*GC*, p. 207). Again and again we see Iorek Byrnison as a model of honesty and faithfulness in the way he behaves. Having given his word to obey Lord Faa, he will not take Lyra to the village where she finds Tony Makarios unless Lord Faa instructs him to. And once Iorek had been commanded to care for Lyra, he keeps doing so until he has accompanied her almost to the very northern tip of Svalbard when a thin ice bridge across a fissure prevented him going any further. There comes a moment when Lyra realizes that the armored bear can read her in an uncanny way. Iorek gives her a startling demonstration that bears cannot be tricked (an incident straight out of Kleist's *On the Marionette Theatre*—see chapter four):

> He seemed to know what she intended before she did, and when she lunged at his head, the great paw swept the stick aside harmlessly, and when she feinted, he didn't move at all. She became exasperated, and threw herself into a furious attack. . . .
>
> Finally, she was frightened and stopped. . . . "I bet you could catch bullets," she said, and threw the stick away. "How do you *do* that?"
>
> "By not being human," he said. "That's why you could never trick a bear. We see tricks and deceit as plain as arms and legs. We can see in a way humans have forgotten." (*GC*, p. 226)

Philip Pullman draws a very stark contrast between Iorek Byrnison and the ursine usurper, Iofur Raknison. Iorek exemplifies all that is good about the noble *panserbjørne* because of his integrity as a bear—he is true to his nature. Iofur, however, has brought about a period of great uncertainty in the Svalbard kingdom as a result of his lack of integrity. He wants to be like the humans and has instituted a program of "modernization" and development that has left his subjects no longer knowing how to act or even how to think—they can no longer be true to themselves. What's more, Iofur wants to *be* a human complete with dæmon, and by denying his bear nature so radically he becomes vulnerable to Lyra tricking him. The great confrontation between the two bears is a powerfully tense moment in which Pullman pits not simply two bears against each other, but two ways of life and two moralities. It's not just a bear hero who wins, but integrity as a way of living. Iorek's great dilemma as to whether he should repair the subtle knife or not comes down to whether or not to do so would be consistent with his bear nature. Afterward he's not sure he's done the right thing:

> "Maybe I should not have mended it. I'm troubled, and I have never been troubled before, never in doubt. Now I am full of doubt. Doubt is a human thing, not a bear thing. If I am becoming human, something's wrong, something's bad. And I've made it worse. . . . I think I have stepped outside bear nature in mending this knife. I think I've been as foolish as Iofur Rakinson. Time will tell. But I am uncertain and doubtful." (*AS*, p. 192)

His deep uncertainty springs from the fact that he is now caught up in affairs that are a long way from the concerns of the bears. He is caught up in a crisis that reaches far beyond the world, never mind his kingdom, and which has implications for all fully conscious creatures in all the worlds. Suddenly he no longer has clear bearlike criteria against which to measure his actions. And yet, he still acts—and worries—with extraordinary integrity.

THE IMPORTANCE OF BEING HONEST

Lyra seems to be strongly affected by her encounters with characters who are so full of integrity—not just John Faa and Iorek Byrnison but others including Farder Coram, Lee Scoresby, Serrafina Pekkala and of course Will. They don't prompt Lyra to have a sudden change of heart about her reliance on lying. But we do see her being challenged, helped and even unnerved by them. What finally does bring about a moment of transformation is her encounter with creatures who seem to be the embodiment of everything that stinks, physically and morally. In what are some of the most heart-wrenching scenes in *His Dark Materials*, Lyra succeeds in getting to the world of the dead, though at great personal cost. She arrives feeling scared, heartbroken and more vulnerable than ever. But when the harpy attacks, she knows she has her great skill to fall back on—some fantastic tale will get her and Will and the spies out of danger:

> "What do you want with us?" said Lyra.
>
> "What can you give me?"
>
> "We could tell you where we've been, and maybe you'd be interested, I don't know. We saw all kinds of strange things on the way here."
>
> "Oh, and you're offering to tell me a story? . . . Try, then," said No-Name.
>
> And even in her sickness and pain, Lyra felt that she'd just been dealt the ace of trumps. . . . [Her] mind was already racing ahead through the story she'd told the night before, shaping and cutting and improving and adding: *parents dead; family treasure; shipwreck; escape* . . . (*AS*, p. 292)

The response from the harpy is rapid, unexpected and terrifying. She flies at Lyra, tearing out some of her hair, and screaming at her:

> *"Liar! Liar! Liar!"*
>
> And it sounded as if her voice were coming from everywhere, and the word echoed back from the great wall in the fog, muffled and changed, so that she seemed to be screaming Lyra's name, so that *Lyra* and *liar* were one and the same thing. (*AS*, p. 293)

Lyra is desolate. Having wrenched herself away from Pantalaimon, now the one skill she felt she could rely on has let her down:

> She gave a shudder and took a long shaky breath, and her eyes focused on him, full of a wild despair.
>
> "Will—I can't do it anymore—I can't do it! I can't tell lies! I thought it was so easy—but it didn't work—it's all I can do, and it doesn't work!" (*AS*, p. 294)

Will is quick to point out that she does have another skill—one that is both extremely rare and hugely significant for the future of all the worlds. She can read the alethiometer. This points out a paradox with which Lyra has been living for some time. On the one hand she prides herself in being an accomplished liar; on the other she has access to—and passes on—truth through her reading of the golden compass. The word *alethiometer* means "truth meter," and almost from the very beginning Lyra has been convinced that it is entirely truthful. Yes, her invented stories have gotten them out of scrapes, but attending to the instructions of the alethiometer may have avoided the need for it in the first place. Now, having realized the failure of lying and the success of truth, she is ready for her transformation. A little later, the ghosts crowd around Lyra and beg her to tell them about the world of life, the sunshine and wind. She is apprehensive but Will, who was always committed to truth, encourages her to be honest. She uses her same story-telling skills to tell true stories, evoking the sensations of living, and at the end is startled to see the harpies all listening intently. The chevalier Tialys quizzes them about what has made the difference:

> "Answer my questions truly, and hear what I say, and then judge. When Lyra spoke to you outside the wall, you flew at her. Why did you do that?"
>
> "Lies!" the harpies all cried. "Lies and fantasies!'
>
> "Yet when she spoke just now, you all listened, every one of you, and you kept silent and still. Again, why was that?"
>
> "Because it was true," said No-Name. "Because she spoke the truth. Because it was nourishing. Because it was feeding us. Because we couldn't help it. Because it was true. Because we had no idea that there was anything but wickedness. Because it brought us news of the world and the sun and the wind and the rain. Because it was true." (*AS*, p. 317)

The Authority had given the harpies "power to see the worst in everyone." The worst has been their constant diet, and now their "blood is rank with it," their "very hearts are sickened" (*AS*, p. 316). But there was no al-

ternative; it was all they had. Now they are incensed at the possibility of
Lyra taking even that away by opening a way out for the ghosts, but they
also realize for the first time that there is something better. Tialys brokers a
deal, by which the harpies will become the guides, rather than guardians,
for the dead, and in return will have the right to demand from people true
stories. The injunction on all future ghosts to "tell them stories" is eventually passed on to Mary Malone by the ghost of an old woman as she leaves
the window that Will ultimately opens into the world of the mulefa. Mary
takes this to heart in her relationship with Will and Lyra. It is her recounting the true story of her past that crystallizes the feelings of the children,
allowing them to express their love for each other and so restoring the inflow of Dust into the worlds. Lyra's economy with the truth is a part of her
impish nature, but perhaps the most important way in which she matures
during the trilogy is her embracing of truthfulness, which happens at the
lowest point of her life. It is a turning point not only for Lyra, but for the
entire narrative of *His Dark Materials*.

FANTASTIC TRUTH

Philip Pullman is clearly a writer who puts an extremely high value on truth
and integrity. This comes through the kinds of characters that many of his heroes are, and through parts of the narrative (especially in *His Dark Materials*),
particularly in some of the transformations that characters experience and in
the focus on the importance of truth telling. But Pullman wants to communicate truth at a deeper level than that—he wants his stories to be truthful.
That doesn't mean that he believes he is writing true stories—he's a fiction
writer, and a writer of fantasy fiction at that—but that he believes the stories
he tells are truthful about human beings. In an interview on the Scholastic
website he referred to *His Dark Materials* as "stark realism."[4] It was a provoc-
ative comment to make about books featuring dæmons, talking bears and
other universes. Philip explains what he meant by it on his own website:

> That comment got me into trouble with the fantasy people. What I mean

by it was roughly this: that the story I was trying to write was about real people, not beings that don't exist like elves or hobbits. Lyra and Will and the other characters are meant to be human beings like us, and the story is about a universal human experience, namely growing up.[5]

Although there are nonhuman characters that play a very prominent part in the story, it is first and foremost about Lyra and Will, and perhaps second about Lord Asriel and Mrs. Coulter. Iorek Byrnison, Serafina Pekkala, Tialys and Salmakia, and others are in supporting roles. Pantalaimon is important too—his animal forms should not distract us from remembering that dæmons are intended to say something important about the nature of human beings, as we discussed in chapter nine. Pullman continues:

> The "fantasy" parts of the story were there as a picture of aspects of human nature, not as something alien and strange. For example, readers have told me that the dæmons, which at first seem so utterly fantastic, soon become so familiar and essential a part of each character that they, the readers, feel as if they've got a dæmon themselves. And my point is that they have, that we all have. It's an aspect of our personality that we often overlook, but it's there. That's what I mean by realism: I was using the fantastical elements to say something that I thought was true about us and about our lives.[6]

Pullman disdains much of the fantasy he has read, including Tolkien's abidingly popular *Lord of the Rings*,[7] because it doesn't seem to him to say anything very interesting about people and their psychology. In a debate on morality in fiction at the 2002 Edinburgh International Books Festival, he said: "Fantasy, and fiction in general, is failing to do what it might be doing. It has unlimited potential to explore all sorts of metaphysical and moral questions, but it is not. . . . My quarrel with fantasy writing is that it is such a rich seam to be mined, such a versatile mode, that is not always being used to explore bigger ideas."[8] He argued that fiction should deal with big issues, including death. On Pullman's own website, however, he appears to contradict this when he says that children's literature *doesn't* have a duty to deal with big issues. "The only duty it has is best expressed in the words of Dr. Johnson: 'The only aim of writing is to help the reader better to enjoy life, or better to endure it.'"[9] But helping people to enjoy or endure life does still fit with his conviction that the business of writing stories is profoundly moral: "You can't leave morality out unless your work is so stupid and trivial and so worthless that [nobody] would want to read it anyway."[10]

So Philip Pullman wants his fiction to be true in that it deals honestly with human psychology and with difficult issues of morality. In many respects he succeeds admirably at this: Lyra and Will are very believable characters who have some very real struggles, for example. But there are weaknesses too. One is Lyra's response to Roger's death. After the trouble to which Lyra goes to rescue Roger from Bolvangar, at the end of *The Golden Compass* she doesn't seem too distraught at his death, more angry with her father. Yes, she felt "wrenched apart with unhappiness" (*GC*, p. 397), but within moments she is fired up at the thought of discovering the source of Dust. This doesn't feel psychologically true—an eleven year old's playmate has just been killed by her father and she jumps off to pursue Dust in another world just five minutes later? Roger's death is referred to quite matter-of-factly in *The Subtle Knife*, and it isn't until *The Amber Spyglass* that we begin to see Lyra's anguish over his fate—and then only because of her drug-induced hallucinatory glimpse into the world of the dead. More seriously for many people, Pullman's portrayal of the church is deeply prejudiced and unfair—a subject we will consider in the next chapter.

Still, despite the weaknesses, *His Dark Materials* and much of Pullman's other work is often very insightful into human nature and does place a high value on some vital human qualities: integrity and honesty are central; curiosity and a love of the physical world are important too. And because the situations within which he places his characters are so full of moral issues, almost anyone who reads his books will find themselves asking some searching questions as a result.

13

THE MAGISTERIUM AND
THE AUTHORITY

His Dark Materials made Philip Pullman the focus of a certain amount of controversy. For some time the three volumes sold strongly without attracting the hostility that was greeting J. K. Rowling's books in some circles. Pullman suspects that Harry Potter initially diverted the general public attention away from him:

> I've been surprised by how little criticism I've got. Harry Potter's been taking all the flak . . . the people—mainly from America's Bible Belt—who complain that Harry Potter promotes Satanism or witchcraft obviously haven't got enough in their lives. Meanwhile, I've been flying under the radar, saying things that are far more subversive than anything poor old Harry has said. My books are about killing God.[1]

Pullman doesn't beat about the bush on this: he says, "I'm trying to undermine the basis of Christian belief,"[2] though elsewhere he claims that he's "not making an argument, or preaching a sermon or setting out a political tract: I'm telling a story."[3] He insists he didn't set out to offend Christians. However, "before too long I realised I was telling a story which would serve as a vehicle for exploring things which I had been thinking about over the years. Lyra came to me at the right stage of my life."[4]

Throughout *The Golden Compass* it seems as though only the church is in Pullman's sights, but early in *The Subtle Knife*, Lord Asriel's manservant Thorold tells Serafina Pekkala that Asriel is "aiming a rebellion against the highest power of all. He's gone a-searching for the dwelling place of the Authority Himself, and he's a-going to destroy him" (*SK*, p. 46).

SECRET HISTORY

A key bone of contention for Pullman is the issue of authority, which is of course why Pullman gives God the title of "the Authority." There is a sense in which the Authority and the Magisterium are just manifestations of misused power. But given Pullman's comments quoted above, it seems clear that he does have religion—rather than authority generally—in his sights. The Authority's title distances him in the reader's mind from the Christian God; it doesn't feel like Pullman is talking about the same being. But in case we fail to make the connection, Balthamos spells it out: "The Authority, God, the Creator, the Lord, Yahweh, El, Adonai, the King, the Father, the Almighty—those were all names he gave himself. He was never the creator. He was an angel like ourselves—the first angel, true, the most powerful, but he was formed of Dust as we are" (*AS*, p. 31). How can "God" be an angel? In Pullman's underlying "creation myth," matter became conscious of itself and generated Dust. Some of it "condensed" into the first angel—a being of pure Dust. This new being was fully conscious, and when he began to see other angels condensing out of the Dust he realized what an opportunity he had. Since he came first, he could tell the subsequent angels that he was God and had created them. The angels loved and obeyed him, but the Sophia (Wisdom), the youngest and most beautiful angel, discovered the truth about the Authority who subsequently expelled her. There was an angelic rebellion, but the Authority defeated it and imprisoned the rebels in one of the many worlds. The Sophia told them about the Authority's lies to human beings (and conscious beings in other worlds), and the rebels escaped to bring enlightenment, wisdom and full consciousness to the poor creatures under the Authority's rule.

This myth draws heavily on second-century Gnosticism, but also inverts it. Gnosticism is all about *gnosis*—knowledge, in particular secret, esoteric knowledge open only to a privileged few. For the early Gnostics, the secret knowledge about reality was that the world was not created by God, but by an evil demiurge (a lesser or false god); the true God is unreachable and unknowable. The Gnostics believed that matter is essentially evil, but Sophia, one of the angelic beings, managed to put a spark of true spiritual nature (*pneuma*) into human beings. Pullman doesn't believe this but sees it as a good story with "immense explanatory power: it offers to explain why we feel . . . *exiled* in this world, *alienated* from joy and meaningfulness and the true connection we feel we must have with the universe."[5] Where Pullman turns this on its head is in the attitude toward the physical. Gnosticism sees it as evil; Pullman sees it as something to be enjoyed and celebrated.

Pullman's myth also draws on *Paradise Lost's* angelic war, Satan's escape from his prison and his tempting of Adam and Eve. By recasting God as the demiurge impostor, Pullman transforms him into the bad guy, and casts the rebels (including the Sophia) as the good guys. On this view, the Fall is a good thing (see chapters ten and eleven). This is an ideal scenario for Pullman: a materialist universe that has found its own wisdom fighting off the deceptions and impositions of a "god" who is really nothing of the sort. Archbishop Rowan Williams points out that "someone [the demiurge or the Authority] is trying to pull the wool over your eyes . . . and wisdom is an unmasking. . . . If you have a view of God which makes God internal to the universe, that's what happens."[6] Williams is saying that if you see God merely as part of the physical universe, then you automatically see him as a deceiver. The historically orthodox Christian understanding of God and the universe only works if God is transcendent.

THE DEATH OF GOD

Pullman says that "the Authority . . . is an ancient *idea* of God, kept alive artificially by those who benefit from his continued existence."[7] He believes that for sensible people, "the old assumptions have withered away . . . the idea of God with which I was brought up is now perfectly incredible."[8] So God should be eliminated. In the real world, Pullman thinks the *idea* of God should be abandoned; in his imagined worlds, where the Authority is merely an angel, he can kill him off. He makes much of the fact that the Authority is getting old—early on he walks in the Garden with Adam and Eve, but eventually he is the "Ancient of Days."[9] So Pullman portrays him as now "demented and powerless," fearful, miserable and light as paper ("in other words he has a reality which is only symbolic"[10]). Will cuts open his crashed crystal litter to help him out:

> The aged being could only weep and mumble in fear and pain and misery, and he shrank away from what seemed like yet another threat. . . . In the open air there was nothing to stop the wind from damaging him, and to their dismay his form began to loosen and dissolve. Only a few moments later he had vanished completely, and their last impression was of those eyes, blinking in wonder, and a sigh of the most profound and exhausted relief. Then he was gone: a mystery dissolving in mystery. (*AS*, pp. 410-11)

In interviews, Pullman stresses the "profound and exhausted relief"—he wants this to be seen as an act of compassion for a being who has had enough. For the being in *His Dark Materials* this is perfectly reasonable. But that being is *not* the God of the Bible.

The Bible is clear that God exists eternally and is unique. He is the creator of everything, and made human beings in his image. That means we are fully conscious not because we have rebelled against an angelic upstart, but because we reflect our Creator. That much comes from the first chapter of the Bible. It's clear from elsewhere in the Bible that God is not simply different in *degree* from the angels—he's not just older and more powerful—but that he is radically different in his very *nature*.[11] It's also clear that he is not remote from his creation, threatened by it, or vindictive toward it; rather, he is intimately involved in it moment by moment,[12] compassionate toward it,[13] and longing for both humans and the whole creation to find redemption.[14]

REPELLENT RELIGION

Rowan Williams writes: "What the story makes you see is that if you believe in a mortal God, who can win and lose his power, your religion will be saturated with anxiety—and so with violence."

In a sense, you could say that a mortal God needs to be killed. . . . And if you see religious societies in which anxiety and violence predominate, you could do worse than ask what God it is that they believe in. The chances are that they secretly or unconsciously believe in a God who is just another inhabitant of the universe, only more powerful than anyone else. And if he is another inhabitant of the universe, then at the end of the day he just might be subject to change and chance like everything else.[15]

The church in Lyra's world—and especially its ruling body, the Magisterium—is indeed "saturated with anxiety and so with violence." It is a singularly repellent institution. The church's "power over every aspect of life" was "absolute" (*GC*, p. 30) and had been since the time of Calvin, who Pullman rather mischievously makes the last pope in Lyra's world. In reality, John Calvin did live in Geneva but far from being pope, he was one of the most significant figures in the Reformation. To have him as the end of the papal line signals clearly that in Lyra's world there was no Reformation. This makes it easy for Pullman to portray the church as authoritarian, with a history of Inquisitions and the kinds of theological maneuvering that provoked the Reformation in our world. Early in *The Golden Compass* we learn about the Magisterium's interference in "experimental theology," and later of its interrogation of Rusakov "under the rules of the Inquisition" (*GC*, p. 371). John Faa also tells Lyra about rumors that the Office of Inquisition is to be re-instituted (*GC*, p. 127). These references to the Inquisition carry connotations of ruthlessness and violence.

The church is responsible for the atrocity of Bolvangar by tacitly accepting the General Oblation Board's Experimental Station. The fact that Mrs. Coulter can insist on the torturing of a captured witch (in the presence of various clerics, including a Cardinal, and Fra Pavel, the Consistorial Court of Discipline's alethiometrist) suggests that the Magisterium is fully supportive of her. But the board and its activities are sufficiently removed from the Magisterium to be denounced if necessary. The feeling evoked by the scenes on the boat is of unmitigated cruelty. Later in *The Subtle Knife*, the troubled times bring Ruta Skadi to meet with Serafina Pekkala and her clan. When Serafina invites her to address their council that evening, the visitor says:

> Sisters . . . let me tell you . . . who it is that we must fight. . . . It is the
> Magisterium, the Church. For all its history . . . it's tried to suppress
> and control every natural impulse. And when it can't control them, it
> cuts them out. Some of you have seen what they did at Bolvangar. And
> that was horrible, but it is not the only such place, not the only such
> practice. Sisters, you know only the north; I have travelled in the
> south lands. There are churches there, believe me, that cut their chil-
> dren too, as the people of Bolvangar did—not in the same way, but
> just as horribly. They cut their sexual organs, yes, both boys and girls;
> they cut them with knives so that they shan't feel.[16] That is what the
> Church does, and every church is the same: control, destroy, obliterate
> every good feeling. So if a war comes, and the Church is on one side
> of it, we must be on the other, no matter what strange allies we find
> ourselves bound to. (*SK*, p. 50)

In *The Amber Spyglass*, we meet Semyon Borisovitch, the disgusting, drunk, witch-hating and possibly pedophilic priest (*AS*, pp. 97-102), and, in an outrageous slur on a real historical figure, we are told that John Calvin was responsible for ordering the deaths of children (*AS*, p. 205).[17] The Mag-isterium also shows callous cruelty with its solution to the problem of Lyra once it learns that she is a second Eve. The president of the Consistorial Court of Discipline, Father Hugh MacPhail, proposes to have her hunted down and killed. The "blazing-eyed" fanatic, Father Luis Gomez is quick to volunteer having already done sufficient masochistic penance in advance to offset the guilt of killing someone (*AS*, p. 71).[18] He is to stop at nothing to achieve his goal—but he's on his own; the Magisterium will disown him if he is ever discovered.

BLURRING FACT AND FICTION

Now, all this is so strongly antichurch as to be offensive to many people within the real-world church. But *His Dark Materials* is *fantasy* literature. The church Pullman describes is in another world; it is not the church in our world. And yet something about the passion with which Pullman denounces it, and the fact that the Magisterium has not one single redeeming feature, leaves one feeling that the contempt is still directed at the real-world church, even if the specific criticism is only within the realm of fiction. Pullman confirms this impression when he says very similar things about the real-world church in interviews. In a discussion on Readerville.com he was asked why all the Magisterium characters are bad. He replied:

> That was due to a flaw in my artistry, no doubt. But I was trying to hit a target that deserved hitting, and there's no merit in pulling punches when important issues are at stake. Anyway, every time I thought I was overdoing it, up came another scandal about brutal monks mistreating children in Irish schools, or sadistic nuns tormenting children in Scottish orphanages, to name but two that came up recently. These things do happen.[19]

Pullman's view of Christian history is profoundly negative. At times he concedes that there have been some very positive aspects: "I'm fascinated by the history of religious thought and the structures of religious life. It was a natural thing to write about, because it encapsulates so much of the best as well as the worst of what human beings have done."[20] He also happily affirms that there are many good Christian people. But the overall tenor of his assessment is still rather jaundiced. He says that his antipathy toward the church comes from history:

> It comes from the record of the Inquisition, persecuting heretics and torturing Jews and all that sort of stuff; and it comes from the other

side, too, from the Protestants burning the Catholics. It comes from the insensate pursuit of innocent and crazy old women, and from the Puritans in America burning and hanging the witches—and it comes not only from the Christian Church but also from the Taliban.

Every single religion that has a monotheistic god ends up by persecuting other people and killing them because they don't accept him. Wherever you look in history, you find that. It's still going on.[21]

Elsewhere he says:

The God who dies is the God of the burners of heretics, the hangers of witches, the persecutors of Jews, the officials who recently flogged that poor girl in Nigeria who had the misfortune to become pregnant after having been forced to have sex—all these people claim to know with absolute certainty that their God wants them to do these things. Well, I take them at their word, and I say in response that that God deserves to die.[22]

Pullman's antagonism toward religion generally, and Christianity in particular, certainly doesn't seem to be motivated by bad personal experiences of it. His grandfather's influence was very positive, and he admits that his early experiences of church gave him a love for the Bible, or at least, the Authorized Version of 1611:

All through my childhood, I went to church every Sunday. I went to Sunday school. I know the Bible very well. I know the hymns and the prayer book very well—and this is the old, authorized King James Version of the Bible, and the 1662 Book of Common Prayer that used to be used in English churches, and the old hymns that used to be sung. When I go into a church now, I don't recognize the language. It's sort of modern and it's flat and it's bureaucratic and it's derivative. . . . In attempting to be inclusive and friendly, it becomes awfully . . . jolly and I can't bear that. But I love the language and the atmosphere of the Bible and the prayer book.[23]

But this does not mean that he believes it. He continues:

> I don't say I agree with it. . . . Since growing up and since thinking about
> it, I've come to realize that the basis on which these belief systems were
> founded isn't there. I no longer believe in the God I used to believe in
> when I was a boy. But I do know the background very well, and I will
> never escape it. So although I call myself an atheist, I'm certainly a Chris-
> tian atheist and even more particularly, a Church of England . . . atheist.
> And very specifically, a 1662 Book of Common Prayer atheist. I can't es-
> cape these influences on my background, and I would not wish to.[24]

It's interesting that he would not wish to escape these influences, but they
are influences at a literary, artistic, perhaps emotional level, rather than at
the level of belief. However, I would argue that this background also continues to have a profound influence on Pullman at a moral level too.

PULLMAN'S CHRISTIAN VALUES?

Many of the values Pullman champions in his books are thoroughly Christian. We saw in the previous chapter how committed he is to notions of truth
and integrity. He is also a great believer in courage, love, freedom, responsibility, duty, curiosity and tolerance.

Pullman is correct to point out that in history and around the world today, there are all too many expressions of Christianity that are far removed
from these values. But these values are nevertheless a core part of Christian
behavior when it is lived with integrity and in faithfulness to God. Everybody—Christian or otherwise—has lapses and fails to live up to his or her
own standards. When so-called Christians depart significantly from Christian values, it shows that their faith is not a heart matter—not a relationship
with a living God—but merely the inspiration for their own invented religion, which superficially looks like genuine Christianity.

Pullman is also correct to say that these values are not *distinctively* Christian. One interviewer, Huw Spanner, asked Philip about the source of values: "Where in a world without God does [the] sense of 'ought' come from?"

Pullman's response was vigorous: "I'm amazed by the gall of Christians. You think that nobody can possibly be decent unless they've got the idea from God or something. Absolute bloody rubbish! Isn't it your experience that there are plenty of people in the world who don't believe who are very good, decent people?"[25] When Spanner pressed him on where the values come from, Pullman continued:

> For goodness' sake! It comes from ordinary human decency. It comes from accumulated human wisdom—which includes the wisdom of such figures as Jesus Christ. Jesus, like many of the founders of great religions, was a moral genius, and he set out a number of things very clearly in the Gospels which if we all lived by them we'd all do much better. What a pity the Church doesn't listen to him![26]

MORALITY IN A GODLESS UNIVERSE

Pullman's comment that Christians "think that nobody can possibly be decent unless they've got the idea from God or something" misses the point. Spanner was not suggesting that each person's moral sense comes *directly* from God; nor was he denying that many non-Christians, including atheists, are deeply moral people. Pullman himself is a good example. The question is, why is there *any* sense of ought, *any* moral value, in a world without God? Why is it possible to talk about "ordinary human decency" at all? How do we give such a phrase any meaning?

Pullman's view is that it is through "accumulated human wisdom." But *human* wisdom, accumulated or otherwise, has nothing transcendent about it. In other words, there's no objective basis for it, nowhere to ground it. On what basis do we decide that "Jesus, like many of the founders of great religions, was a moral genius"? Which "founders of great religions" do we include in the category of "moral genius," and which do we exclude—and why? Is it simply that we *like* the moral positions of Jesus, Zarathustra, Siddharta Gautama, Muhammad or Guru Nanak,[27] but we don't like the moral positions of Sun Myung Moon,[28] Joseph Smith Jr.,[29] Charles T. Russell[30] or L. Ron Hubbard?[31]

Perhaps it is the *accumulation* of wisdom over the centuries that allows us to see that some moral positions work well and others don't. But if we really were accumulating wisdom, surely we should be seeing an improvement in the moral foundations of society. Yet as I write this chapter it's exactly ten years since the genocide in Rwanda—800,000 people killed in a hundred days. Since then we've seen massacres in the former Yugoslavia, East Timor, Sierra Leone, Liberia and elsewhere. The supposedly morally upstanding forces of the West are currently facing allegations of abusing Iraqi prisoners. How much did we learn from the slaughter of six million Jews at the hands of the Third Reich? Why doesn't our "accumulated human wisdom" prevent such things from happening? Simply because it is human wisdom with no objective basis.

If morality is simply determined by humans, then why should one powerful group listen to the rest of the world? Or why should one individual listen to anyone else, when self-interest clashes with the "herd morality" of society? If moral principles are simply the customs of wise human beings, then someone who chooses to reject those morals is doing nothing more serious than being an individualist, a nonconformist. Pullman himself is against the moral anarchy that would result from people making their own moral decisions without reference to everybody else—he believes there are genuine moral principles. But in a world without God it seems to be extremely difficult to find any objective basis for those principles; they become arbitrary.

Christians are not claiming a monopoly on morality and values. But they believe that morality only functions because it has an objective basis in the character of God, *whether or not* anybody believes in him. Pullman rejects the existence of God yet clings to moral principles—but basing these simply on "accumulated human wisdom" isn't good enough. Besides which, Pullman is a materialist—he believes this world is all there is. So where does his cherished freedom come from? If there is nothing other than a physical universe, then *everything* Pullman does or thinks is a result of physical processes. Everything is a result of his genetic inheritance or of physical influences from outside his body. But these two are a result of prior physical processes.

Everything is deterministic—there is no freedom. As Will Provine, professor of biological sciences and the history of biology at Cornell University, insists:

> Humans are comprised only of heredity and environment, both of which are deterministic. There is simply no room for the traditional concepts of human free-will. That is, humans do make decisions and they go through decision-making processes, but all of these are deterministic. So from my perspective as a naturalist, there's not even a possibility that human beings have free will.[32]

It's not sufficient to bring in quantum effects within the human brain to answer this problem either—all that does is introduce complete randomness into the mix. The only way humans can be genuinely free to make real moral choices is if something outside the physical system of the universe gives us that freedom—if there is a God.

But Pullman doesn't believe there is a God—or at least, he says he's seen no evidence of God; he doesn't rule out the possibility that God may exist somewhere very remote from human life. The Christian response is that the evidence is all around—a world of magnificent beauty and diversity; a world of freedom and moral responsibility; a world in which even today the vast majority of people believe in the existence of the supernatural;[33] and in particular there is the historical textual evidence of the life, death and resurrection of Jesus of Nazareth. It is possible to explain such things away with alternative theories, but the question is, which explanation best fits *all* the evidence—a materialistic, deterministic universe, or a God who is intimately involved with his creation? A rationalist man like Philip Pullman sees the idea of God as "now perfectly incredible,"[34] but as Will says, "You think things have to be *possible*? Things have to be *true*!" (*SK*, p. 322).

14

THE REPUBLIC OF HEAVEN

To the characters within the story, Lord Asriel is the hero, mounting a justifiable rebellion against a malevolent and sadistic usurper. By the time Mrs. Coulter joins him, we have still not learned what he has in mind to replace the Authority's regime. Interestingly, we never hear it from Asriel himself; it is King Ogunwe who reveals the aims to Mrs. Coulter as they descend the staircase deep into the adamant tower.[1] After shocking her with news that the Authority was not eternal (*AS*, pp. 209-10), Ogunwe explains to her:

> We haven't come to conquer, but to build. . . . I am a king, but it's my proudest task to join Lord Asriel in setting up a world where there are no kingdoms at all. No kings, no bishops, no priests. The kingdom of heaven has been known by that name since the Authority first set himself above the rest of the angels. And we want no part of it. This world is different. We intend to be free citizens of the Republic of Heaven. (*AS*, pp. 210-11)

REPUBLIC OR REVOLUTION?

King Ogunwe is committed to the ideals of the new republic, but I wonder whether he has perhaps been taken in by Lord Asriel. As we noted in chapter four, Lord Asriel's high-handed attitude toward his manservant seems stereotypically aristocratic rather than republican. Thorold can only guess at his master's plans despite nearly forty years of service (*SK*, p. 46). Even in his relationship with his commanders, although they are free to speak their minds, Asriel is very much in charge. Ruta Skadi tells Serafina Pekkala that

Lord Asriel "lives at the center of so many circles of activity, and he directs them all" (*SK*, p. 271). It feels less like a democracy in the making than an embryonic tyranny. Perhaps I'm doing Lord Asriel a disservice, but he has shown that he will do anything to get what he wants (think of little Roger "crying and pleading, begging, sobbing and Lord Asriel [taking] no notice except to knock him to the ground" (*GC*, p. 391)). Why does the heroic visionary leader never once articulate what his vision is? Ruta Skadi's breathless report of her visit to Asriel emphasizes not the great future ahead, but that to rebel "right and just" because of the "hideous cruelties . . . all designed to destroy the joys and the truthfulness of life" (*SK*, p. 272). The Gallivespians also seem more focused on defeating the Authority than on what follows. Lord Asriel's aim does seem to be conquering, not building.

Most major characters seem distanced from Lord Asriel's cause, being concerned to protect Lyra above everything: Lee Scoresby, Serafina Pekkala and Iorek Byrnison (who also wants to avenge Lee Scoresby's death—*AS*, p. 43) are involved in the war but there's no sense of them thinking ahead to the republic of heaven. When Mrs. Coulter changes sides, she too wants only to protect Lyra. Even Lord Asriel finally sees that the future of the republic depends on his daughter remaining alive (*AS*, p. 378), and wonders whether it might actually exist primarily to serve a higher cause: helping her (*AS*, p. 379).

AN ORGANIC REPUBLIC

The one significant character who clearly believes in the republic of heaven ideal is Stanislaus Grumman. From the perspective of the whole narrative, the shaman shows himself to be the most insightful man in the story. He tells Will and Lyra:

> Your dæmon can only live its full life in the world it was born in. Elsewhere it will eventually sicken and die. We can travel, if there are openings into other worlds, but we can only live in our own. Lord Asriel's great enterprise will fail in the end for the same reason: we have

to build the Republic of Heaven where we are, because for us there is no elsewhere. (*AS*, p. 363)

This is the first time that Will and Lyra hear the phrase "republic of heaven." Far from being committed to "Lord Asriel's great enterprise," their minds are entirely on other things—Dust, Will's father, rescuing Lyra, reaching the world of the dead, bringing "salvation" to the ghosts[2]—before at last becoming wrapped up with each other. Later, when Will and Lyra are trying to come to terms with the traumatic realization that they cannot stay together, Will recalls his father's words: "He said we have to build the Republic of Heaven where we are. He said that for us there isn't any elsewhere. . . . I thought he just meant Lord Asriel and his new world, but he meant us, he meant you and me. We have to live in our own worlds" (*AS*, p. 488).

Despite their distress they recognize that, for the good of each other and of all the dead, they must part. And every window except the one for the dead must be closed. Will and Lyra both assume that their duty is to build the republic of heaven. Though this is not spelled out explicitly, the final words of the story drive home its importance.

"The republic of heaven" is a powerful phrase[3] that Pullman has used extensively in real life (suggesting that he *does* see *His Dark Materials* as having a message despite claiming the contrary). In one interview he said:

The most important questions of all are the big religious ones: Is there a God? What is our purpose? And so on. . . . If there are lessons to be learned in the fantasy world, we have to see how to put them to use in our real lives . . . the theme, if you like, of *His Dark Materials* is the search for a way of looking at . . . big religious questions which might be called republican. My own belief is that God is dead, but that we need heaven nonetheless; and since it's no longer possible to believe in a Kingdom of Heaven, we shall have to create a republic.[4]

Or take these comments from another interview:

We're used to the kingdom of heaven; but you can tell from the general thrust of the book that I'm of the devil's party, like Milton. And I think it's time we thought about a republic of heaven instead of the kingdom of heaven. The king is dead. That's to say I believe that the king is dead. I'm an atheist. But we need heaven nonetheless, we need all the things that heaven meant, we need joy, we need a sense of meaning and purpose in our lives, we need a connection with the universe, we need all the things that the kingdom of heaven used to promise us but failed to deliver. And, furthermore, we need it in this world where we do exist— not elsewhere, because there ain't no elsewhere.[5]

These remarks clearly show that when Pullman writes about Will and Lyra building the republic of heaven, he thinks it is something we should do in the real world. Again he blurs the boundary between fiction and reality, as with his critique of the church and of God. But what does "the republic of heaven" really mean?

STAY IN YOUR OWN WORLD

Several aspects come out of Xaphania's conversation with Will and Lyra (*AS*, 491-96). I have already touched on the first: they must build the republic of heaven in their own worlds. Pullman feels strongly about this in the real world too—"there ain't no elsewhere." There are two sides to this. First, Pullman (strongly echoing Blake[6]) is celebrating the physical world. In passage after passage in *His Dark Materials*, Pullman brilliantly evokes different worlds and stresses the importance of their physical natures. One example is Will's and Lyra's exit from the world of the dead: "It was the sweetest thing they had ever seen. The night air filled their lungs, fresh and clean and cool; their eyes took in a canopy of dazzling stars,[7] and the shine of water somewhere below" (*AS*, p. 363). Part of Pullman's celebration of the physical is his focus on growing up, especially with regard to sexuality (see chapter nine). Pullman rejoices in all the physical sensations that come with Will and Lyra's love—their kisses, the feelings within them, even the sensations of their picnic (*AS*, pp. 465-66).

In his essay "The Republic of Heaven," Pullman says, "The republic of Heaven . . . enables us to see this real world, our world, as a place of infinite delight, so intensely beautiful and intoxicating that if we saw it clearly then we would want nothing more, ever. We would know that this earth is our true home, and nowhere else is."[8] The other side of "there ain't no elsewhere" is the denial of any spiritual reality or afterlife. It's the corollary of his denial of God's existence. Pullman says that "the most important subject I know . . . is the death of God and its consequences."[9] I find it fascinating that Pullman finds what he doesn't believe in "the most important subject" he knows. By the death of God, he means the death of the *idea* of God. He continues: "The idea that God is dead has been familiar, and has felt true, to many of us for a long time now . . . the old assumptions have all withered away . . . the idea of God with which I was brought up is now perfectly incredible."[10] There are many highly intelligent people who would find such comments patronizing since they do not find it remotely incredible.

FACE UP TO RESPONSIBILITIES

A second aspect of the republic of heaven is the importance of bearing responsibilities even at great personal cost. "A great wave of rage and despair" (*AS*, p. 493) sweeps over Will but he still faces the "bleak rocks" of his obligations (*AS*, p. 493). Responsibilities require commitment, and Lyra now faces a lifetime of relearning to read the alethiometer. Will and Lyra could learn to travel to other worlds "in spirit" as Will's father did in his trances (*SK*, p. 215; *AS*, p. 494). But it will require long practice and work—a familiar theme in Pullman's stories. The windows must be closed partly so that Will and Lyra don't waste their lives: "If you thought that any [windows] still remained, you would spend your life searching for one, and that would be a waste of the time you have. You have other work than that to do, much more important and valuable, in your own world" (*AS*, p. 495).

This all entails selflessness and sacrifice. After they have parted, Lyra reflects on this—she or Will would gladly have lived in an alien world. "But then we wouldn't have been able to build [the republic of heaven]. No one could if they put themselves first" (*AS*, p. 518). Nicholas Tucker remarks that this is a "final temptation for Will and Lyra to put their own good above everything else. . . . Lyra, the second Eve, resists the temptation of selfishness, and this time Pullman is on her side."[11] The need for selflessness is one of the most powerful moral lessons of the trilogy as well as several of his other stories. He says, "Putting your own feelings first and insisting on expressing them, no matter what the cost, is not a republican virtue."[12]

MAKE MORE DUST

The third aspect that Xaphania highlights is the particular responsibility to make more Dust:

> Conscious beings make Dust—they renew it all the time, by thinking and feeling and reflecting, by gaining wisdom and passing it on.
>
> And if you help everyone else in your worlds to do that, by helping them to learn and understand about themselves and each other and the way everything works, and by showing them how to be kind instead of cruel, and patient instead of hasty, and cheerful instead of surly, and above all how to keep their minds open and free and curious . . . Then they will renew enough to replace what is lost through one window. (*AS*, pp. 491-92)

It's worth noting that all this is very close to what Pullman sees as the process of growing up. The children must help others grow so that Dust is constantly replenished. Growth involves thinking and feeling (rational and intuitive), self-analysis and understanding. This is the search for meaning, which is the central theme of *Lyra's Oxford*. We'll return to this shortly. "Gaining wisdom" is discovering the right way to live. Pullman singles out kindness, patience, cheerfulness and having open, inquiring minds. Lyra reflects on this in the Botanic Garden: "We have to be all those difficult things like cheerful and kind and curious and brave and patient, and we've got to study and think and work hard, all of us, in all our different worlds" (*AS*, p. 518). Pullman frequently stresses the importance of belonging: "In the re-

public we're connected in a moral way to one another, to other human beings. We have responsibilities to them, and they to us. We're not isolated
units of self-interest in a world where there is no such thing as society; we
cannot live so."[13] These values are as important to citizens of the kingdom
of heaven as they are to citizens of the republic. As Pullman said on British
television program *The South Bank Show,* "An honest reading of the story
would have to admit that the qualities that the stories celebrate and praise
are those of love, kindness, tolerance, courage, open-heartedness, and the
qualities that the stories condemn are: cruelty, intolerance, zealotry, fanaticism . . . well, who could quarrel with that?"[14] These good qualities are indeed seen throughout the trilogy. But is it really true that the stories condemn "cruelty, intolerance, zealotry, fanaticism"? Well, up to a point. I have
commented before on Lord Asriel's ambiguity. He shows little of these positive qualities, except courage, but he exemplifies cruelty (to Roger), zealotry
and fanaticism. The church is accused of these things but Asriel is equally
guilty. He's guilty of intolerance too. Thorold tells Serafina he's "seen a spasm
of disgust cross his face when they talk of the sacraments, and atonement,
and redemption, and suchlike" (*SK*, p. 45).

Many commentators have seen Pullman's own attack on Christianity as
fanatical and intolerant. It's hard to escape the feeling from some passages in
His Dark Materials that Pullman is expressing his own deep hatred of the real
church. Pullman seems to register a spasm of disgust himself when he blasts
C. S. Lewis's stories. He calls the Chronicles of Narnia (based on Christian
ideas) "one of the most ugly and poisonous things I've ever read," "vile,"
"life-hating," "nauseating drivel," "loathsome,"[15] "disgusting,"[16] and "con-
taining a view of life so hideous and cruel I can scarcely contain myself when
I think of it."[17] When I first witnessed Pullman talking about Lewis I was
startled at the anger with which he spoke. It's a very strong reaction to a mere
story, even if it is perhaps over-revered by some. Yes, it contains some serious
flaws, but the real problem seems to be that it is a story that expresses a
worldview completely antithetical to Pullman's. His "paroxysm of loathing"[18] feels distinctly intolerant.[19]

MAKE YOUR OWN CHOICES

The republic of heaven also includes the need to make one's own choices. Will and Lyra reluctantly choose to part without Xaphania laying it on them as their duty. Will later tells Xaphania:

> I shall decide what I do. If you say my work is fighting, or healing, or exploring, or whatever you might say, I'll always be thinking about it. And if I do end up doing that, I'll be resentful because it'll feel as if I didn't have a choice, and if I don't do it, I'll feel guilty because I should. Whatever I do, I will choose it, no one else. (*AS*, p. 496)

Will has responsibilities to build the republic of heaven, but he insists on his absolute autonomy. Xaphania (who at this point seems to represent the highest wisdom) underlines the importance of autonomy when she replies to Will that he has "already taken the first steps toward wisdom." This is a key lesson within the story—you must freely choose your own path because you are answerable only to yourself. Will and Lyra are both fiercely independent and insist on making their own decisions. Will made the same point in his final conversation with his father's ghost: "You said I was a warrior. You told me that was my nature, and I shouldn't argue with it. Father, you were wrong. I fought because I had to. I can't choose my nature, but I can choose what I do. And I *will* choose, because now I'm free" (*AS*, p. 418). Here Pullman touches on the tension between our genes determining who we are, and the freedom to act differently. For Pullman, not only can we transcend our genetic inheritance, we have a responsibility to do so. But as I noted in chapter thirteen, in a materialist universe (which Pullman believes in) such freedom is an illusion. There is a further tension in Pullman's thinking here. Lyra can only fulfill her destiny by acting freely. This kind of destiny is not at all the predetermined outcome of a purely physical universe, since Lyra could fail to fulfill her destiny if she knew what it was. Pullman has to smuggle in this kind of destiny with the witches' prophecies and the alethiometer's leadings. These things are tied in with the intentions of Dust, which becomes a dualistic substitute for God. God, as the Bible describes him, is not found in *His Dark Materials*, while the god substitute that Pullman puts in his place is so much part of the system that he cannot act sovereignly over the whole of it (and is not eternal). So to bring a sense of destiny without God, Pullman presents Dust as omnipresent and omniscient. While not omnipotent, Dust can still direct the affairs of material creatures in order to fulfill its intentions and desires. Dust may be godlike but there is no sense of accountability to this pseudodeity. Xaphania endorses Will's autonomy rather than instruct him in "interrogating the universe" so he can find out what Dust would have him do.[20]

MYTH AND MEANING

There is another important dimension to the republic of heaven that does not come out in the conversation with Xaphania, but that underpins the whole of *His Dark Materials*. That dimension is *myth*, which is related to the issue of *meaning*.[21] Pullman wrote his underlying "creation myth" to help him get the story of *His Dark Materials* right. But myths are needed in the real world too: "We need a story, a myth that does what the traditional religious stories did. It must *explain*. It must satisfy our hunger for a *why* . . . there are two kinds of *why*, and our story must deal with both. There's the one that asks *What brought us here?* and the other that asks *What are we here for?*"[22] For Pullman, the answer to the first question is evolution by natural selection, which he recognizes as a purposeless process. But his response is to say that purpose has arisen through consciousness: "Now we are here, now we are conscious, we make a difference."[23] Again, in a materialist universe, how can you ever know if consciousness includes freedom?[24] And if not, how can we make a difference? Part of the second question has to do with how we discern good and bad, right and wrong. He says that "what shuts out knowledge and nourishes stupidity is wrong; what increases understanding and deepens wisdom is right."[25] Another part of the question has to do with what happens when we die. That issue is very much bound up with the issue of the meaning of life.

Pullman says, "I think we need this thing which I've called joy. I might also have called it Heaven."

What I'm referring to is a sense that things are right and good, and we are part of everything that's right and good. It's a sense that we're connected to the universe. This connectedness is where meaning lies; the meaning of our lives is their connection with something other than ourselves.[26] The religion that's now dead did give us that, in full measure: we were part of a huge cosmic drama, involving a Creation and a Fall and a Redemption, and Heaven and Hell. What we did *mattered*, because God saw everything, even the fall of a sparrow. And one of the most deadly and oppressive consequences of the death of God is this sense of meaningless[ness] or alienation that so many of us have felt in the past century or so.[27]

CONNECTION REGAINED

Pullman admits that a Christian worldview makes sense of life. So where does meaning come from if there is no God? Later he adds: "Part of the *meaning* that I've suggested we need, the sense that we belong and we matter, comes from the moral and social relations that the republic of heaven must embody."[28] The importance of belonging, and of being part of a bigger story, shapes the end of *His Dark Materials*: Will returns to his world with Mary who tells him, "If you'll let me, I'll be your friend for the rest of our lives" (*AS*, p. 510). Lyra returns home with Serafina Pekkala; later she can develop a new kind of relationship with the Master and Dame Hannah Relf. But it's more than human relations: "Part of the sense of wider meaningfulness that we need comes from seeing that we have a connection with nature and the universe around us, with everything that is *not* human as well."[29] Mary Malone realizes what Christianity offered:

> This was the very thing she'd told Will about when he asked if she missed God: it was the sense that the whole universe was alive, and that everything was connected to everything else by threads of meaning. When she'd been a Christian, she had felt connected, too; but when she'd left the Church, she felt loose and free and light, in a universe without purpose. (*AS*, p. 449)

But then comes her realization that the physical world was trying to hold back the flood of Dust:

> Matter *loved* Dust. It didn't want to see it go. That was the meaning of this night, and it was Mary's meaning, too.
>
> Had she thought there was no meaning in life, no purpose, when God had gone? Yes, she had thought that.
>
> "Well, there is now," she said aloud, and again, louder: "There is now!" (*AS*, p. 452)

Both Mary's conclusion and Pullman's own comments have a distinctly mystical, spiritual feel—it sounds like New Age monism.[30] Pullman is a convinced materialist, but he does nevertheless seem to be drawn toward the mystical with his reliance on Gnostic and other esoteric ideas, and references to shamans, voodoo and angels.

EMBRACING OBLIVION

The same sense comes in the description of ghosts' atoms merging again into the cosmos. Pullman is clear that there is no continuation of existence beyond death, but he smuggles in the same mystical feeling to mask the bleakness of this materialist view.

The ghost of a martyred girl denounces the faith by which she lived and died, and welcomes Lyra's message as one of hope:

> Even if it means oblivion . . . I'll welcome it, because it won't be nothing. We'll be alive again in a thousand blades of grass, and a million leaves; we'll be falling in the raindrops and blowing in the fresh breeze; we'll be glittering in the dew under the stars and the moon out there in the physical world, which is our true home and always was. (*AS*, p. 320)

And at the end of the story, Will tells Lyra: "I *will* love you forever. . . . And when I find my way out of the land of the dead I'll drift about forever, all my atoms, till I find you again." She replies:

I'll be looking for you, Will, every moment, every single moment. And when we do find each other again, we'll cling together so tight that nothing and no one'll ever tear us apart. Every atom of me and every atom of you . . . We'll live in birds and flowers and dragonflies and pine trees and in clouds and in those little specks of light you see floating in sunbeams. (*AS*, p. 497)

To talk about atoms being conscious in this kind of way—since they are not particles of Dust—is mystical nonsense, which serves only to make the prospect of oblivion more palatable.

The ideals of the republic of heaven (celebrating and making the most of this world, responsibility, wisdom, moral behavior, selflessness) sound great, but the underlying framework—the myth—is a worldview of materialist determinism with no genuine freedom (despite the claims for autonomy) and a destiny of oblivion, however much it is dressed up in mystical ideas. We will unpack this a little more in the next chapter.

15

ONCE UPON A TIME
LASTS FOREVER

Pullman, as we have seen, is a master storyteller above all else. From the deceptively simple retelling of classic fairy tales through to the epic of *His Dark Materials*, Pullman revels in the joy of storytelling and writing about stories:

> My intention is to tell a story—in the first place because the story comes to me and wants to be told. . . . I am the servant of the story—the medium in a spiritualist sense, if you like—and it feels as if, unless I tell this story, I will be troubled and pestered and harried by it and worried and fretted until I do something about it. The second reason I do it is that I enjoy the technical business of putting a story together in a way that excites and gives pleasure to an audience. The third reason is that I need to earn a living—and there is another range of reasons beyond that which might include at some point the desire to make sense of the world and my experience of it and give a sort of narrative account of why things are as they are.[1]

But Pullman also contends, "All stories teach, whether the storyteller intends them to or not. They teach the world we create. They teach the morality we live by."[2] His stories teach the things included in what he refers to as "another range of reasons." We have considered Pullman's insistence that stories must have some truth about them—they must be psychologically true, telling us about ourselves and our place in the world. When Lyra finally tells true stories in the world of the dead, the harpies find themselves drawn to it. This is something they have longed for and needed all their long lives without ever realizing it, but their deep, unsatisfied hunger had spewed out in venom and filth and hatred. Tialys persuades them to guide every ghost to the window to oblivion in return for true stories. Pullman comments: "The implication is that we have to engage with life, or else. We have to notice the world. If we spend our lives doing nothing but watching television and playing computer games, we will have nothing to tell the harpies in the world of the dead, and there we will stay."[3]

Pullman loves life, and through his stories he urges all of us to engage with it. He wants readers who are still in the process of growing up to discover the focus of their lives, and to pursue their ambitions with determination and hard work, making the most of their talents and every opportunity life throws at them. He wants them to develop their autonomy, setting their own course and seeking all the wisdom the world can offer. This is the world Pullman creates in his books, and the morality he lives by. It's an extremely positive vision of life.

A CONVINCING MISTAKE?

But while Pullman's stories are life affirming, he faces up to the hard side of life too—including the harsh realities of separation and of death. The way his protagonists respond teaches important lessons about handling difficulty and tragedy. But as we saw in the previous chapter, Pullman tries to put a very positive spin on his materialist convictions in the oblivion of death. John Faa summarizes this: "To know that after a spell in the dark we'll come out again to a sweet land like this, to be free of the sky like the birds, well, that's the greatest promise anyone could wish for" (*AS*, p. 502). How can this be the greatest promise anyone could wish for? Which is a greater promise— the republic of heaven's promise of complete nothingness, or the kingdom of heaven's offer of eternal life? But Pullman has rejected the possibility of king or kingdom and all that comes with it.

His Dark Materials is a narrative of extraordinary scope and brilliance, but those critics who claim that he loses his focus in the third volume do perhaps have something of a point. There are times when the story feels uneasily like the background for the philosophical and theological ideas, rather than the ideas forming the backdrop to the story. Now and again Pullman seems to take his eyes off his overriding goal of telling the story, rather than teaching a message. Leonie Caldecott claims that "he commits the cardinal sin of fiction, whereby an author, instead of embedding the moral of his story in the text as a whole, contents himself with putting it on the lips of a protagonist."[4] This is certainly true when Pullman has Mary Malone describe her loss of faith to Will and Lyra: "I thought physics could be done to the glory of God, till I saw there wasn't any God at all and that physics was more interesting anyway. The Christian religion is a very powerful and convincing mistake, that's all" (AS, p. 441). It feels like he strains a little too hard to keep emphasizing his humanist views in opposition to Christian ideas. As I suggested in chapter thirteen, the picture of both God and the church that Pullman paints in His Dark Materials is a straw man, which would matter far less if he didn't keep saying the same things in interviews. While Pullman is deeply critical— and rightly so—of the many failings of the Christian church over the years, he does have a strong tendency to stress only the negative aspects and to downplay the positives. In his interview for Third Way, he agrees with Mary Malone that Christianity is a "powerful and convincing mistake," saying:

> It's a very good story. It gives an account of the world and what we're doing here that is intellectually coherent and explains a great deal. . . . The Christian story gives us human beings a very important and prominent part. We are the ones who Jesus came to redeem from the consequences of sin. . . . It is a very dramatic story and we are right at the heart of it, and a great deal depends on what we decide.[5]

But then he dismisses this story on the grounds that it doesn't "gel at all with the more convincing account that is given by Darwinian evolution— and the scientific account is far more persuasive intellectually."[6] He quickly moves on to argue that belief in a single God is a "very good excuse for people to behave very badly." It is certainly true that belief in God has been—

and continues to be—used as a good excuse to justify oppression, warfare and genocide. But this is true of *any* powerful belief system—or, indeed, of any system at all. There are always people who will attempt to use a system to their own ends, regardless of how consistent or inconsistent they may be with the underlying ethics. In fact, the history of the last century includes terrifying atrocities at the hands of explicitly atheistic regimes—atrocities that are out of all proportion to anything the Christian church has ever done.[7] On the other hand, the impact of Christianity on the world's education, health care and social reforms has been incalculable.[8] On one side we see "the general human tendency to exalt one doctrine above all others,"[9] and on the other we see the committed followers of Christ making an impact on their world.

A Tale of Two Kingdoms

In Pullman's attack on the kingdom of heaven, then, he misrepresents history and misreads the Bible to create a caricature of Christianity, inverting all the categories in the process. He makes God out to be a cruel and vindictive impostor who is part of the universe, not its transcendent Creator; he presents the rebellious human grasping after autonomy as a search for wisdom; and thus he redefines "sin" as good. Within the narrative world of *His Dark Materials* this is internally coherent, if rather overplayed. As Rowan Williams points out, this is what happens if you have a "mortal God, who can win and lose his power."[10] But when Pullman plays this card so frequently and blatantly within the story, and then makes exactly the same points in interviews, it all feels rather intolerant, as I suggested in chapter fourteen. The irony is that this is the exact opposite of one of the major moral lines of *The Amber Spyglass*. Scott Masson, an English lecturer at Durham University, writes:

> Lyra and Will *personally* exhibit the courage, loyalty, honesty and fairness that incite our genuine admiration. . . . However, . . . these virtues seem to bear no relation to the idea of ultimate good, which is only really revealed in the final instalment of the trilogy. The powers

of good and evil . . . give way to the "higher virtue" of tolerance in Pullman's earthly eschatology. And this leaves the reader ice-cold, the dull sensation that is the residue of a virtue divested of sacrificial, atoning love. Much as one would expect of one enamoured of the virtue of the Enlightenment god (which Pullman tries to foist onto Christianity), we are left with a complacent, abstract and wholly intellectual virtue. The irony is heavy indeed, though I suspect that it will escape most readers.[11]

Nicholas Tucker writes that "at base *His Dark Materials* is a strongly humanist text, celebrating the abiding existence of human courage and essential goodness."[12] Well, yes, but the worldview underpinning *His Dark Materials* is bleak. The physical world is all there is; there ain't no elsewhere. So we are here through the purposeless, deterministic processes of evolution by natural selection and nothing more. Somehow, this process has led to us having consciousness, personality and genuine freedom of thought and action, although *every* physical process involved is deterministic. That consciousness brings purpose and meaning to us—and perhaps to the entire universe. We must live good lives, connected to other people and the universe; in particular we must be open-minded and tolerant, which is seeking after wisdom. We must live in such a way that we have a story to tell. When we die, our personal consciousness ceases to exist but our atoms can be reused in a beautiful world of which we are already a vital part. This rather reminds me of the Authority—emaciated, weak, fragile, paper-thin and offering no real hope.

It's hard to see how this gives much of a base for those Pullmanic virtues of curiosity, kindness, courage and determination. And it's hard to see the grounds for Pullman's optimism in human nature, especially given our history—why do we have any essential goodness? It all relies on that leap of "There is now"—meaning and purpose has come, in Pullman's view because of consciousness. We are back at the Fall with Milton, Blake and Kleist again, and Pullman's conviction that moving from innocence to experience, seizing autonomy, declaring independence, becoming masters of our own destiny was the best possible thing we could—or can—do.

As Pullman concedes in the quotation above, the Christian worldview is an "intellectually coherent" view of the world. I strongly dispute his claim that the "scientific account is far more persuasive intellectually" because that scientific account is so limited. Science cannot *begin* to answer fundamental questions like "Is there a God beyond the physical universe?" or "Why are we here?" Science deals in mechanisms, not metaphysics. The Christian worldview includes the reality of a spiritual realm;[13] it sees humans as created by God in his image, giving us consciousness, personality, *genuine* freedom, purpose, meaning and a spiritual dimension. Kleist was right that we cannot return to Paradise, we can only go forward, but wrong to suggest that we can come to it again through a back door, and eat again of the tree of knowledge of good and evil. The second decisive moment in human history is not a second Fall, but the undoing of the first Fall in the death and resurrection of Jesus Christ.

There's a curious parallel between this and the "Fall" of Lyra and Will. I commented in chapter ten that it didn't *seem* like a Fall—responding to Mary's account of her own experiences, they discover the emotional language and freedom to both recognize and express their love for each other. From the point of view of the story's sympathies, they do *exactly the right thing,* and it brings about a new age in human history. From the point of view of the Christian story, Jesus did exactly the right thing when he gave himself up to be killed on a cross, also bringing about a new age in human history.[14]

Pullman sees Jesus as little more than a teller of great stories, and dismisses his claims to be God's Son. Yet for Christians, Jesus' death and resurrection open up the possibility of redemption through a relationship with him, and the prospect of eternity with him, rather than oblivion. The Christian conviction is that God the Father has given all authority to the risen Jesus, not to an angelic Regent; Jesus is the King and the Bible contrasts his Kingdom not with a republic, but with another kingdom: "the kingdom of darkness" (Colossians 1:13 NLT). Many Christians reading *His Dark Materi-*

als want to distance themselves from both the Magisterium and the Authority, but believe that wisdom is ultimately found in the person of the King of heaven, not in building the republic of heaven.

Nevertheless, despite these objections to the underlying worldview of *His Dark Materials*, there is much to be enthusiastic about. Philip Pullman's books are, as I have said repeatedly, fabulous, wonderful celebrations of some of the richest aspects of life—the "absolute preciousness of the here and now,"[15] the innate qualities of human beings, the values that should be part of every good life, the need to keep on growing in wisdom and understanding because we're not yet what we can be. These are common to the vast majority of Pullman's work so far. His editor, David Fickling, quotes Pullman as saying, "Telling and listening to stories is what makes us human," and adds, "It defines us . . . stories are at the foundation of what we call civilisation."[16] Philip Pullman's stories will be chewed over for years. While the philosophical and theological issues pass many readers by, nobody can fail to be inspired by his stories of gutsy heroines and heroes exemplifying values that sadly often feel in short supply. As Pullman himself says, "Once upon a time lasts forever."[17]

APPENDIX
The Science of *His Dark Materials*

Philip Pullman loves science. He says it "was one of those things . . . that I was fascinated by at home, and turned off by at school."[1] He struggles with mathematics so could never be a scientist, but he loves science "for the stories that are told about it."[2] His fascination with the subject and its stories led him to include quite a lot of science in *His Dark Materials*. He sees it in terms of the background to the story he's really trying to tell, and it was important to him that he got it sufficiently right to "make the reader feel that the background was solid enough not to fall over when anyone leant against it."[3] At the same time, he didn't want to be overzealous about it—he wanted the freedom to invent things too. He says: "My test was always: 'I don't know very much about this, but I do know something, and if I read this in a novel, would it make me think that the writer knew at least as much as I did, and wasn't a complete fool?'"[4] He has done remarkably well to include so much science and to give it that sense of solidity. This is confirmed by the fact that highly respected science writers Mary and John Gribbin were able to write an entire book on the subject: *The Science of Philip Pullman's His Dark Materials*.[5] Their book is written at a level to suit teenage readers of the trilogy and is therefore very accessible.

Despite the existence of the Gribbins' excellent book, I wanted to include an appendix on the science here, partly because with a background in physics myself I would feel it was missing otherwise, but more importantly because the Gribbins have not really dealt with some of the philosophical ideas that are associated with the science, and certainly haven't dealt with the objections to some of them. There is much more to be said than can be written in one short appendix, so I have concentrated briefly on just two physics-related aspects of the science that play a significant role in *His Dark Materials*.

DARK MATTER

Dark matter has been one of the greatest mysteries of modern science for three decades. Since the 1970s scientists have been trying to track down vast quantities of the universe, which our telescopes and detectors can't see. We know it's there somewhere from studying the behavior of galaxies—they just don't behave in a way that fits what we can see. The only way of making it all work is if there's a lot of matter that is currently invisible to us. The searchers divided into two main camps. At one extreme, astronomers busied themselves looking for MACHOs (Massive Astrophysical Compact Halo Objects)—big lumps of stuff like small, dense stars (brown dwarfs) or enormous black holes, or even large numbers of planets. All these things are difficult to see at any distance because they don't radiate much, if any, electromagnetic radiation—hence the name "dark matter." As the sensitivity of our equipment increased significantly, some enormous but far-off objects were identified.[6] They do make some contribution to the missing mass of the universe, but nowhere near enough.

At the other extreme, physicists started looking for tiny particles that could make up the missing mass. There were two rival ideas—hot dark matter and cold dark matter. The particles at the center of the hot dark matter theory are large neutrinos, huge numbers of which must have been created in the Big Bang. They are thought of as "hot" because they must be traveling at nearly the speed of light. Cold dark matter theorists—who now seem to be winning the day[7]—were looking for a new kind of particle altogether: WIMPs—Weakly Interacting Massive Particles. If WIMPs behaved like the ordinary matter that makes up everything we see, they would be easy to find—but they don't. Normal (baryonic) particles interact with each other in four ways: the strong and weak nuclear forces, electromagnetism, and gravity. Gravity isn't generally a big deal with tiny particles because they don't have much mass—the other three forces are what stick everything together. Gravity only becomes significant when a lot of matter is collected in one place—except when it comes to WIMPs. WIMPs are nonbaryonic and they *only* interact with normal baryonic matter by gravity, which is why they are *weakly interacting*. They are *massive* particles because they have a much greater mass than that of a proton or neutron. In the world of particle physics, that makes them enormous—but because they only interact by gravity they're just about impossible to spot.

Therein lies the problem: the only time we can detect one is if it bumps into the nucleus of an atom in the detector, and because both WIMPs and nuclei are rather minuscule, that won't happen very often. While we're waiting for one to make its presence felt, all kinds of other particles and cosmic rays could be smashing into the detection equipment and obscuring the results. The solution is to place the detectors deep underground. That way the earth's crust shields out all the more obvious particles, leaving only the WIMPs shooting deep underground. In the United States, the Cryogenic Dark Matter Search (CDMS II) is carrying out its research at the bottom of a mine in Minnesota,[8] while Britain has the Boulby Underground Laboratory,[9] also in a mine more than a kilometer deep. At the time of writing, CDMS II has failed to find evidence of WIMPs, though their first results showed that there would be less than one WIMP interaction every twenty-five days within each kilogram of the detector material.[10]

Although WIMPs became the main contender for an explanation of dark matter, in the last few years the situation has become more complicated. In the late 1990s cosmologists started to realize that the expansion of the universe was accelerating, not slowing down. Some cosmic force was driving it apart. They began to think in terms of dark energy as well as dark matter. In 2001 NASA launched a new satellite—the Wilkinson Microwave Anisotropy Probe (WMAP)—to measure the cosmic microwave background radiation more accurately than ever before. This background radiation is the "echo" of the Big Bang, and by studying it closely scientists expect to clarify much of their understanding about the early universe. WMAP results from 2003 confirm that a mere 4 percent of the universe is composed of atoms, and only 23 percent is dark matter. Which leaves a colossal 73 percent of the universe in the form of *dark energy*[11] (energy and matter are, of course, intricately linked in Einstein's famous equation, $E=mc^2$). This is an even bigger mystery than dark matter.

There are dissenters who claim that our models of how the universe began and developed (a Big Bang followed by a period of rapid inflation) are completely wrong. They see dark matter and dark energy as a quick fix, which avoids revising the widely held inflationary theory. If WIMPs can't be found it may begin to look as though they have a point. The difficulty for the objectors is that there don't seem to be any good alternatives to inflationary theory at present. Mainstream cosmologists are reluctant to drop their current model of the origin of the universe without having something else to replace it with. They also point to the impressive accuracy of WMAP results and claim that "dark energy is unassailable now."[12]

MULTIPLE UNIVERSES

The idea of multiple universes is very trendy in the worlds of cosmology and quantum physics at present. But many people don't realize that the multiple universe ideas in these two branches of physics are quite different.

Cosmology. The first area of physics in which people are talking about multiple universes is in cosmology. Some models of the early inflation of the universe suggest that the Big Bang gave rise to a number of universes, rather like bubbles coming off the surface of a boiling liquid. We live in one bubble but there could be many more beyond the limits of ours. They remain entirely separate (though Michio Kaku suggests that "dark matter may be the presence of a neighbouring universe that we cannot see"[13]). But there are also many good inflationary theories that *don't* predict multiple universes, and we're not yet at a point where we can say that one model rather than another is right. Among others, Stephen Hawking and the Astronomer Royal Martin Rees believe that there are other bubble universes besides our own that are different in a few, or maybe in many, respects.

In his book *Just Six Numbers: The Deep Forces That Shape the Universe*,[14] Rees explores some of the amazingly delicate balances of the universe that make it possible for us to be here. For example, he discusses the ratio of the electromagnetic forces between atoms to the force of gravity between them. If this ratio was only very slightly lower, only a tiny universe could exist for a very short period of time. There's exactly the right amount of material in the universe to enable stars and galaxies to form without the whole thing collapsing back on itself. The rate of expansion is just right. Rees focuses on six, but astrophysicist Hugh Ross lists many more.[15]

The idea that the universe is finely balanced to make human life on earth possible is called the *anthropic principle*. The *strong* version of the anthropic principle says that the universe has been *designed* this way to make life possible. The *weak* anthropic principle says we just *happen* to live in a universe that is balanced in this way.[16] It may be that we were just lucky that it all worked, or it may be that there are other universes where things are a little different. One universe might be expanding just a little too fast to produce conditions favorable for life. Another may expand more slowly and collapse back on itself before life ever formed. After examining these anthropic balances, Rees has to decide which way he's going—with the strong or weak versions of the anthropic principle. He presents the choice starkly: either he has to accept the existence of God, or he has to assume there are other universes and we just happen to live in the one that resulted in us. He admits that he chooses the latter because he doesn't want to believe in the former: "If one doesn't accept the 'providence' argument, there is another perspective, which—though still conjectural—I find compellingly attractive. . . . This may not seem an 'economical' hypothesis—indeed, nothing might seem more extravagant than invoking multiple universes—but it is a natural deduction from some (albeit speculative) theories."[17] It rather seems that his emotional—or theological—preference for bubble universes, rather than design, is what makes him lean toward some inflationary models rather than others.

Quantum physics. The second area in which the idea of multiple universes comes up is in quantum physics. As with the bubble universes of cosmology, the idea only arises in *some* interpretations of quantum physics, not all. The mathematics of the quantum world have never been seriously challenged since the 1920s and 1930s when it was developed—although it has been significantly refined since then. But there are a number of ways of *interpreting* what the mathematics mean in practice. The standard way of understanding quantum physics is called the Copenhagen interpretation because it was developed by physicists working there, and others who came to meet with them, in the late 1920s—Werner Heisenberg, Niels Bohr, Max Born and Erwin Schrödinger being the most notable. Two of its key features are:

- Heisenberg's uncertainty principle, which says that there's a fundamental limit to how accurately we can measure certain pairs of quantities at the quantum level. For example, it's impossible to measure both the position and the speed of a particle accurately. You can pin down its position but you won't have a clue about the speed, or you can know how fast it's going but not know quite where it is.

- Bohr's complementarity of waves and particles, which says that, at a quantum level at least, everything can be thought of as waves *or* particles. We think of light as waves and can do many experiments that demonstrate this (a diffraction grating like the surface of a CD, for example, produces bands of color because the waves are split by the grating and then interfere with each other as they recombine). But there are also experiments that show just as clearly that light is particles—photons (Einstein first demonstrated this with the photoelectric effect). On the other hand, different experiments can show electrons behaving as particles or as waves.

The solution was to start thinking of everything as a wave that doesn't exist in one particular position. It has a "wave function," which describes the probability of finding a particle at each position. The particle could be anywhere along the wave but we don't know where. When the detecting apparatus spots a particle, the wave function collapses—it has a 100 percent probability of being where it is, and a 0 percent probability of being anywhere else. It's impossible to really understand this. Richard Feynman, one of the greatest geniuses ever in the world of physics and winner of a Nobel Prize for his further development of quantum theory, said that "nobody understands quantum mechanics. . . . Do not keep saying to yourself . . . 'But how can it be like that?' because you will go down the drain into a blind alley from which nobody has yet escaped. Nobody knows how it can be like that."[18] So, we haven't got much of a clue what's really going on at a quantum level. Quantum physics is riddled with paradoxes, both mathematically and experimentally. Bohr's interpretation of it all was that nothing was real until you looked at it, or measured it.

But in 1957 Hugh Everett proposed a radically different interpretation of quantum mechanics. He suggested that there is a parallel universe for every quantum possibility. So a wave function collapses one way, to leave a particle in position X, in our world. But at that moment another world comes into existence in which *everything* is exactly the same *except* the wave function collapses differently to leave a particle in position Y. And since quantum effects are a crucial part of the workings of the brain, each time we make a decision, reality splits into more parallel universes. We are only aware of the decision we did take, and the path we are on. But on Everett's view, there are other versions of me who are only aware of *their* decisions. Once a world splits off, it goes on a path of its own, and the two worlds become increasingly divergent. Time is no longer going in a straight line, but branches off into a tree that is constantly expanding. Some of the scientists who advocate this "many worlds interpretation," including Stephen Hawking, see it as just a way of doing the mathematics, rather than as a real situation of a rapidly mushrooming number of universes. Others believe these other universes really do come into existence. One of the most enthusiastic exponents of the many worlds interpretation is Oxford physicist David Deutsch, who says, "Physical reality is the set of all universes evolving together." He calls it the *multiverse*. This is the interpretation of quantum physics that you will recognize from *His Dark Materials*.[19]

It's important to understand that this is a radically different notion from the bubble universes of cosmology. The bubbles all arise out of the initial inflation of the universe. The parallel universes of the many worlds interpretation are constantly coming into existence. There may be only one inflationary bubble universe among many that has the right conditions to support life, but in the many worlds interpretation there are uncountable billions of parallel universes almost identical to ours.

MANY WORLDS, FIVE PROBLEMS

However, it seems to me that there are some very fundamental questions that need to be asked about these multiple universe ideas. First, how can we ever know? Science writer Martin Gardner wrote, "The stark truth is that there is not the slightest shred of reliable evidence that there is any universe other than the one we are in. No multiverse theory has so far provided a prediction that can be tested."[20] How *could* a prediction of other universes ever be tested (and no, a really sharp knife won't actually help us on this)? By definition, we cannot scientifically verify anything beyond this universe. And if there's no way of testing the predictions, how useful a theory is it? Karl Popper, the philosopher of science, argued that all good scientific theories must be capable of being proved false—and there's no way of falsifying an idea about something that is inaccessible to us.

Second, science has an important principle known as Occam's razor,[21] which says that simple explanations are preferable to complicated ones. Occam's razor is often misused by not taking into account all the available evidence, so a simple explanation at one point may turn out to be oversimplistic when other evidence is included. However, an exponentially increasing number of universes seems to violate this principle to an extraordinary degree.

Third, and related to this, is the problem about where all the stuff comes from. Two principles of physics are the conservation of mass and the conservation of energy. In the day-to-day world, the amount of stuff you have remains the same no matter what processes you put it through. You may melt some ice into water and then boil it into steam, which you then lose into the air, but the same molecules are still around somewhere. Energy is conserved in a similar way. When you put fuel into your car, it has a certain amount of energy stored in it. Some of that energy gets turned into the kinetic (moving) energy of the car, a small amount becomes sound energy, and a lot is wasted as heat energy (note that this isn't talking about *saving* energy, but that the amount of energy in the system is conserved, or remains the same). We can combine the two for the universe as a whole with Einstein's famous equation $E=mc^2$, but still the total amount of mass-energy remains the same. Where does the mass-energy for a rapidly increasing number of new universes come from?

Fourth, if you have countless billions of universes, you can use it to explain absolutely anything because there are always other worlds where things are different. It provides such an easy way out of finding explanations that the whole process of science becomes devalued—all the results, all the conclusions and theories are particular to some universes and not others. It actually begins to render science *unintelligible*.

Fifth, most proponents of the many worlds interpretation admit that it excludes any idea of free will. You never really make a choice, the universe splits so that one of you is in a universe in which you took one course of action, and another of you is in a universe in which you took the other course. Although terrorists flew airplanes into the World Trade Center in the world(s) in which you are reading this book, there are other worlds in which they did not do such a heinous thing. They didn't *choose*, they just *felt like* they were choosing. Note the statement of value I included—why is it right to describe the events of 9/11 as "heinous"? Why do we see the action of the terrorists as morally reprehensible? If there are many worlds, they *did not choose* to do what they did, and therefore their actions *have no moral value*. We cannot say that a world in which the Holocaust never happened is preferable to a world in which it did, because both outcomes must have happened; the state of affairs *just is*. All our talk about morality is just words and we have no choice about saying them or thinking them. But the words mean nothing, on this view, because everything is determined—including what you think about morality and multiple universes. It's my conviction that morality does matter, that it's not illusory, and neither is my perception of having genuine freedom. And the only way I see that the universe can be nondeterminist and include genuine freedom is if there is a God to whom we are morally accountable.

Martin Gardner summarizes, "Surely the conjecture that there is just one universe and its Creator is infinitely simpler and easier to believe than that there are countless billions upon billions of worlds, constantly increasing in number and created by nobody. I can only marvel at the low state to which today's philosophy of science has fallen."[22] Philip Pullman, however, isn't trying to argue for the science, or an interpretation of it. He's simply telling a story and using some current ideas of science to give him stage scenery that has some substance. Fantasy writers have written about alternative worlds for a long time, and will continue to do so regardless of whether or not real science supports their ideas.

Notes

Preface

[1] Nicholas Tucker, *Darkness Visible: Inside the World of Philip Pullman* (London: Wizard, 2003).

[2] Claire Squires, *Philip Pullman's His Dark Materials Trilogy: A Reader's Guide* (New York: Continuum, 2003).

[3] Michael Brunton, "You Don't Know How Famous You Are Until Complete Strangers Stop You in the Street to Talk," *Time* (www.time.com/time/europe/arts/article/0,13716,579063,00.html).

Chapter 1: The Once upon a Time Business

[1] Nicholas Tucker, "Paradise Lost and Freedom Won," *Independent*, October 28, 2000.

[2] Quoted on the back cover of *The Amber Spyglass* (London: Point, 2001 edition).

[3] Peter Kemp, "Master of His Universe," *The Sunday Times*, October 19, 1997.

[4] Peter Hitchens, "This Is the Most Dangerous Author in Britain," *Mail on Sunday*, January 27, 2002.

[5] Anna Weinberg, "Are You There, God? It's Me, Philip Pullman," *Book*, November/December 2002.

[6] Deborah Ross, "Philip Pullman: Soap and the Serious Writer," *Independent*, February 4, 2002.

[7] Alona Wartofsky, "The Last Word," *Washington Post*, February 19, 2001.

[8] Harry Potter had stirred up strong opposition from the Christian Right in America—wrongly, in her view. Since it was close to Guy Fawkes Night (an annual celebration in Britain marked with fireworks and bonfires), she "joked in a regular column . . . for the Catholic Herald that any bookburners out there could find many other stories far more 'worthy of the bonfire' than Harry Potter. I went on to use Pullman's books as an example of something that was far more likely to harm a child's capacity for faith. . . . I pointed out that, in these books, everything we normally associate with safety and security—parents, priests, and even God himself—is evil, is indeed 'the stuff of nightmares.'" Since this was before *The Amber Spyglass* was published, Leonie Caldecott also speculated that Pullman might turn it all around in the final installment (Leonie Caldecott, "Paradise Denied: Philip Pullman and the Uses and Abuses of Enchantment," *Touchstone*, 2003 <www.touchstonemag.com/docs/issues/16.8docs/16-8pg42.html>).

[9] *Publishers Weekly* (www.reviews.publishersweekly.com/searchDetail.aspx?id=0679879242).

[10]Robert McCrum, "Not for Children," *Observer*, October 22, 2000.

[11]Andrew Marr, "Pullman Does for Atheism What C. S. Lewis Did for God," *Daily Telegraph*, January 24, 2002.

[12]Commander of the Order of the British Empire.

[13]Julia Eccleshare, "Letter from London," *Publishers Weekly*, December 2, 2002.

[14]Philip Pullman, "An Introduction to . . . Philip Pullman," in *Talking Books: Children's Authors Talk about the Craft, Creativity and Process of Writing,* ed. James Carter (New York: Routledge, 1999), pp. 187-88.

[15]Pullman, "Introduction to . . . Philip Pullman," p. 190.

[16]The change in name came about because Pullman provisionally titled the trilogy *The Golden Compasses* (from Book VII of *Paradise Lost* where it refers to compasses for drawing circles with). Someone at the American publishers, Knopf, mistakenly thought this referred to the alethiometer and that became their working title for the first volume. When Philip informed them that he had changed the trilogy's title to *His Dark Materials*, Knopf refused to change the title of the first volume. Pullman says, "Their obduracy in this matter was accompanied by such generosity in the matter of royalty advances, flattery, promises of publicity, etc, that I thought it would be churlish to deny them this small pleasure" (www.bridgetothe stars.net/index.php?p=FAQ#4).

[17]Pullman says, "It's a mistake really to call it a trilogy as it's one story, one book in three volumes. It has to be published in three volumes for various financial, physical and marketing reasons" ("Introduction to . . . Philip Pullman," p. 192). Since the *Cambridge Advanced Learners Dictionary* defines a *trilogy* as "a series of three books or plays written about the same situation or characters, forming a continuous story," this seems a rather curious protest to be making.

[18]Sophie recounts the story herself at www.darkmaterials.com/archive/0005.htm.

[19]Some of the best sites are www.bridgetothestars.net, www.hisdarkmaterials.org, www.dark materials.com and www.geocities.com/darkadamant.

[20]For example, "Tell Them Stories" at www.inkypot.com/tts.

[21]See www.nationaltheatre.org.uk.

[22]Rowan Williams, "A Near-Miraculous Triumph," *Guardian*, March 10, 2004.

[23]In first and second place were J. R. R. Tolkien's *The Lord of the Rings* and Jane Austen's *Pride and Prejudice*, which consistently came out on top of other polls—even before the films of *The Lord of the Rings* came out.

[24]The Carnegie Medal is the United Kingdom's highest honor specifically for children's literature.

[25]At the 2001 British Book Awards.

[26]David Lister, "Children's Book Wins Whitbread Top Prize," *Independent*, January 23, 2002.

[27]Boyd Tonkin, "Whitbread Award: An Inevitable Victory for a Dark and Complex Fable," *Independent*, January 23, 2002.

[28]Millicent Lenz, "Philip Pullman," in Peter Hunt and Millicent Lenz, *Alternative Worlds in Fantasy Fiction* (New York: Continuum, 2001), pp. 122-23.

[29]Nick Thorpe, "The Anti-Christian Fundamentalist," *The Sunday Times*, August 4, 2002.

[30]Hitchens, "This Is the Most Dangerous Author." A copy of the article is online at pers-www.wlv.ac.uk/~bu1895/hitchens.htm.

[31]Sarah Johnson, "On the Dark Edge of Imagination," *The Times*, October 18, 2000.

[32]Minette Marin, "What Happens to the Kingdom of Heaven When God Is Killed?" *Daily Telegraph*, October 21, 2000.

[33]Susan Roberts, "A Dark Agenda?" (www.surefish.co.uk/culture/features/pullman_interview.htm).

[34]Philip Pullman, "About the Books" (www.philip-pullman.com/about_the_books.asp).

[35]Quoted in Bel Mooney, *Devout Sceptics—Conversations on Faith and Doubt* (London: Hodder & Stoughton, 2003), p. 123.

[36]Roberts, "A Dark Agenda?"

[37]Ibid.

[38]Naturalism as a worldview is the belief that everything has purely natural causes; it is a denial of the supernatural.

[39]Steve Meacham, "The Shed Where God Died," *Sydney Morning Herald*, December 13, 2003 (www.smh.com.au/articles/2003/12/12/1071125644900.html?from=storyrhs).

[40]James W. Sire, in his book *How to Read Slowly*, 2nd ed. (Downers Grove, Ill.: InterVarsity Press, 1988), argues that to read well means being alert for, and taking account of, the worldview that is being communicated through the writing.

[41]Philip Pullman, "The Republic of Heaven," *Horn Book Magazine*, November/December 2001, p. 667.

[42]Quoted in Mooney, *Devout Sceptics*, p. 132.

Chapter 2: Philip Pullman: Places and People

[1]Philip Pullman says, "I was told that there was some family connection with the General Sir James Outram of the Indian Mutiny, but it turns out that we're not related . . . it's just that my great-grandfather was Outram's godson" (personal e-mail to the author, May 13, 2004).

[2]Philip Pullman, "I Have a Feeling This All Belongs to Me" (www.philip-pullman.com/pages/content/index.asp?PageID=84).

[3]Kathleen Odean, "The Story Master," *School Library Journal*, October 1, 2000 (www.schoollibraryjournal.com/article/ca153054).

[4]Pullman, "I Have a Feeling."

[5]Ibid.

[6]Philip Pullman, "From Exeter to Jordan," in the Exeter College Association *Register* for 2001, p. 18. This article is available online at www.oxfordtoday.ox.ac.uk/archive/0102/14_3/03.shtml.

[7]Ibid.

[8]Ibid.

[9]"Achuka Interview" (www.achuka.co.uk/archive/interviews/ppint.php).

[10]Ted Dewan, "Lots More about Ted" (www.wormworks.com/tedpages/tdbioex.htm).

[11]These are all reproduced on Philip Pullman's website with a little explanation about each one (www.philip-pullman.com/pages/content/index.asp?PageID=90).

[12]Philip Pullman, "Medtner," *Granta* 76, January 9, 2002 (www.granta.com/extracts/1469).

[13]Pullman, "I Have a Feeling."

[14]Ibid.

[15]First broadcast October 6, 2002.

[16]Kerry Fried, "Darkness Visible: An Interview with Philip Pullman" (www.amazon.com/exec/obidos/tg/feature/-/94589/103-2179560-1236619).

[17]Nick Curtis, "Spotlight on Pullman's Dark," *Evening Standard*, January 2, 2003.

[18]Pullman, "I Have a Feeling."

[19]Ibid.

[20]Andrew Billen, "A Senile God? Who Would Adam and Eve it?" *The Times*, January 21, 2003.

[21]As chaplain of the prison, one of his roles was to accompany condemned prisoners to their execution—a role that he found very difficult.

[22]Pullman, "I Have a Feeling."

[23]Roberts, "Dark Agenda?" (www.surefish.co.uk/culture/features/pullman_interview.htm).

[24]Billen, "Senile God?"

[25]Odean, "Story Master."

Chapter 3: Storytelling and Other Stories

[1]Kerry Fried, "Darkness Visible: An Interview with Philip Pullman" (www.amazon.com/exec/obidos/tg/feature/-/94589/103-2179560-1236619).

[2]Philip Pullman, "Let's Write it in Red: The Patrick Hardy Lecture," *Signal* 85 (January 1998): 44-62.

[3]Philip Pullman, "Carnegie Medal Acceptance Speech" (www.randomhouse.com/features/pullman/philippullman/speech.html).

[4]Philip Pullman, "An Introduction to . . . Philip Pullman," in *Talking Books: Children's Authors Talk about the Craft, Creativity and Process of Writing,* ed. James Carter (New York: Routledge, 1999), p. 185.

[5]Philip Pullman, "I Have a Feeling This All Belongs to Me" (www.philip-pullman.com/pages/content/index.asp?PageID=84).

[6]Philip Pullman, interview on Kidsreads.com, December 12, 2001 (www.kidsreads.com/authors/au-pullman-philip.asp).

[7]Pullman, "I Have a Feeling."

[8]Ibid.

[9]Ibid.

[10]Pullman, "Introduction to . . . Philip Pullman," p. 182.

[11]Claire Squires, *Philip Pullman's His Dark Materials Trilogy: A Reader's Guide* (New York: Continuum, 2003), p. 13.

[12]Amanda Mitchison, "The Art of Darkness," *Daily Telegraph*, November 3, 2003.

[13]Squires, *Philip Pullman's His Dark Materials Trilogy*, p. 13.

[14]Having been out of teaching for some years, Pullman says, "I have maintained a passionate interest in education, which leads me occasionally to make foolish and ill-considered remarks alleging that not everything is well in our schools. My main concern is that an over-emphasis on testing and league tables has led to a lack of time and freedom for a true, imaginative and humane engagement with literature" (www.philip-pullman.com/about_the_author.asp).

[15]Pullman, "Let's Write it in Red."

[16]Pullman, "Introduction to . . . Philip Pullman," pp. 182-83.

[17]Mitchison, "Art of Darkness."

[18]Ibid.

[19]Ibid.

[20]Charles N. Brown, "An Interview with Philip Pullman" (www.avnet.co.uk/amaranth/Critic/ivpullman.htm).

[21]See Tony Watkins, "A Study Guide for *The Ruby in the Smoke*" (www.damaris.org/content/content.php?type=1&id=197).

[22]Pullman, "Introduction to . . . Philip Pullman," p. 182.

[23]*The Ruby in the Smoke* (Oxford: Oxford University Press, 1986); *The Shadow in the North* (as *The Shadow in the Plate*, Oxford University Press, 1986); *The Tiger in the Well* (London: Penguin, 1991); and *The Tin Princess* (London: Penguin, 1994).

[24]*The New Cut Gang: Thunderbolt's Waxwork* (London: Viking, 1994), and *The New Cut Gang: The Gas Fitters' Ball* (London: Viking, 1995). Note that these are set in Lambeth rather than the East End—the atmosphere feels much less dangerous.

[25]Philip Pullman, personal e-mail to the author, May 2004.

[26]Most prominently, Hangman's Wharf is the location of the ghastly Mrs. Holland's lodging house in *The Ruby in the Smoke*, but it is also mentioned in *Spring-Heeled Jack*. It returns much later in *The Golden Compass* where it has moved from Wapping to Limehouse (p. 42).

[27]In *Clockwork* (illustrated by Peter Bailey), the pictures are used as a "counterpoint" to the text—adding to the appreciation of the story without being quite part of it. In *Count Karlstein* (illustrated by Patrice Aggs), the pictures are mostly used to tell parts of the story in place of the text.

[28]Philip Pullman, "The Firework-Maker's Daughter, and How She Became a Play, and Then a Book, and Then Another Play" (www.sheffieldtheatres.co.uk/education/productions/fireworkmaker/pullman.shtml).

[29]*Clockwork* was the Smarties Book Prize Silver Award winner in 1997, and was also turned into an opera by composer Stephen McNeff and librettist David Wood for the Unicorn Theatre at the Royal Opera House, London.

[30]See Tony Watkins, "Stories Run like Clockwork" (www.damaris.org/content/content.php?type=5&id=351).

[31]Pullman, "Let's Write it in Red."

[32]Philip Pullman, *Clockwork or All Wound Up* (London: Corgi Yearling, 1997), p. 36.

[33]See Tony Watkins, "Firework-Makers and Fairy Tales" (www.damaris.org/content/content.php?type=5&id=346).

[34]*The Firework-Maker's Daughter* became a play again at Sheffield's Crucible Theatre (adapted by Stephen Russell and directed by Paul Hunter and Hayley Carmichael) in March 2003, and Anthony Minghella is producing a film version.

[35]Pullman, "Firework-Maker's Daughter."

[36]Ibid.

[37]Philip Pullman, *The Firework-Maker's Daughter* (London: Corgi Yearling, 1996), p. 10.

[38]*I Was a Rat* was televised by the BBC in 2001, and in spring 2004 was turned into a stage play by Oxford Youth Theatre.

[39]Jim seems to have been named after Pullman's friend in Exeter College who discovered the "gutter crawl."

[40]See Tony Watkins, "A Study Guide for *The Butterfly Tattoo*" (www.damaris.org/content/content.php?type=1&id=183).

[41]See Tony Watkins, "A Study Guide for *The Broken Bridge*" (www.damaris.org/content/content.php?type=1&id=186).

[42]See Steve Tilley, "A Study Guide for *His Dark Materials*" (www.damaris.org/content/content.php?type=1&id=142); Tony Watkins, "A Study Guide for *Northern Lights*" (www.damaris.org/content/content.php?type=1&id=198); "A Study Guide for *The Subtle Knife*" (www.damaris.org/content/content.php?type=1&id=199); and "A Study Guide for *The Amber Spyglass*" (www.damaris.org/content/content.php?type=1&id=200).

[43]Philip Pullman, "About the author" (www.randomhouse.com/features/pullman/philippullman/index.html).

[44]*Myth* is used here in its technical sense of a story that explains origins—whether or not the story is true is not relevant to its designation as a myth in this sense.

[45]Pullman, "Carnegie Medal Acceptance Speech."

Chapter 4: His Raw Materials

[1]Philip Pullman, acknowledgments in *The Amber Spyglass*, p. 521.

[2]One throwaway reference in this respect is to "the house of the great magician Dr. Dee" (*GC*, p. 40). This is John Dee (1527-1608), physician to Queen Elizabeth I and alchemist. He was the founder of "Enochian Magick," which, based on Gnostic sources, was all about talking to angels.

[3]See the appendix for more on dark matter and many worlds. For more on other aspects of science within the trilogy, I recommend Mary and John Gribbin, *The Science of Philip Pullman's His Dark Materials* (London: Hodder, 2003).

[4]The boatman named Charon ferries the souls of the dead across the River Styx to Hades, the underworld.

[5]See Virgil's *Aeneid* Book III, for example.

[6]Philip Pullman, author interview on Jubilee Books (www.jubileebooks.co.uk/jubilee/magazine/authors/philip_pullman/interview.asp).

[7]Mary Malone's "Cave" takes its name from Plato.

[8]Mary Malone is thinking about Augustine's comments on angels (*SK*, p. 249).

[9]The World of the Dead has echoes of the great plain of the vestibule of hell in Dante's *Inferno* (Canto III), where the inhabitants are tormented by hornets and gadflies. Perhaps there is deliberate irony in having the stinging Gallivespians riding dragonflies trying to torment the harpies. It's also interesting that the name Gallivespian may come from *vespa* meaning *wasp*. The common hornet is *vespa crabro*. Dante also features Charon the boatman, but the boat crossing comes after the great plain.

[10]When telling Lyra about the state of mind necessary for interacting with the "Cave" (*SK*, p. 88), Mary Malone quotes from a letter that John Keats (1795-1821) wrote in 1817 (www.mrbauld.com/negcap.html). Lyra calls this state of mind "negative capability" (*AS*, p. 458), a phrase borrowed from Keats's letter, although Mary Malone never uses the phrase. Keats's poem "Ode to a Nightingale" is also quoted as the epigraph for chapter twenty-eight in the British edition of *The Amber Spyglass*.

[11]The epigraph for chapter twenty-one of the British edition of *The Amber Spyglass* quotes Lord Byron (1788-1824) in a letter he wrote from Venice in 1817. Byron's sentiments at this point underpin Pullman's approach to writing fiction. Byron says, "But I hate things all fiction. . . . There should always be some foundation of fact for the most airy fabric, and pure invention is but the talent of a liar" (engphil.astate.edu/gallery/byron7.html).

[12]The reforging of the subtle knife perhaps has echoes of Siegfried reforging Siegmund's sword, which had been broken by Wotan in Wagner's *Ring des Niebelungen*.

[13]The epigraphs for three of the chapters in the British edition of *The Amber Spyglass* come from Emily Dickinson's poems: "She lay as if at play" in chapter four, "A shade upon the mind" in chapter nine, and "I gained it so" in chapter twenty.

[14]Six of the epigraphs from the British edition of *The Amber Spyglass* are drawn from the Authorized Version (1611) of the Bible: Job 4:15 in chapter two, Exodus 18:3 in chapter eight, 1 Kings 18:44 in chapter ten, Genesis 3:1 in chapter seventeen, John 8:32 in chapter twenty-three and Ezekiel 16:44 in chapter twenty-four.

[15]The idea has its roots in the New Testament but it was developed and embellished in the apocryphal Gospel of Nicodemus (dating from the second or third century A.D.). For more on this, see "Harrowing of Hell" in *Catholic Encyclopedia* (www.newadvent.org/cathen/07143d.htm).

[16]There are some useful *Paradise Lost* resources on the Internet, including www.paradiselost.org, which has the text of the poem, summaries, essays and other material.

[17]Philip Pullman in an interview with Charles N. Brown at the Lexicon literary convention in Oxford, August 2000. An edited version appeared in "Philip Pullman: Storming Heaven," *Locus* 45:6 no. 479. A longer version of the interview is available online at www.avnet.co.uk/amaranth/Critic/ivpullman.htm.

[18]It comes in Book II, line 916.

[19]The myth is never made explicit in *His Dark Materials*, but Pullman developed it and wrote it down as he went along. It has not been made public, although Pullman has divulged some parts of it in interviews. He intends to include it in *The Book of Dust*.

[20]William Blake, *The Marriage of Heaven and Hell*, in *William Blake Collected Poems*, ed. W. B. Yeats (London: Routledge, 2002), p. 165.

[21]Ed Vulliamy, "Author Puts Bible Belt to the Test," *Observer*, August 26, 2001.

[22]John Milton, *Paradise Lost*, Book VI, line 200.

[23]Ibid., lines 327-43.

[24]Philip Pullman says that "Lewis is a contradictory sort of character for me. I loathe the Narnia books, and I loathe the so-called space trilogy, because they contain an ugly vision. But when he was talking about writing for children, and about literature in general, Lewis was very, very acute and said some very perceptive and wise things. As a critic . . . I rate him very highly, but I do detest what he was doing in his fiction" (Huw Spanner, "Heat and Dust," *Third Way* 25, no. 2: 22-26; www.thirdway.org.uk/past/showpage.asp?page=3949).

[25]C. S. Lewis, *A Preface to Paradise Lost* (London: Oxford University Press, 1960), p. 99.

[26]Philip Pullman, personal e-mail to the author, June 16, 2004.

[27]The "lonely fen" is actually mentioned in "Little Boy Found" in the *Songs of Innocence*, but since he is rescued *from* it, the setting seems to belong with *Experience*.

[28]William Blake, *Songs of Experience,* in Yeats, ed., *William Blake Collected Poems,* pp. 67-71.

[29]Ibid., pp. 65-66.

[30]Ibid., p. 78.

[31]Especially *The First Book of Urizen* (1794), *The Song of Los* (1795), *The Book of Ahania* (1795) and *The Book of Los* (1795).

[32]Nicholas Marsh, *William Blake: The Poems* (New York: Palgrave, 2001), p. 186.

[33]Philip Pullman, personal e-mail to the author, June 16, 2004.

[34]Blake, *Songs of Experience,* p. 71.

[35]Ibid., p. 75.

[36]Marsh, *William Blake,* p. 123.

[37]A reference to the angel who blocked a return to Eden for Adam and Eve in Genesis 3:24.

[38]Blake, *Marriage of Heaven and Hell,* p. 170.

[39]We will consider whether or not this is valid in chapter thirteen.

[40]He had made a suicide pact with a young married society woman, Henriette Vogel, who was suffering from cancer. They checked into a hotel and went out for a picnic; Kleist shot Henrietta before killing himself. Ironically, it was the ensuing scandal that finally brought his writing to prominence across Europe.

[41]Idris Parry's 1981 translation of Heinrich von Kleist's *On the Marionette Theatre* can be found at the back of Nicholas Tucker, *Darkness Visible: Inside the World of Philip Pullman* (London: Wizard, 2003), pp. 197-207. It is also available online at www.southerncrossreview.org/9/kleist.htm.

[42]Kleist uses the word *grace* in relation to movement rather than in its theological sense of God's kindness to people who don't deserve it.

[43]Kleist tells the story in the first person, but it is not clear whether or not this is an account of a real conversation.

[44]Kleist, *On the Marionette Theatre.*

[45]Ibid.

[46]Ibid.

[47]Ibid.

[48]Which armored bears have never done because they have no soul.

[49]Kleist, *On the Marionette Theatre.*

[50]Blake, *Marriage of Heaven and Hell,* p. 166.

[51]Kleist, *On the Marionette Theatre.*

[52]Philip Pullman, BBC webchat (www.bbc.co.uk/radio4/arts/hisdarkmaterials/pullman_webchat.shtml).

[53]Not necessarily sexually—see the discussion on this in chapter eleven.

Chapter 5: *The Golden Compass*

[1]Philip Pullman, "About the Writing" (www.philip-pullman.com/about_the_writing.asp).

[2]Philip Pullman, "Philip Pullman's Interview Transcript" (www2.scholastic.com/teachers/authorsandbooks/authorstudies/authorhome.jhtml?authorID=78&collateralID=6472&displayName=Interview+Transcript).

[3]William Blake, *Songs of Experience,* in *William Blake Collected Poems,* ed. W. B. Yeats (London:

Routledge, 2002), pp. 67-71.

[4]We will consider truth, integrity and the part played by the alethiometer in chapter twelve.

[5]We will look at dæmons in detail in chapter nine.

[6]Pullman often mentions Pan taking on an ermine form. This was partly inspired by Leonardo da Vinci's *Lady with an Ermine.*

[7]Philip Pullman, "From Exeter to Jordan," in Exeter College Association *Register* of 2001, p. 18. This article is available online at www.oxfordtoday.ox.ac.uk/archive/0102/14_3/03.shtml.

[8]Pullman, "From Exeter to Jordan," p. 18.

[9]One website on word origins claims that the origin of *chocolate* is a little more complicated than the dictionaries make out. See www.takeourword.com/Issue016.html if you're interested.

[10]Naphtha is the name for a group of colorless flammable liquids produced in petroleum or coal tar distillation.

[11]For example, www.bridgetothestars.net (HisDarkMaterials.tk) and www24.brinkster.com/ menthapiperita/tgc.htm (HisDarkMaterialsAnnotated.tk).

[12]Pullman writes, "Heaven forfend that the rector of Exeter should feel obliged to serve opium after dinner, but this is an alternative universe, after all. I lifted that dainty detail from the diary of an English lady living in India before the Mutiny, which I'd come across 10 years before while I was looking for something else entirely. I knew I could use it somewhere" ("From Exeter to Jordan," p. 18).

[13]Philip Pullman in an interview on the Scholastic Teachers website. It has been removed from that site but is available at www.geocities.com/torre_degli_angeli/scholasticinterview.htm.

[14]C. S. Lewis, *The Lion, the Witch and the Wardrobe* (New York: HarperCollins, various editions).

[15]Philip Pullman in a discussion on Readerville.com (www.readerville.com/WebX?14 @65.93OcaX9YecM^7@.ef6c70e/59).

[16]Snow leopards are, sadly, in danger of extinction. For more information about snow leopards, see www.snowleopard.org.

[17]The Tartars (or Tatars) originally came from Siberia, but the name is used to describe the Mongol invaders of Europe and Asia in the thirteenth century.

[18]Muscovy was the predecessor of Russia and existed from the fourteenth to the eighteenth centuries.

[19]Skraeling was the Viking name for the Native Americans they encountered in Newfoundland. They were probably Beothuk people, and possibly Miqmac. Since the Skraeling wars in *His Dark Materials* took place in Beringland, it might suggest that the word applies to all natives of North America in the trilogy.

[20]*Magisterium* is the word used by the Roman Catholic Church to refer to the authority of the church.

[21]We will look at the church in some detail in chapter thirteen.

[22]The background to this phrase is that theology (the study of God) was once thought of as the "queen of the sciences"—*science* in that sense meaning an area of knowledge. Perhaps also in the background is the famous saying of the astronomer Kepler, who referred to his scientific work as "thinking God's thoughts after him."

[23]Marina Warner, *Fantastic Metamorphoses, Other Worlds* (Oxford: Oxford University Press, 2002).

[24]Philip Pullman, "There Has to Be a Lot of Ignorance in Me When I Start a Story," *Guardian*, February 18, 2002.

[25]She is not literally magnetic, but it seems somehow more than simply her personality. For some curious reason, Pullman twice refers to Mrs. Coulter having a "metallic" smell (*GC*, 87, 91). Why? "Now you've got me. I haven't the faintest idea. I think I was trying to convey her powerfully physical presence" (Philip Pullman, personal e-mail to the author, May 28, 2004).

[26]Warner, *Fantastic Metamorphoses*, p. 207.

[27]Pullman says that *panserbjørne* is a "word I made up from the Nordic languages: the *bjørne* part is bear[s], and *panser* means armour. So putting the two bits together, it was easy to make the word I have now."

[28]John Faa is based on a historical Scottish gypsy family. In 1540 a document of King James V of Scotland mentions "oure lovit Johnne Faa, Lord and Earle of Littill Egipt." In 1611 in Edinburgh, another John Faa was hanged along with three other family members. In 1624 Captain John Faa and some relatives, described as "all Egyptians, vagabonds, and common thieves," were also hanged in Edinburgh. Their wives and daughters were sentenced "to be drowned till they be deid," but the King settled for banishing them from Scotland. The descendants of Johnne Faa were the Romany kings and queens, the last being King Charles Faa-Blythe, who died in 1902. For more on the Faas, see www.electricscotland.com/history/scotsman/gypsies.htm, www.kittybrewster.com/ancestry/anstruther.htm, www.ayrwritersclub.co.uk/the _gypsy_laddie.htm and www.contemplator.com/child/gypsylad.html.

[29]Note Pullman's use of an epic simile on page 350. What begins with "Like two great masses of rock . . ." gets developed for half a paragraph.

Chapter 6: *The Subtle Knife*

[1]Though it is, of course, a fictional version of it, and therefore in a sense not the world we know at all. It is, however, a world that is familiar, in that it is like ours in almost all respects.

[2]No offense intended to residents of Winchester. I live near it and it's a fine place, but it doesn't quite compare with Lyra's Oxford or Svalbard for excitement.

[3]Psychosis is having a distorted perception of reality.

[4]We'll return to the subject of Dust in chapter ten.

[5]The Pitt-Rivers Museum in South Parks Road, Oxford (www.prm.ox.ac.uk), which is accessed through the Oxford University Museum of Natural History (www.oum.ox.ac.uk). See *SK*, p. 76.

[6]"Latrom" is "mortal" backward. This doesn't seem greatly significant since everybody in Pullman's stories—including the Authority—is mortal, but perhaps when Lord Boreal chose his pseudonym, he was aware of the need to keep returning to his own world if he wasn't going to sicken and die.

[7]There's more on Mary in the next chapter, and on dark matter in chapter eleven and the appendix.

[8]Cittàgazze was inspired by Venice—Pullman has Canaletto's *Portico with Lantern* hanging on his study wall (see www.upenn.edu/ARG/archive/venice/CaMeB10big.jpeg).

[9]J. K. Rowling, *Harry Potter and the Prisoner of Azkaban* (London: Bloomsbury, 2000).

[10]Philip Pullman, personal e-mail to the author, May 28, 2004.

[11]Quoted in Marina Warner, *Fantastic Metamorphoses, Other Worlds* (Oxford: Oxford University Press, 2002), p. 130.

[12]"String theory" and later "superstring theory" viewed all fundamental particles as vibrating strings—either loops or open-ended lines. Each string is ten-dimensional with the six extra dimensions (those that we cannot perceive) wrapped up inside the string.

[13]Superstring theory has now evolved into M-theory, which works in eleven dimensions. These multidimensional theories are necessary to be able to find some way of combining quantum physics with relativity to arrive at a "theory of everything." For more information, see "M-theory, the Theory Formerly Known as Strings" on the Cambridge Relativity website (www.damtp.cam.ac.uk/user/gr/public/qg_ss.html).

[14]In *The Subtle Knife*, Yambe-Akka is the goddess who comes to witches when they die (*SK*, p. 39).

[15]He's described as a "New Dane" (*GC*, p. 178). New Denmark was the name used for Canada by the early settlers, so the fact that Lee Scoresby is a New Dane from Texas suggests that in Lyra's world the United States doesn't exist as such. Lee's name comes from Lee Van Cleef, the actor in westerns, and William Scoresby, who was a real Arctic explorer (www.whitby -yorkshire.co.uk/scoresby/scoresby.htm).

[16]Is this a tacit—perhaps even subconscious—admission on Pullman's part that Milton really does show Satan as a failure in *Paradise Lost*?

[17]Pullman says, "I made it up from two Norse words meaning God and death" (BBC webchat— www.bbc.co.uk/radio4/arts/hisdarkmaterials/pullman_webchat.shtml).

[18]Novaya Zemlya, an island off the northern coast of Russia.

[19]The Pakhtars appear to be invented by Pullman, as does the Semyonov range of mountains near which they are located (note the similarity of name with the odious Russian priest in *The Amber Spyglass,* who is called Semyon Borisovitch; *AS*, p. 98). The Yenisei River, however, is one of the major rivers in Siberia, which passes through the Sayan mountains (from which Stanislaus Grumman's dæmon gets part of her name). For information, see www.en.wikipedia .org/wiki/Yenisei_River.

[20]The process is called trepanning or trephination, and in Lyra's world it was to let more Dust in. It is not entirely clear why ancient peoples in our world carried out this practice—whether it was for medical or spiritual reasons. There are a small number of people in our times who have trepanned themselves in order to achieve an altered state of consciousness. For one person's account of this, see "The People with Holes in Their Heads" (from John F. Michell, *Eccentric Lives and Peculiar Notions* [San Diego: Harcourt Brace Jovanovich, 1984]) at www.noah.org/trepan/people_with_holes_in_their_heads.html.

[21]This comes from the Siberian shamans' belief that they can travel to the underworld and the overworld while in a trance.

Chapter 7: *The Amber Spyglass*

[1]The quotation at the beginning of chapter one of the British edition of *The Amber Spyglass* is from William Blake's "Little Girl Lost," one of the poems in *Songs of Experience* (W. B. Yeats, ed., *William Blake Collected Poems* [London: Routledge, 2002], p. 68). Pullman leaves out the first line of the stanza, which reads, "Sleeping Lyca lay . . ."

[2]As I suggested in chapter four, this seems to me to be a gross misreading of John Milton's work.

[3]Philip Pullman, "Discussion on Readerville.com" (www.readerville.com/WebX?14@65 .93OcaX9YecM^7@.ef6c70e/59).

[4]Ibid. Pullman worked some of his ideas about angels into the text of *His Dark Materials*, but included some more in the *Liber Angelorum*, which is found on the Random House website (www.randomhouse.com/features/pullman/subtleknife/liber.html).

[5]For a thorough examination of the idea of angels, see Peter S. Williams, *The Case for Angels* (Milton Keynes, U.K.: Paternoster, 2003).

[6]Jesus is mentioned twice in *His Dark Materials*. Both references are from Mary Malone explaining her loss of faith (pp. 465, 466).

[7]The idea of Jesus being at the "right hand" of God, that is, in the position of utmost importance, occurs frequently in the Bible.

[8]Sally Vincent, "Driven by Daemons," *Guardian*, November 10, 2001.

[9]Interestingly, Mrs. Coulter seems to have managed the journey of several thousand miles in a matter of a few days, whereas Will has to travel at a more modest pace.

[10]We never hear what happens to Lyra's death—does he cease to accompany her throughout life?

[11]There is a strong echo of *Paradise Lost* here that describes Satan's hordes in hell as "His Legions, Angel Forms, who lay intrans't / Thick as Autumnal Leaves that strow the Brooks / In Vallombrosa" (Book I, lines 301-3).

[12]Pullman writes: "I remember a day with my younger son, who was then 15, when we were on holiday in Slovenia, and we were speculating about the business of why no animals had wheels. What would be necessary, biologically, physiologically, for that to be possible? We were walking around Lake Bled, which is a very pretty lake all surrounded by trees, and in two or three hours we had invented the mulefa. At least, we'd got the creatures and the trees and the seed-pods and the wheels. But on their own they would have meant little and added nothing to the story; so then the connection had to be made with Dust and the basic theme of the story, which of course is the difference between innocence and experience" (www .readerville.com/WebX?14@65.93OcaX9YecM^7@.ef6c70e/92).

[13]She says that this is predicted by quantum theory (p. 90). This idea is examined in the appendix.

[14]A recurrence of Pullman's common theme of the need for talent, hard work and luck (see chapter three).

[15]Nicholas Tucker, *Darkness Visible: Inside the World of Philip Pullman* (London: Wizard, 2003), p. 179.

Chapter 8: Beyond *The Amber Spyglass*

[1]Philip Pullman, *His Dark Materials* (London: Cover to Cover, 2002). The three volumes each won Audio Publishers Association Audie awards (in 2000, 2001 and 2002).

[2]*Philip Pullman: His Dark Materials Trilogy* (London: BBC Radio Collection, 2003).

[3]Philip Pullman, BBC webchat (www.bbc.co.uk/radio4/arts/hisdarkmaterials/pullman _webchat.shtml).

[4]Philip Pullman, "Discussion on Readerville.com" (www.readerville.com/webx?14@20 .iHImaaLtrtL.0@.ef6c70e/92).

[5]See www.nationaltheatre.org.uk. For more information on staging the production, see Robert Butler, *The Art of Darkness: Staging the Philip Pullman Trilogy* (London: National Theatre, 2003) and www.stagework.org.uk.

[6]Quoted in Robert Butler, *The Art of Darkness*, p. 76.

[7]Ibid., p. 6.

[8]Sarah Lyall, *New York Times*, January 25, 2004.

[9]Quoted in Butler, *Art of Darkness*, p. 36.

[10]Michael Brunton, "You Don't Know How Famous You Are Until Complete Strangers Stop You in the Street to Talk," in *Time* (www.time.com/time/europe/arts/article/0,13716,579063,00 .html).

[11]"Philip Pullman Answers Your Questions" (www.bbc.co.uk/gloucestershire/getfresh/2003/ 10/philip_pullman_qa.shtml).

[12]Rupert Kaye, "Association of Christian Teachers Attacks the National Theatre for Staging "Blasphemous" Philip Pullman Play" (www.christianteachers.org.uk/news/HisDarkMaterials .htm).

[13]Aleks Sierz, "Philip Pullman and Nicholas Hytner: Enter the Dæmons," *Independent*, December 12, 2003.

[14]Brunton, "You Don't Know How Famous You Are."

[15]"Northern Weitz," *Empire Online*, May 25, 2004 (www.empireonline.co.uk/site/news/news story.asp?news_id=15875).

[16]Philip Pullman, personal e-mail to the author, June 16, 2004.

[17]Quoted in Julia Eccleshare, "Letter from London," *Publishers Weekly*, March 5, 2001.

[18]Philip Pullman, "About the Books: Lyra's Oxford" (www.philip-pullman.com/pages/content/ index.asp?PageID=61).

[19]Vanessa Thorpe and Jonathan Heawood, "Pullman Brings Back Lyra for Oxford Mystery," *Observer*, April 6, 2003.

[20]Ibid.

[21]Ibid.

[22]Philip Pullman, *Lyra's Oxford* (Oxford: David Fickling Books, 2003), introductory pages.

[23]Some voodoo traditions are thought to originate with the Dahomey people of Benin.

[24]There is no connection between Jotham Santelia and the city of Sant'Elia in the world of Cittàgazze—Pullman says he was "just being careless. It's a name I like, and I came back to it forgetting that I'd used it before" (personal e-mail to the author, May 28, 2004).

[25]Pullman, *Lyra's Oxford*, postcard.

[26]Pullman, *Lyra's Oxford*, introductory pages.

[27]St. Sophia's may possibly have this name because this is the place where Lyra will continue her process of learning true wisdom. Or it may not.

[28]This is rather a hostage to fortune—if Makepeace doesn't appear in *The Book of Dust* I'll look rather silly. I have *tried* to get Pullman to spill the beans on what's going into *The Book of Dust*, but he remains tight-lipped, saying, "No clues at all. I'm not going to give away the slightest hint" (personal e-mail to the author, June 16, 2004).

Chapter 9: Dæmons and Growing Up

[1]Kirjava means "multicolored."

[2]"Achuka Interview" (www.achuka.co.uk/archive/interviews/ppint.php).

[3]*Webster's Revised Unabridged Dictionary.*

[4]See also David Maybury-Lewis, *Millennium: Tribal Wisdom and the Modern World* (New York: Viking Penguin, 1992).

[5]James George Frazer, *The Golden Bough* (1922); available online at www.bartleby.com/196/169.html.

[6]Sally Vincent, "Driven by Dæmons," *Guardian*, November 10, 2001.

[7]The way we resolve this tension is to see the wave in terms of the probability of where a particle is at any moment. See the appendix for more on this.

[8]Quoted in Bel Mooney, *Devout Sceptics—Conversations on Faith and Doubt* (London: Hodder & Stoughton, 2003), p. 130.

[9]For example, Fra Pavel has a frog dæmon (*AS*, p. 69), Father MacPhail has a lizard (*AS*, p. 70) and Father Gomez has a beetle (*AS*, p. 77).

[10]Charles N. Brown, "An Interview with Philip Pullman" (www.avnet.co.uk/amaranth/Critic/ivpullman.htm).

[11]Kerry Fried, "Darkness Visible: An Interview with Philip Pullman" (www.amazon.com/exec/obidos/tg/feature/-/94589/103-2179560-1236619).

[12]Brown, "Interview with Philip Pullman."

[13]Helena de Bertodano, "I Am of the Devil's Party," *Daily Telegraph*, January 29, 2002.

[14]This raises the question of why Will didn't see his dæmon when he entered Lyra's world while searching for her.

[15]Brown, "Interview with Philip Pullman."

[16]Philip Pullman, "An Introduction to . . . Philip Pullman," in *Talking Books: Children's Authors Talk About the Craft, Creativity and Process of Writing*, ed. James Carter (London: Routledge, 1999), p. 190.

[17]Millicent Lenz, "Philip Pullman," in Peter Hunt and Millicent Lenz, *Alternative Worlds in Fantasy Fiction* (New York: Continuum, 2001), p. 140.

Chapter 10: Dust, Sin and the Fall

[1]In our world, diseases were once thought to have come from space in a constant inflow—which is where we get the word *influence* from, as well as *influenza*.

[2]Pullman says, "I know the Bible very well. I know the hymns and the prayer book very well—and this is the old, authorized King James Version of the Bible, and the 1662 Book of Common Prayer that used to be used in English churches. . . . I love the language and the atmosphere of the Bible and the prayer book" (Kathleen Odean, "The Story Master," *School Library Journal*, October 1, 2000 <www.schoollibraryjournal.com/article/ca153054>). Elsewhere he talks of the "dreadful, barren language that disfigures the forms of service they have now" (Huw Spanner, "Heat and Dust," *Third Way* 25, no. 2: 22-26 <www.thirdway.org.uk/past/showpage.asp?page=3949>).

[3]Interestingly, this last change suggests that, although Philip is scathing about modern translations of the Bible, he evidently sees at least *some* need for updating the language for a modern audience.

[4]See "Sin" in Sinclair Ferguson and David Wright, eds., *New Dictionary of Theology* (Downers Grove, Ill.: InterVarsity Press, 1988), pp. 641-43; and Henri Blocher, *Original Sin* (Leicester, U.K.: Apollos, 1997).

[5]Cornelius Plantinga, *Not the Way It's Supposed to Be: A Breviary of Sin* (Leicester, U.K.: Apollos, 1995), p. 33.

[6]Some commentators do disagree with the majority in that they take "to dust you will return" as something that was always inevitable for Adam, even before his rebellion. In other words, he would have died whether he sinned or not, and the judgment on him is that work will now be difficult for him until that time. Most see physical death as being part of God's judgment and a consequence of being expelled from Eden. But this difference of opinion is over what the words imply, not over the translation itself. See Gordon Wenham, *Word Biblical Commentary: Genesis 1-15* (Waco, Tex.: Word, 1987), p. 83, for more details.

[7]The square root of any number, when multiplied by itself (squared) gives you the number you started with. The square root of 9 is 3, so 3 x 3 = 9. But what number, when multiplied by itself, gives the answer -1? It's impossible, since multiplying two positive numbers gives a positive result as does multiplying two negative numbers. The square root of -1 is therefore called an "imaginary number" and it's vital for solving certain equations.

[8]"Faith and Fantasy," Australian Broadcasting Company Radio National, March 24, 2002 (www.abc.net.au/rn/relig/enc/stories/s510312.htm). The same ideas come at the end of his "Republic of Heaven" essay (Philip Pullman, "The Republic of Heaven," *Horn Book Magazine*, November/December 2001, pp. 655-67).

[9]Tony Watkins, "In Conversation with Philip Pullman" (www.damaris.org/content/content .php?type=5&id=357).

[10]There is nothing to suggest that it was an apple tree—this is a common misconception.

[11]For example, see Helena de Bertodano, "I Am of the Devil's Party," *Daily Telegraph*, January 29, 2002.

Chapter 11: Consciousness, Wisdom and the Second Fall

[1]Celia Dodd, "Debate: Human Nature: Universally Acknowledged," *The Times*, May 8, 2004.

[2]Pierre Gehmlich, "Dark Matter 'Found within Decade,'" April 9, 2004 (news.bbc.co.uk/1/hi/ sci/tech/3614127.stm).

[3]The opening was on April 28, 2003.

[4]For more information, see David Whitehouse, "Science in the Underworld," April 28, 2003 (news.bbc.co.uk/1/hi/sci/tech/2981837.stm).

[5]The appendix of this book has more on the real science of dark matter.

[6]Philip Pullman, personal e-mail to the author, May 13, 2004.

[7]Reply by Pullman in a discussion on the Readerville website (www.readerville.com/ WebX?14@216.M6d8aZSiqFu.17@.ef6c70e/28).

[8]The responses Mary gets confirm that it is Shadows/Dust/dark matter that is communicating with her, but then they call themselves angels—"structures" or "complexifications" of Dust (*SK*, p. 249).

[9]Reply by Pullman in a discussion on the Readerville website (www.readerville.com/ webx?14@207.TcfXaajhstu.0@.ef6c70e/92).

[10]Charles N. Brown, "An Interview with Philip Pullman" (www.avnet.co.uk/amaranth/Critic/ivpullman.htm).

[11]Philip Pullman, personal e-mail to the author, May 13, 2004.

[12]Self-consciousness in the positive sense of self-awareness, rather than awkwardness.

[13]"Faith and Fantasy," Australian Broadcasting Company Radio National, March 24, 2002 (www.abc.net.au/rn/relig/enc/stories/s510312.htm).

[14]Dave Weich, "Philip Pullman Reaches the Garden" (www.powells.com/authors/pullman.html).

[15]Ibid.

[16]"Ah! Marchpane!" exclaims Lyra (AS, p. 443). Marchpane was the Old English name for marzipan.

[17]Huw Spanner, "Heat and Dust," Third Way 25, no. 2: 22-26 (www.thirdway.org.uk/past/showpage.asp?page=3949).

[18]Philip Pullman in a discussion on the Readerville website (www.readerville.com/WebX?14@216.M6d8aZSiqFu.18@.ef6c70e/30).

[19]Spanner, "Heat and Dust."

Chapter 12: Truth, Integrity and the Alethiometer

[1]Ogunwe is, in fact, a king, not a prince (AS, p. 63).

[2]Peter Hitchens, "A Labour of Loathing," Spectator, January 18, 2003.

[3]Giving up on one's faith.

[4]"Philip Pullman in His Own Words" (www.scholastic.co.uk/zone/spyglasshome/amber_philip.html). Terry Pratchett says that referring to His Dark Materials as "stark realism" rather than fantasy shows "that Mr. Pullman—a nice chap, by the way—has certainly grasped one requisite for being a successful fantasy writer" (www.dcs.gla.ac.uk/SFArchives/Ansible/a175.html).

[5]Philip Pullman, "About the Writing" (www.philip-pullman.com/about_the_writing.asp).

[6]Ibid.

[7]"When I think about the fantasy that I've read . . . I have to say that it's pretty thin. . . . Inventiveness a-plenty—no shortage of strange creatures and made-up languages and broad landscapes . . . but that kind of thing is not hard to make up. . . . But there isn't a character in the whole of The Lord of the Rings who has a tenth of the complexity, the interest, the sheer fascination, of even a fairly minor character from Middlemarch, such as Mary Garth. Nothing in her is arbitrary; everything is necessary and organic, by which I mean that she really does seem to have grown into life, and not to have been assembled from a kit of parts. She's surprising. It's not just character drawing, either; it's moral truthfulness. I can't remember anything in The Lord of the Rings, in all that vast epic of heroic battles and ancient magic, that titanic struggle between good and evil, that even begins to approach the ethical power and the sheer moral shock of the scene in Jane Austen's Emma when Mr. Knightley reproaches the heroine for her thoughtless treatment of poor Miss Bates. Emma's mortification is one of those eye-opening moments after which nothing is the same. Emma will grow up now, and if we pay attention to what's happening in the scene, so will we. That's what realistic fiction can do, and what fantasy of the Tolkien sort doesn't" (Philip Pullman, "Writing Fantasy Realistically,"

Sea of Faith National Conference 2002 <www.sofn.org.uk/Conferences/pullman2002.htm>).

[8]Quoted in Angelique Chrisafis, "Pullman Lays Down Moral Challenge for Writers," *Guardian*, August 12, 2002.

[9]Pullman, "About the Writing."

[10]Quoted in Chrisafis, "Pullman Lays Down Moral Challenge."

Chapter 13: The Magisterium and the Authority

[1]Steve Meacham, "The Shed Where God Died," *Sydney Morning Herald*, December 13, 2003.

[2]Alona Wartofsky, "The Last Word," *Washington Post*, February 19, 2001.

[3]Huw Spanner, "Heat and Dust," *Third Way* 25, no. 2:22-26.

[4]Meacham, "Shed Where God Died."

[5]Philip Pullman, "The Republic of Heaven," *Horn Book Magazine*, November/December 2001, p. 657.

[6]Philip Pullman and Rowan Williams, "The Dark Materials Debate: Life, God, the Universe . . . ," *Daily Telegraph*, March 17, 2004.

[7]Philip Pullman, "Discussion on Readerville.com" (www.readerville.com/WebX?14@216 .M6d8aZSiqFu.17@.ef6c70e/28).

[8]Pullman, "Republic of Heaven," p. 655.

[9]Philip Pullman, *His Dark Materials: The Myth* (unpublished).

[10]Pullman and Williams, "Dark Materials Debate."

[11]See Hebrews 1 for one discussion of Jesus the Son of God's superiority to angels.

[12]See Hebrews 1:3, for example.

[13]For example, see Psalm 111 and Psalm 145.

[14]See Romans 8:19-23.

[15]Rowan Williams, "A Near-Miraculous Triumph," *Guardian*, March 10, 2004.

[16]Male circumcision is a central part of the religious practices of Jews and Muslims; it is generally performed expertly and carries little or no health risk. Female circumcision, also known as female genital mutilation (FGM), is a cultural practice, *not* a religious one (though there is some controversy within Islam about two sayings of Muhammad that are interpreted as approving of the practice). It is a barbaric practice intended to preserve a girl's virginity by preventing or reducing any sexual feeling, and it carries severe health risks. For more information, see www.religioustolerance.org/fem_cirm.htm.

[17]Since John Calvin is a real historical figure in our world, it's important to remember at this point that Pullman is writing about a fictional John Calvin in another world. The Calvin in our world was never guilty of such a thing.

[18]The idea of preemptive absolution is Pullman's invention—it is not an idea accepted in any orthodox, mainstream church.

[19]Pullman, "Discussion on Readerville.com" (www.readerville.com/WebX?14@216 .M6d8aZSiqFu .18@.ef6c70e/30).

[20]Pullman, "Discussion on Readerville.com" (www.readerville.com/WebX?14@216.M6d8a ZSiqFu.11@.ef6c70e/111).

[21]Spanner, "Heat and Dust."

[22]Pullman, "Discussion on Readerville.com" (www.readerville.com/WebX?14@216.M6d8a ZSiqFu.17@.ef6c70e/28).

[23]Kathleen Odean, "The Story Master," *School Library Journal*, October 1, 2000 (www.school libraryjournal.com/article/ca153054).

[24]Odean, "Story Master."

[25]Spanner, "Heat and Dust."

[26]Pullman says: "Jesus is a very interesting character, whom the Christian church in all its branches has completely misunderstood—more truthfully, misrepresented—for two thousand years. In almost every respect his actual words directly contradict what churches tell us—about the family, to take one obvious and current example. To hear the church, you'd think that Jesus was completely obsessed by the question of homosexuality and what a threat it was to the family. But he never mentions homosexuality, and his view of families was that you should leave them behind entirely. And so on. My view of him, of course, would say that he was not God at all, but a man—a man of genius, a great moral teacher and storyteller, but only a man—who died. The resurrection was a story made up later in order to consolidate the authority of the new and shaky structure of the church, and to bolster the fantasies of Paul about the imminent end of the world" (personal e-mail to the author, June 16, 2004).

[27]Zarathustra (Zoroaster in Greek) (probably around 1500 B.C.) was the founder of Zoroastrianism; Siddharta Gautama (563-483 B.C.) was the founder of Buddhism; Muhammad (A.D. 570-632) was the founder of Islam; and Guru Nanak (A.D. 1469-1539) was the founder of Sikhism.

[28]Sun Myung Moon (born 1954) is the founder of the Unification Church. Moon and his followers have frequently been accused of manipulative recruiting techniques, deception and brainwashing. Moon was convicted of tax fraud in 1982 and is alleged to have links with extremist right-wing organizations and arms manufacturers. While I was writing this chapter, it was announced that Moon, while in the U.S. Senate, had declared himself Messiah, and claimed that "communist leaders such as Marx and Lenin, who committed all manner of barbarity, and dictators such as Hitler and Stalin, have found strength in my teachings, mended their ways and been reborn as new persons" (Julian Borger, "Moonie Leader 'Crowned' in Senate," *Guardian*, June 24, 2004). See also en.wikipedia.org/wiki/Sun_Myung_Moon.

[29]Joseph Smith Jr. (1805-1844) was the founder of the Church of Jesus Christ of Latter-Day Saints (Mormons). He was accused of being a charlatan, and many of his early associates turned against him, not least because of his practice of polygamy. The Mormon Church is accused of being authoritarian, deceptive and oppressive of women, as well as secretly continuing to encourage polygamy. See en.wikipedia.org/wiki/Church_of_Jesus_Christ_of_Latter day_Saints and www.irr.org/mit/Default.html.

[30]Charles T. Russell (1852-1916) was the founder of the Jehovah's Witnesses (although this is disputed by some). He too is accused of being a charlatan and not only lost a libel suit when contesting such allegations, but perjured himself in the process. It has a history of failed prophecies (it has prophesied the end of the world at least six specific dates). See en.wikipedia .org/wiki/Jehovah's_Witnesses and www.watchtowerinformationservice.org.

[31]L. Ron Hubbard (1911-1986) was the founder of the Church of Scientology. Hubbard, a science fiction writer and convicted thief, is said to have been a pathological liar, fraud, cheat,

wife beater, alcoholic and drug addict. The Church of Scientology has repeatedly been accused of mind control, exploitation, espionage, intimidation, violence and even murder. See en.wikipedia.org/wiki/Scientology and www.clambake.org.

[32]Quoted in Russell Stannard, *Science and Wonders: Conversations about Science and Belief* (Boston: Faber & Faber, 1996), p. 60.

[33]Victoria Nelson argues that many secular people have a deep, unconscious belief in the transcendent, which is why science fiction and fantasy are such popular genres in both literature and film. See her *The Secret Life of Puppets* (Cambridge, Mass.: Harvard University Press, 2003).

[34]Pullman, "Republic of Heaven," p. 655.

Chapter 14: The Republic of Heaven

[1]The double meaning of *adamant* is surely intentional—Lord Asriel's fortress is both made of an exceptionally hard stone and is immovable, unshakable and impenetrable.

[2]While dissolving into the cosmos may not seem like salvation, within the framework of the narrative it is certainly presented in this way—the ghosts experience a liberating release.

[3]The idea is not original to Pullman. A book called *The Tableau or, Heaven as a Republic* by a John George Schwahn was published in America in 1892. More recently, David Boulton's *Gerrard Winstanley and the Republic of Heaven* was published in 1999—a year before *The Amber Spyglass*.

[4]Philip Pullman, interview on Kidsreads.com, December 12, 2001 (www.kidsreads.com/authors/au-pullman-philip.asp).

[5]Charles N. Brown, "An Interview with Philip Pullman" (www.avnet.co.uk/amaranth/Critic/ivpullman.htm).

[6]In "The Republic of Heaven" (*Horn Book Magazine*, November/December 2001, p. 664), Pullman calls Blake "one of the founding fathers of the republic of Heaven" and quotes some lines from *The Marriage of Heaven and Hell*: "How do you know but ev'ry Bird that cuts the airy way, / Is an immense world of delight, clos'd by your senses five?" Blake also wrote, "To see a world in a grain of sand, / And a heaven in a wild flower; / Hold infinity in the palm of your hand, / And eternity in an hour" ("Auguries of Innocence," in *William Blake Collected Poems*, ed. W. B. Yeats [London:Routledge, 2002], p. 88).

[7]Dante also comments on the stars when he leaves hell: "I beheld through a round aperture / Some of the beauteous things that Heaven doth bear; / Thence we came forth to rebehold the stars" (Dante Alighieri, *Inferno*, Canto XXXIV).

[8]Pullman, "Republic of Heaven," p. 664.

[9]Ibid., p. 655.

[10]Ibid.

[11]Nicholas Tucker, *Darkness Visible: Inside the World of Philip Pullman* (London: Wizard, 2003), p. 181.

[12]Pullman, "Republic of Heaven," p. 663.

[13]Ibid., p. 664.

[14]Philip Pullman, *The South Bank Show*, March 9, 2003 (www.southbankshow.com/coming_shows/show/17).

[15]All from Philip Pullman, "The Darkside of Narnia," *Guardian*, October 1, 1998.

[16]Helena de Bertodano, "I Am of the Devil's Party," *Daily Telegraph*, January 29, 2002.

[17]Erica Wagner, "Courageous and Dangerous: A Writer for All Ages," *The Times*, January 23, 2002.

[18]Ibid.

[19]For an evaluation of Pullman's critique of C. S. Lewis, see www.damaris.org/Pullman.

[20]Brown, "Interview with Philip Pullman."

[21]Myth in this sense means a story (which may or may not be true) that explains a worldview, or some feature of the world.

[22]Pullman, "Republic of Heaven," p. 665.

[23]Ibid.

[24]If the universe is a purely physical system, the only factors that affect the movement of electrical signals in my brain are my genes and my environment (both of which are deterministic in a purely physical system), and quantum fluctuations (which are entirely random). Therefore, my thoughts are either *determined* or *random*. In either case, how can I possibly know whether my thoughts are *true* or *reliable*? My beliefs about the nature of the universe, my brain and determinism (or randomness) would themselves be completely determined or completely random. As the biologist J. B. S. Haldane remarked, "In order to escape from the necessity of sawing away the branch on which I am sitting, so to speak, I am compelled to believe that mind is not wholly conditioned by matter." And that is possible *only* if there is something beyond the material.

[25]Pullman, "Republic of Heaven," p. 666.

[26]This is a key idea within *Lyra's Oxford*—see chapter eight.

[27]Pullman, "Republic of Heaven," p. 656.

[28]Ibid., p. 664.

[29]Ibid.

[30]Monism can mean two things. First, the belief that everything is the same kind of stuff. Pullman is a monist in this sense in that he believes only in the physical world and rejects any spiritual dimensions. The second is more mystical: the belief that "reality is one unitary organic whole with no independent parts" (Merriam-Webster Online Dictionary <www.m-w.com/cgi-bin/dictionary?book=Dictionary&va=monism>).

Chapter 15: Once Upon a Time Lasts For Ever

[1]Huw Spanner, "Heat and Dust," *Third Way* 25, no. 2:22-26.

[2]Philip Pullman, "Carnegie Medal Acceptance Speech" (www.randomhouse.com/features/pullman/philippullman/speech.html).

[3]Philip Pullman, "Writing Fantasy Realistically," Sea of Faith National Conference 2002 (www.sofn.org.uk/Conferences/pullman2002.htm). It is interesting to note that when Bel Mooney asked Pullman if he believes in any form of life after death, he replied, "I believe pretty well what I've described. . . . I believe in something like what happens in the world of the dead" (Bel Mooney, *Devout Sceptics—Conversations on Faith and Doubt* [London: Hodder & Stoughton, 2003], p. 131).

[4]Leonie Caldecott, "Paradise Denied: Philip Pullman and the Uses and Abuses of Enchant-

ment," *Touchstone*, 2003 (www.touchstonemag.com/docs/issues/16.8docs/16-8pg42.html).

[5]Spanner, "Heat and Dust."

[6]Ibid. When I interviewed Pullman, he seemed surprised that there are Christians who see a process of evolution as compatible with belief in God as a Creator. This is a contentious issue within Christian circles—especially in the USA. Some argue that the scientific theories of origins are an explanation of the way God works; some argue that aspects of the science point clearly to the need for some original creative act; others argue that the science is completely wrong and needs to be completely reinterpreted.

[7]Nazism may have made use of Christian ideas, but its heart was thoroughly atheistic (based as it was on the thinking of Nietzsche and a misreading of Darwin's theory of evolution by natural selection), and it was responsible for the deaths of six million Jews; Stalin had millions of people killed; Pol Pot had a million or more killed in Cambodia. Pullman's response to this is fascinating: "They functioned psychologically in exactly the same way [as religions]. They had a sacred book that provided an explanation of history which so far transcended every other explanation as to be unquestionable. There were the great prophets—Marx, Engels, Lenin, Stalin, Mao Tse-Tung—men so far above the human race that they might as well be exalted as gods. They were treated in just the same way as the Pope. Every word they said, every thing they touched, was holy; their bodies had to be preserved and filed past in reverential silence. The fact that they proclaimed that there was no God didn't make any difference: it was a religion, and they acted in the way any totalitarian religious system would" (Spanner, "Heat and Dust").

[8]See, for example, the summaries of the actions of many individuals at www.spartacus.school net.co.uk/religion.htm.

[9]Spanner, "Heat and Dust."

[10]Rowan Williams, "A Near-Miraculous Triumph," *Guardian*, March 10, 2004.

[11]Scott Masson, "Philip Pullman's His Dark Materials Trilogy," *Glass* 15 (spring 2003): 19-23.

[12]Nicholas Tucker, *Darkness Visible: Inside the World of Philip Pullman* (London: Wizard, 2003), p. 167.

[13]Materialist theologian Don Cupitt chides Pullman for "clinging to the apparatus of supernaturalism" (www.sofn.org.uk/Conferences/ pullman2002.htm).

[14]In some ways, the voluntary self-sacrifice of Mrs. Coulter and Lord Asriel also parallels Jesus' sacrificial death: they realize that it is only through their death that Lyra can be safe and the ultimate victory won. It is also their death that brings about the destruction of their greatest enemy, Metatron.

[15]Helena de Bertodano, "I Am of the Devil's Party," *Sunday Telegraph*, January 27, 2002.

[16]David Fickling, "Narrative Heaven: The Editor's Tale—The Patrick Hardy Lecture 2001," *Signal* 97 (January 2002).

[17]Pullman, "Carnegie Medal Acceptance Speech."

Appendix

[1]Philip Pullman, "Science: A Very Short Introduction," in Mary Gribbin and John Gribbin, *The Science of Philip Pullman's His Dark Materials* (London: Hodder, 2003), p. xv.

[2]Ibid., p. xvi.

[3]Ibid., p. xviii.

[4]Ibid., pp. xviii-xix.

[5]Gribbin and Gribbin, *Science of Philip Pullman's His Dark Materials*.

[6]See, for example, "First Sighting of Dark Matter," March 22, 2001 (physicsweb.org/article/news/5/3/10/1).

[7]See "Hot Gas Reveals Cold Dark Matter," *CERN Courier* 43, no. 6 (www.cerncourier.com/main/article/43/6/12).

[8]See the CDMS II website (cdms.berkeley.edu/experiment.html).

[9]See the UK Dark Matter Collaboration website (hepwww.rl.ac.uk/UKDMC/ukdmc.html).

[10]"Dark Matter Remains at Large," May 5, 2004 (physicsweb.org/article/news/8/5/3/1).

[11]See the very informative WMAP website for more information (map.gsfc.nasa.gov/index.html); the results are summarized at map.gsfc.nasa.gov/m_mm/mr_limits.html.

[12]Carlos Frenk, quoted in "Biggest Map of Universe Clinches Dark Energy," *New Scientist*, October 28, 2003 (www.newscientist.com/news/news.jsp?id=ns99994314).

[13]Michio Kaku, "Parallel Universes Live Chat," BBC (www.bbc.co.uk/science/space/spacechat/livechat/michio_kaku.shtml).

[14]Martin Rees, *Just Six Numbers: The Deep Forces That Shape the Universe* (New York: HarperCollins, 1999).

[15]See Hugh Ross, "Design and the Anthropic Principle" (www.reasons.org/resources/apologetics/design.shtml?main).

[16]For more on this, see William Lane Craig, *Barrow and Tipler on the Anthropic Principle vs. Divine Design* (www.leaderu.com/offices/billcraig/docs/barrow.html).

[17]Rees, *Just Six Numbers*, p. 150.

[18]Quoted in Gribbin and Gribbin, *Science of Philip Pullman's His Dark Materials*, p. 77.

[19]Deutsch talks about "shadow particles," which are the counterparts of "tangible particles" in our world, but Mary Malone uses the term "shadow particles" only to talk about dark matter.

[20]Martin Gardner, "Multiverses and Blackberries," *Skeptical Inquirer,* September/October 2001 (www.csicop.org/si/2001-09/fringe-watcher.html).

[21]The principle is named after William of Ockham (c.1285-1349), a Franciscan monk who said, "*Entia non sunt multiplicanda praeter neccessitatem*"—"Entities are not to be multiplied beyond necessity."

[22]Gardner, "Multiverses and Blackberries."

BIBLIOGRAPHY

This is a select bibliography, listing just a few of the many books and articles related to Philip Pullman. A fuller bibliography is available from Damaris Publishing's *Dark Matter: A Thinking Fan's Guide to Philip Pullman* website: www.damaris.org/Pullman.

Due to the nature of the Internet, we cannot guarantee that the URLs given for online articles will remain correct, or even that the articles will remain accessible via the Internet. All URLs were correct as of October 2005.

Books by Philip Pullman

The Haunted Storm. London: NEL, 1972.

Galatea. New York: Dutton, 1979.

Using the Oxford Junior Dictionary: A Book of Exercises and Games. Oxford: Oxford University Press, 1979.

Ancient Civilizations. Exeter, U.K.: Wheaton, 1981.

The Ruby in the Smoke. New York: Knopf, 1985.

Shadow in the North. New York: Knopf, 1988.

Frankenstein. Oxford: Oxford University Press, 1990.

How to Be Cool. London: Macmillan, 1990.

The Tiger in the Well. New York: Knopf, 1990.

Count Karlstein or The Ride of the Demon Huntsman. London: Doubleday, 1991.

Spring-Heeled Jack. New York: Knopf, 1991.

The Broken Bridge. New York: Knopf, 1992.

Sherlock Holmes and the Limehouse Horror. Walton-on-Thames, U.K.: Thomas Nelson, 1992.

The Butterfly Tattoo. London: Macmillan Children's Books, 2001. First published as *The White Mercedes*. New York: Knopf, 1993.

The New Cut Gang: Thunderbolt's Waxwork. London: Viking, 1994.

The Tin Princess. New York: Knopf, 1994.

The New Cut Gang: The Gas-Fitter's Ball. London: Viking, 1995.

The Golden Compass. New York: Knopf, 1996.

The Subtle Knife. New York: Knopf, 1997.

Clockwork, or All Wound Up. New York: Levine, 1998.

Detective Stories chosen by Philip Pullman. New York: Kingfisher, 1998.

Mossycoat. London: Scholastic, 1998.

The Firework-Maker's Daughter. New York: Levine, 1999.

The Amber Spyglass. New York: Knopf, 2000.

I Was a Rat! New York: Knopf, 2000.

Puss in Boots. New York: Knopf, 2000.

Lyra's Oxford. New York: Knopf, 2003.

The Scarecrow and the Servant. New York: Knopf, 2004.

Aladdin and the Enchanted Lamp. New York: Levine, 2005.

Other Works

"Achuka Interview: Philip Pullman" (www.achuka.co.uk/archive/interviews/ppint.php).

Alderson, Brian. "Compass, Knife and Spyglass." *New York Times*, November 19, 2000.

Barger, Jorn. "Philip Pullman Resources on the Web" (www.robotwisdom.com/jorn/pullman.html).

BBC webchat (www.bbc.co.uk/radio4/arts/hisdarkmaterials/pullman_webchat.shtml).

Bobby, Susan. "What Makes a Classic? Dæmons and Dual Audience in Philip Pullman's *His Dark Materials*." *Alice's Academy* 8, no. 1 (www.the-looking-glass.net/rabbit/v8i1/academy1.html).

Brown, Charles N. "An Interview with Philip Pullman" (www.avnet.co.uk/amaranth/Critic/ivpullman.htm). An edited version appeared in "Philip Pullman: Storming Heaven." *Locus* 45:6, no. 479.

Brunton, Michael. "You Don't Know How Famous You Are Until Complete Strangers Stop You in the Street to Talk." *Time* (www.time.com/time/europe/arts/article/0,13716,579063,00.html).

Butler, Robert. *The Art of Darkness: Staging the Philip Pullman Trilogy*. London: National Theatre, 2003.

Caldecott, Leonie. "Paradise Denied: Philip Pullman and the Uses and Abuses of Enchantment." *Touchstone*, 2003 (www.touchstonemag.com/docs/issues/16.8docs/16-8pg42.html).

Chabon, Michael. "Dust and Dæmons." *New York Review of Books*, March 25, 2004.

Couchman, David. "Philip Pullman's *His Dark Materials*: A Not-So-Subtle Knife." *Facing the Challenge* (www.facingthechallenge.org/pullman.htm).

———. "The Empty Vision." *Facing the Challenge* (www.facingthechallenge.org/lewis.htm).

Dirda, Michael. "The Amber Spyglass." *Washington Post*, October 29, 2000.

Eccleshare, Julia. "Letter from London." *Publishers Weekly*, December 2, 2002.

Faith and Fantasy. Australian Broadcasting Company Radio National, March 24, 2002 (www.abc.net.au/rn/relig/enc/stories/s510312.htm).

Flesch, William. "Childish Things." *Boston Globe*, June 13, 2004.

Fried, Kerry. "Darkness Visible: An Interview with Philip Pullman" (www.amazon.com/exec/obidos/tg/feature/-/94589/103-2179560-1236619).

Gevers, Nick. "*Northern Lights* by Philip Pullman." *Infinity Plus*, July 24, 1999 (www.iplus.zetnet.co.uk/nonfiction/northern.htm).

———. "*The Subtle Knife* by Philip Pullman." *Infinity Plus*, July 24, 1999 (www.iplus.zetnet.co.uk/nonfiction/subtle.htm).

Grenier, Cynthia. "Philip Pullman's Dark Materials." *Crisis*, October 2001 (www.crisismagazine.com/october2001/feature4.htm).

Gribbin, Mary, and John Gribbin. *The Science of Philip Pullman's His Dark Materials*. London: Hodder Children's Books, 2003.

Harnett, Seán. "Fast Food Fantasy." *Spike* (www.spikemagazine.com/0602amberspyglass.htm).

Hitchens, Peter. "This Is the Most Dangerous Author in Britain" (pers-www.wlv.ac.uk/~bu1895/hitchens.htm).

Hunt, Peter. *Children's Literature*. Oxford: Blackwell, 2001.

Jefferson, Margo. "On Writers and Writing: Harry Potter for Grown-Ups." *New York Times*, January 20, 2002.

Jones, Dudley. "Only Make-Believe? Lies, Fictions, and Metafictions in Geraldine McCaughrean's *A Pack of Lies* and Philip Pullman's *Clockwork*." *The Lion and the Unicorn* 23, no. 1: 86-96.

Kaye, Rupert. "Association of Christian Teachers Attacks the National Theatre for

Staging 'Blasphemous' Philip Pullman play" (www.christian-teachers.org.uk/news/HisDarkMaterials.htm).

———. "Association of Christian Teachers Critiques Philip Pullman's Attempt to Besmear Christianity, Undermine the Church and Attack God" (www.christianteachers.org.uk/news/PhilipPullman.htm).

von Kleist, Heinrich. *On the Marionette Theatre* (www.southerncrossreview.org/9/kleist.htm).

Krehbiel, Greg. "Philip Pullman's His Dark Materials," *Journeyman* 1, no. 1 (www.crowhill.net/journeyman/Vol1No1/Darkmaterials.html).

Langton, Jane. "What Is Dust?" *New York Times*, May 19, 1996.

Lenz, Millicent. "Philip Pullman," pp. 122-69. In Peter Hunt and Millicent Lenz. *Alternative Worlds in Fantasy Fiction*. London: Continuum, 2001.

Lopez, Barry. *Arctic Dreams: Imagination and Desire in a Northern Landscape*. London: Harvill Press, 1999.

Lyall, Sarah. "The Man Who Dared Make Religion the Villain." *New York Times*, November 7, 2000.

———. "Staging the Next Fantasy Blockbuster." *New York Times*, January 25, 2004.

Masson, Scott J. "Philip Pullman's *His Dark Materials* Trilogy." *The Glass* 15 (spring 2003): 19-23 (www.freenetpages.co.uk/hp/clsg/Glass15.pdf).

McSporran, Cathy. "The Kingdom of God, the Republic of Heaven: Depictions of God in C. S. Lewis's *Chronicles of Narnia*, and Philip Pullman's *His Dark Materials*" (www.sharp.arts.gla.ac.uk/e-sharp/articles/autumn_2003/Cathy_McSporranKingdom_of_God.htm).

Meacham, Steve. "The Shed Where God Died." *Sydney (Australia) Morning Herald*, December 13, 2003 (www.smh.com.au/articles/2003/12/12/1071125644900.html?from=storyrhs).

Milton, John, *Paradise Lost* (www.dartmouth.edu/~milton/reading_room/pl/note/index.shtml).

Moloney, Daniel P. "An Almost Christian Fantasy." *First Things* 113 (May 2001): 45-49 (www.firstthings.com/ftissues/ft0105/reviews/moloney.html).

Mooney, Bel. *Devout Sceptics—Conversations on Faith and Doubt* (London: Hodder & Stoughton, 2003), pp. 122-33.

Nelson, Victoria. *The Secret Life of Puppets* (Cambridge, Mass.: Harvard University Press, 2003).

Odean, Kathleen. "The Story Master." *School Library Journal*, October 1, 2000 (www.schoollibraryjournal.com/article/ca153054).

Parsons, Wendy, and Catriona Nicholson. "Talking to Philip Pullman: An Interview." *The Lion and the Unicorn* 23, no. 1: 116-34.

Pattison, Darcy. Letter to the editor in *Horn Book Magazine*, March/April 2002, p. 333.

"Philip Pullman Answers Your Questions" (www.bbc.co.uk/gloucestershire/getfresh/2003/10/philip_pullman_qa.shtml).

"Philip Pullman" in *Jubilee Books* (www.jubileebooks.co.uk/jubilee/magazine/authors/philip_pullman/interview.asp).

"Philip Pullman" in *Kidsreads.com*, December 12, 2001 (www.kidsreads.com/authors/au-pullman-philip.asp).

"Philip Pullman in Readerville," February 5-9, 2001 (www.readerville.com/webx?14@223.shZGaf9Fsuu.0@.ef6c70e/0).

"Philip Pullman Scholastic Interview Transcript" (www.geocities.com/torre_degli_angeli/scholasticinterview.htm).

Pullman, Philip. "An Introduction to . . . Philip Pullman." In *Talking Books: Children's Authors Talk about the Craft, Creativity and Process of Writing,* edited by James Carter. London: Routledge, 1999, pp.178-95.

———. "Fire and Ice: Children's Literature in the New Millennium." *Youth Library Review* 28 (spring 2000) (www.la-hq.org.uk/groups/ylg/archive/ylr28_4.htm).

———. "From Exeter to Jordan," *Register* (www.oxfordtoday.ox.ac.uk/archive/0102/14_3/03.shtml).

———. "Invisible Pictures." *Signal* 60 (September 1989): 160-86.

———. "Let's Write It in Red: The Patrick Hardy Lecture." *Signal* 85 (January 1998): 44-62.

———. "Picture Stories and Graphic Novels." In Kimberley Reynolds and Nicholas Tucker, eds. *Children's Book Publishing Since 1945.* Aldershot: Scholar Press, 1998, pp. 110-32.

———. "Responsibility and the Storyteller." *New Humanist*, March 1, 2002 (www.newhumanist.org.uk/volume117issue1_more.php?id=296_0_14_0_C).

———. *The Firework-Maker's Daughter, and How She Became a Play, and Then a Book, and Then Another Play* (www.sheffieldtheatres.co.uk/education/productions/firework maker/pullman.shtml).

————. "The Republic of Heaven." *Horn Book Magazine*, November/December 2001, pp. 655-67.

————. "Why I Don't Believe in Ghosts." *New York Times*, October 31, 2003.

————. "Writing Fantasy Realistically." Sea of Faith National Conference, 2002 (www.sofn.org.uk/Conferences/pullman2002.htm).

Roberts, Susan. "A Dark Agenda?" (www.surefish.co.uk/culture/features/pullman_interview.htm).

Snelson, Karin. "It's No Fantasy" (www.amazon.com/exec/obidos/tg/feature/-/79470/104-2884940-7655910).

Spanner, Huw. "Heat and Dust." *Third Way* 25 no. 2: 22-26 (www.thirdway.org.uk/past/showpage.asp?page=3949).

Squires, Claire. *Philip Pullman's His Dark Materials Trilogy.* London: Continuum, 2003.

Thompson, Bob. "'Dark Materials,' Bright Promise." *Washington Post*, December 14, 2003.

Tucker, Nicholas. *Darkness Visible: Inside the world of Philip Pullman.* Cambridge: Wizard Books, 2003.

Veith, Gene Edward. "Atheism for Kids." *World*, June 22, 2002.

Warner, Marina. *Fantastic Metamorphoses, Other Worlds.* Oxford: Oxford University Press, 2002.

Wartofsky, Alona. "The Last Word." *Washington Post*, February 19, 2001.

Weich, Dave. "Philip Pullman Reaches the Garden" (www.powells.com/authors/pullman.html).

Welborn, Amy. "His Dark Materials" (www.amywelborn.com/reviews/pullman.html).

Yeats, W. B., ed. *William Blake Collected Poems.* London: Routledge, 2002.

Useful Websites

Philip Pullman's website—www.philip-pullman.com—contains a number of articles (and links to more) that have been cited in this book and are not relisted here.

The Random House website—www.randomhouse.com/features/pullman—contains much information about Pullman and his books, including his additional material about the alethiometer, the *Liber Angelorum* and his Carnegie Medal acceptance speech.

Damaris Publishing's *Dark Matter: A Thinking Fan's Guide to Philip Pullman* website:

www.damaris.org/pullman (see also articles and study guides on Damaris's CultureWatch site—www.CultureWatch.org).

National Theatre—www.nationaltheatre.org.uk and www.stagework.org.uk.

Bridge to the Stars—www.bridgetothestars.net.

His Dark Materials—www.hisdarkmaterials.org.

His Dark Materials: An Unofficial Fansite—www.darkmaterials.com.

Dark Adamant—www.geocities.com/darkadamant.

His Dark Materials Annotated—www24.brinkster.com/menthapiperita/tgc.htm.